SNAKE BIT

Carroll Shelby's
Controversial *Series 1* Sports Car

SNAKE BIT

Carroll Shelby's
Controversial *Series 1* Sports Car

Eric Davison

Foreword by David E. Davis

MOTORBOOKS
INTERNATIONAL

First published in 2004 by Motorbooks International, an imprint of
MBI Publishing Company, Galtier Plaza, Suite 200, 380 Jackson Street,
St. Paul, MN 55101-3885 USA

Motorbooks International titles are also available at discounts in bulk quantity for
industrial or sales-promotional use. For details write to Special Sales Manager at
Motorbooks International Wholesalers & Distributors,
Galtier Plaza, Suite 200, 380 Jackson Street, St. Paul, MN 55101-3885 USA.

ISBN 0-7603-1781-X

On the front cover : The Shelby Series I. *David Newhardt*

Edited by Peter Bodensteiner
Designed by Stephanie Michaud

Printed in China

CONTENTS

Foreword

I have known Carroll Shelby since 1956, and Eric Davison since 1953. Eric grew up in a household that was precipitously skewed toward sports car enthusiasm, and his father, Charlie Davison, was my treasured friend and unindicted co-conspirator in a variety of automotive adventures. It is therefore appropriate that my friend Eric Davison should write a book about our mutual friend Carroll Shelby and his attempt to create and sell a new sports car—the Shelby Series 1—powered by a high-performance version of the V-8 engine from the Oldsmobile Aurora.

Eric was intimately involved in this project and is thus able to show us, in microcosm, exactly how complicated, difficult, and expensive it is to build a new car in today's ferociously competitive automotive market. It didn't help that Carroll Shelby sought components and technical support from General Motors at a time when that great corporation was desperately trying to extricate itself from several years of botched reorganizations and bad personnel decisions. In a word, GM had its own problems, and after agreeing to give Shelby the support he requested, lost interest in the project and began to regret the whole thing. This was not a promising beginning.

Carroll Shelby had to deal with botched organizational schemes and bad personnel decisions of his own. His huge success with the Shelby GT350s and Shelby Cobras, accomplished 30 years earlier with the support of a very enthusiastic and accommodating Ford Motor Company, did nothing to prepare him for the worst-case scenario he'd be up against trying to bring the oversized and underdeveloped Shelby Series 1 to his eager public.

Eric Davison was there. Eric saw and heard the interplay among a shaky cast of characters. Like Carroll Shelby, he wanted very badly for the Shelby Series 1 to be the car Shelby envisioned, and he was just as heartsick as Shelby himself when it all started to come apart. It's a sad story that goes back before Ned Jordan and the Jordan Playboy, Harry Stutz and the Stutz Bearcats and DV-32s, Preston Tucker and his memorably ugly Tuckers, John DeLorean and his shell-game DeLoreans, and Henry Kaiser, who demonstrated that not even the vast fortune he'd made building Liberty Ships during World War II could begin to make his Kaisers and Frazers competitive against Detroit's Big Three. Losers all, these men and dozens like them were broken by the fact that the automobile business is a tough business.

Neither Carroll Shelby nor Eric Davison had any illusions about the odds against success for the Shelby Series 1, but neither of them could have predicted what a bizarre case study the rise and fall of this particular automotive venture would turn out to be. But something else must be said. Carroll Shelby and all of the other colorful and flamboyant figures who've suffered bloody noses in their attempts to at least fight the automotive business to a draw did it because they loved the game, because it's more fun than any other business, and because there's always the possibility, in the public mind, that the next colorful and flamboyant figure with a big automotive idea will turn out to be the real thing, with an automotive idea that will, no kidding folks, revolutionize personal transportation.

Eric Davison tells how Carroll Shelby lost this round. But despite that bloody nose, and despite the fact that Shelby recently celebrated his 81st birthday, we come away from this book pretty certain that we haven't heard the last from Carroll Shelby.

—David E. Davis
Founder and Editor Emeritus of *Automobile*

Preface

Love him or not, Carroll Shelby is arguably America's best-known living automotive personality. He has been enshrined in the Automotive Hall of Fame. His career has lasted through five decades and is now in its sixth. He is both a legend and a legendary character.

This is not Carroll Shelby's biography; this is the story of an automobile that should have been the greatest success story of the 1990s. It had everything going for it—a brilliant concept that gave birth to a well-engineered vehicle, with the name of an automotive legend behind it. So what happened?

In 1994, I became a player in the development of the business that came up with the Shelby Series 1. Nevertheless, my part was enough to give me a perspective that allows me to tell its story in a reasonably fair and objective way. We can all learn from it.

* * *

While Carroll Shelby earned his reputation as a race car driver and car builder, the reasons for his fame go well beyond anything to do with wheels. They have more to do with the nature of the man. Carroll Shelby has an indomitable nature. He refuses to accept anything other than his own goal and refuses to back off when challenged. He sinks his teeth in and does not let go until he is satisfied with the results of any endeavor in which he has a stake, whether financial or emotional. It is almost as if he can make things happen through sheer willpower.

Do not get in his way. Walls will crumble before Shelby gives in.

This was his way on the racetrack. In photographs, Carroll Shelby was a man on the way to the front. His posture behind the wheel was one of looking ahead, far down the track—looking for a way to pass and anticipating anything and anyone that might be in his path.

He achieved success in his first attempt as a race car driver when he was 30, an age when most drivers are at or past their peak. Through guile, persuasion, and talent, he received offers to drive faster and more competitive cars until he achieved the ultimate honor for an American sports car driver of his day. He was named Sports Car Driver of the Year by *Sports Illustrated* in both 1956 and 1957, and his smiling Texan face on the cover widened his fame well beyond the norm for sports car drivers of his time.

Carroll Shelby was committed to success through racing sports cars even though sports car racing was, at that time, only an amateur sport.

Carroll needed money, so he headed for England where money (albeit pennies) was to be made racing sports cars. His obvious abilities and the fame provided by *Sports Illustrated* enabled him to gain a seat with the prestigious Aston Martin team, and in 1959 he teamed with Englishman Roy Salvadori to win the Le Mans 24-hour race, the most important sports car race in the world. His victory at Le Mans added a European flair to his already rising American stardom.

His active racing career ended less than two years later when a congenital heart condition made it too dangerous for him to continue racing. Starting at age 30 in an obscure race in Texas and then, just seven years later, winning the most prestigious race in the world, driving for one of the most prestigious race teams of the day, was the stuff of folklore.

He accomplished this all despite a heart condition that forced him to drive with a nitroglycerin capsule under his tongue—a last-ditch fail-safe measure in case his heart skipped a beat.

Consider, too, that sports car drivers of that day had little or no physical protection. Crash helmets were barely capable of deflecting stones from the skull. Roll bars were nonexistent. Gas tanks were merely containers of explosive fuel that could rupture and ignite. Fire-resistant driving suits had not yet been invented. Bravery and a macho attitude were the basic requirements. Shelby still has the scars to prove the perilous nature of sports car racing in the 1950s.

Carroll Shelby lived through it all, won races, and made friends around the world, yet came out of it with a bad heart and little money.

The idea of a true American sports car had been in the back of his mind for some time. When he learned that the English AC Cars, Ltd. was facing closure because its source of engines had dried up, he concieved the idea of installing an American V-8 in the lightweight AC roadster and creating an extremely fast sports car.

AC was interested, and the perfect engine appeared to be the new Chevrolet V-8 that was light, powerful, and would shoehorn into the AC engine compartment. Chevrolet was not interested. It already had the Corvette and did not want to supply engines to a potential competitor.

More challenged than angry, Shelby headed to Lee Iacocca, the head man at Ford. Reportedly, Iacocca promised him engines with the desire to help, but also to rid himself of the persistent Texan.

Carroll and his Ford-powered hybrid became one of the most successful sports racing cars of all time. Shelby Cobras laid waste to the best that Corvette could offer and whipped Ferrari for the World Championship for sports cars in 1965. Carroll Shelby's Cobra was the poisonous snake that would bite the competition at every opportunity. Today, original Shelby Cobras are rare and expensive collector cars, reaching prices in excess of $200,000.

Carroll Shelby's friendship with Iacocca endured, as did his relationship with Goodyear, whose racing tire development was vital to the success of the Shelby Cobra. To this day, Shelby remains a Goodyear Racing Tire distributor, and he and Iacocca live near each other in Southern California.

Due to Shelby's racing success with his Ford-powered Cobra, Iacocca asked him to take over the Ford GT racing program that had foundered in company politics despite its superior equipment. Under Shelby's leadership, Ford captured the Le Mans 24-hour race in 1966 and 1967.

Also at the behest of Iacocca, Shelby worked his magic on their anemic 1965 Ford Mustang, turning the Shelby Cobra Mustang into a much-sought-after and highly successful performance car.

* * *

Shelby eventually took a hiatus from most things automotive and explored a multitude of businesses, attacking each one with the same fervor and intellectual curiosity that he used to achieve success in the automotive arena.

When Lee Iacocca became president of Chrysler, he called Carroll Shelby back to infuse some life into the bland little automobiles that were the backbone of Dodge. Between 1986 and 1989, Shelby responded with a series of Dodge cars that were blindingly fast and performed far beyond anyone's expectations.

Eventually, Shelby's heart condition became so perilous that he was forced to keep within a short time and distance of the hospital where a heart transplant could take place as soon as a suitable donor was located. In 1990 he received a heart from a reported gambler—which seemed more than appropriate—and within a few years, Carroll was back playing golf and charging ahead.

The heart transplant medication didn't take long to destroy his kidneys and, once again, Shelby needed surgery to extend his life. The kidney donor was his son Michael. By 1996 Carroll Shelby had once again beaten the odds and was back to business as usual.

Through all of the years and all of his exploits, Carroll Shelby has become a controversial figure. Many people love him; many do not. However, Carroll Shelby remains a vital and energetic man despite the years and his health problems. He remains, at 81, inquisitive, aggressive, and relentless.

The story of the Series 1, as strange as it is, will merely be a footnote or a brief chapter in the full story of Carroll Shelby's extraordinary life. Carroll's original involvement in the creation of the Series 1 was less than one might expect from a company that carried his name on its door. He footed the bills and sold off some property in Texas as well as his beloved and legendary Cobra Daytona Coupe for the program. However, it was the intention of his business partner, Don Rager, to use the Shelby name and reputation to recreate the Shelby American Automobile Company with himself as both the president and the new Carroll Shelby.

Don's aims were realistic, albeit ambitious. Had he been Carroll Shelby, he might have succeeded. The financial concept he pushed, having dealers and customers finance the car and vendors do the technical development, had great merit and might have worked if not for the fact that he was *not* Carroll Shelby.

Carroll was kept minimally informed of details throughout the early Series 1 process. He knew about the car. He knew what the Series 1 was to be and what the final selling price was intended to be. From my vantage point in the project, I do not believe that he was aware of all the deals that were cut and the promises that were made in his illustrious name.

Because of the precarious condition of his health when the project started, Carroll appeared to be more of a spectator to the event. As such, he was locked into an untenable position. If the project succeeded, it would be another Shelby triumph with the glory shared by Don Rager. If it failed, while it would have been Don's fault, the name on the door was Carroll's. However, as the program progressed Carroll stood back and let whatever was going to happen happen.

The only thing for sure about the Series 1 program is that it did not have the full attention of Carroll Shelby. His personal track record is one of doing absolutely everything necessary to assure victory. Don Rager seemed to think that the Shelby name alone would carry the day.

Carroll Shelby had the name, but with drive and ambition to back it up. He knew how to use his name and his reputation to his advantage. Don Rager had no name, and he didn't fully understand how to use Carroll's.

As you will see, "snake bit" is an apt description of all that happened along the way. Everything that could possibly go wrong did. Even some things that couldn't have gone wrong went wrong as well. It was a comic example of Murphy's Law gone wild.

Through some matter of the fates, I was able to have a front-row seat for most of the program. It became too unbelievable to explain to friends and too much of a circus to be forgotten, so I began to write it down as it happened.

Chapter One

First Steps into the Snake Pit

I first heard the name Carroll Shelby in the late 1950s when I was a young sports car racing fan. Carroll was the most notable American race car driver, and his success attracted me to him. In the early 1980s, a business meeting in Los Angeles brought me face to face with him. I wish I could report that I made an immediate and lasting impression on him, but that would be a lie. I am sure he forgot me within the hour. I did not forget him, however, and a combination of fate and good fortune permitted our paths to cross again several years later.

In the mid-1990s, Carroll Shelby began to enjoy the benefits of his heart transplant. He was physically active and was traveling, playing golf, and enjoying life after living at the edge of heart failure for many years. However, he soon began to suffer kidney failure as a result of the massive doses of heart transplant medication that he needed to take. Personal survival was once again foremost in his mind.

Also in the 1990s, General Motors created a new engine specifically for its Cadillac division. It aimed to have the engine, named the Northstar V-8, put Cadillac back into the same league of luxury cars as Mercedes, Lexus, Infiniti, and BMW.

The Northstar was a modern engine in every sense. It was a 4.6-liter V-8 with aluminum cylinder heads and block, making it light. It carried four overhead camshafts, two per cylinder bank. The overhead camshafts operated four valves per cylinder, the current state of the art for efficient engine operation.

The new Cadillac Northstar V-8 was equal, if not superior, to any other luxury car engine, and it was designed and manufactured in America.

This was not lost on Don Landy, the then-president and chief operating officer of Shelby American—the company that was the backbone of Carroll Shelby's many businesses. Because of Carroll's health, Landy was more than president. He effectively was *the company*, and the idea of the Northstar V-8 and its performance potential inspired his imagination. While Carroll nursed his health, Landy took over and made deals.

Carroll Shelby had never built a car from the ground up. His most famous car, the Shelby Cobra, had been an amalgamation of the English AC Ace and a Ford engine. Shelby's imagination, guts, and energy had blended the out-of-date English chassis with a powerful Ford V-8 and created a car that bested Ferrari in 1965.

The availability of the new Cadillac Northstar V-8 from General Motors was of significance, as it provided the chance to complete a hat trick—a Shelby automobile from each of Detroit's Big Three. It appeared to be the perfect time to revive the Shelby name in a big way, to create an all-new, all-Shelby Cobra for the 1990s—the first Shelby car that was Carroll Shelby's from the ground up.

Landy figured that the ideal candidate for the new car was Cadillac. The time was right and the Northstar engine was ideal. With Cadillac's support, he would create the new Shelby sports car. The combination of wealthy Cadillac buyers and a potentially high-performance engine was perfect. It would be the Shelby for the 1990s. At least that is what Landy hoped.

Cadillac even had a brief history in racing. In 1950, sportsman Briggs Cunningham entered a Cadillac sedan and a unique Cadillac roadster in the Le Mans 24-hour race with moderate success. The sedan finished 10th, and the roadster, dubbed "le monstre" because of its ungainly looks, finished 11th despite going off the road and burying itself in a sandbank at one point. The Cadillac engine was subsequently used in a variety of successful sports racing cars, even though Cadillac backed away from further support of Briggs Cunningham, who switched to the new Chrysler Hemi as the engine of choice for his next car.

Unfortunately, Cadillac was not interested in Landy's concept. The idea of a Shelby sports car was not something it needed to enhance its image. Cadillac's mission was to prove to the world that it made luxury cars to compete with the best. A high-performance sports car was not on its list of priorities. Its own dive into high-speed automobiles would come later with pure Cadillac sports racing cars designed to compete at Le Mans.

Shortly after the Cadillac rejection, Oldsmobile announced that a 4.0-liter version of the Northstar would be built for the new Oldsmobile Aurora sedan.

John Rock had recently taken over as general manager of the moribund Oldsmobile division. He was convinced that Oldsmobile could fight its way back from near death by injecting life and enthusiasm through motorsports. He figured that the Aurora V-8 would give the company the needed boost. The new Aurora with its Northstar-derived Aurora V-8 would become the symbol of Oldsmobile's resurgence.

John Rock was a GM success story. He rose through the ranks, earning executive positions at Buick and General Motors' Truck & Coach division. He also served as executive director of sales at General Motors Corporation. While director of sales for GM's Holden operation in Australia, he used auto racing to recharge that company's image.

The fact that there was to be a 4.0-liter version of the Northstar was testament to Rock's powers of persuasion. Cadillac and the GM powertrain group had no intention of making a separate engine for Oldsmobile. With the recent sales performance of the Oldsmobile division, the limited numbers that could be expected to sell would make the 4.0 Aurora V-8 a costly proposition. Although the engine was built, it remained a stepchild, even though it was almost identical to the Northstar except for displacement. Cadillac retained an exclusive on the larger 4.6-liter version. The special 4.0-liter version that was developed for the Indy Racing League series was subsequently adapted for the Cadillac attempt at Le Mans in 2000.

His last assignment, a corporate sales job, proved to be a bore for the energetic John Rock, and his dissatisfaction with GM corporate life led him to tender his resignation. Rather than lose John's energy, GM management offered him the assignment of resurrecting the dying Oldsmobile division.

At one point in its recent past, the Oldsmobile division had sold more than 1,000,000 automobiles. Subsequently, poor quality control, emerging Japanese competition, a poorly conceived diesel engine, and myriad other ailments had pushed Oldsmobile to near death. It was an ideal situation for John Rock, the chance to break the rule book and do anything that made sense to try to save Oldsmobile.

One of John Rock's first tasks was to investigate participation in the newly formed Indy Racing League. The IRL was a breakaway organization from CART (Championship Auto Racing Teams), the organization that dominated open-wheel auto racing in the United States.

The IRL was to be an open-wheel, oval-track racing series. Founder Tony George was the grandson of Tony Hulman, the man who brought the Indianapolis 500-mile race back to life after World War II. George believed that CART had become too powerful and that the cornerstone of auto racing in the United States was his Indianapolis 500. He felt that if he could break the CART stranglehold on open-wheel racing, his new IRL series with the Indy 500 as the centerpiece could surpass CART as the leader in American racing.

Engines based on passenger car engines of 4.0-liter displacement would be the basis of the new racing cars. The new IRL and the new Oldsmobile Aurora V-8 would become partners. The rebirth of American oval-track racing and Oldsmobile would happen together.

Tony George would have an American race engine to highlight his race series, and John Rock would have a showcase for his engines. The starting point for the union would be the Indy 500 in 1997, the first year and the first race in which the new engines would compete. And it would be the first event in a yearlong centennial celebration for Oldsmobile.

An Oldsmobile-powered sports car would also be a fitting part to the Oldsmobile Aurora performance story. Olsmobile would race in the World Sports Car series, an international sports car racing program that included Daytona, Sebring, and Le Mans.

Armed with the knowledge of Rock's goals at Oldsmobile, Landy took his Shelby sports car proposal to John Rock at Oldsmobile. While Rock was intrigued with the idea of a Shelby-Oldsmobile, he was not impressed with Landy. Landy has been described as a "pitchman," and Rock was a bigger-than-life, straight-from-the-shoulder car executive. John believed in straight talk. He had little time for what he perceived to be bullshit and never let his opinions go unstated.

At 6 feet 5 inches and about 250 pounds, John Rock looked exactly like what one would imagine a man named John Rock would look like. He was a cowboy, hunter, fisherman—the personification of the man's man. Simply put, he was the John Wayne of the car business, riding into Lansing, Michigan, in a white Oldsmobile to save the beleaguered car division from the sharp pencils of the GM accountants.

Later, when news leaked that Oldsmobile was to be discontinued, John announced at a press conference, "I am one pissed-off cowboy. I just got here and someone is trying to steal my horse."

John Rock and Don Landy were oil and water. Mixing the two was a bad idea.

While Rock let the idea of an Olds sports car sit, Landy used the press to generate interest and excitement for his proposal. Photographs of a scale model of the proposed car appeared in *Automotive News* and on the cover of *Automobile* magazine. Hints of the possible union appeared in many of the car enthusiast magazines. The *Automobile* magazine article, which appeared in December 1995, was particularly spectacular. It was a spread with a large color illustration of Landy's scale model and a description of what the car might be.

The article was filled with the usual colorful quotes from Carroll Shelby. It would cost no more than $75,000, "because if I can't sell it for $75,000, I won't build it," he said. He planned to use Oldsmobile's Aurora V-8 because it is "the only engine out there worth a shit."

However, even if Rock was not committed to the idea, two of his motorsports engineers were smitten enough with the concept to do some preliminary analysis. Dennis Weglarz and Vic Ide, the two Olds engineers charged with overseeing the IRL and World Sports Car programs, developed a prototype chassis of the same approximate weight as the proposed Shelby sports car. Together with Bilmar Engineering in Florida, a company that was doing engine development work for Oldsmobile, they determined that there was potential for a fast sports car.

With other things on his mind, Carroll sat on the sidelines. He wasn't sure if he really wanted to go back into the rigors of car building, and his patience with Landy was thinning. Other Shelby ventures that Landy was directing were not working out to Carroll's satisfaction, and more and more Carroll needed to get his own financial situation in order. His ailing kidney and the uncertainty of his new heart made it extremely important that his financial future be secured. His wife, Lena, had two daughters, and Carroll had to provide for his own children and grandchildren.

SNAKE BIT

Sometime in 1994, with his compromised physical condition on his mind, Carroll began to have discussions with Don Rager about how the Shelby companies should be structured. Don was a car enthusiast and an accountant by education. He and Carroll had become acquainted through support groups for organ transplant organizations. Carroll already had a heart transplant and was looking for a suitable kidney donor. Rager had received a liver transplant. Both men were active in promoting organ donation, and Carroll had created a charity expressly to generate funds to help needy children obtain organ transplants.

As Carroll realized that Landy would have to go, Rager became more and more involved in the operations of the various Carroll Shelby companies. The concept of the new Shelby sports car was still up in the air. Carroll did not have a full understanding of the level of Oldsmobile interest. Although there was some at the lower levels of Oldsmobile, John Rock had given no indication of serious intent. Under normal conditions, Carroll Shelby could pick up the phone and call just about anyone, from King Edward to Charles De Gaulle, but his health problems were serious. If he called, he would have to become directly involved.

Toward the end of 1994, Carroll approached Vic Olesen about getting some answers to the Oldsmobile question. Vic was a semi-retired marketing executive who knew his way around General Motors. Carroll and Vic had become friends at Bel-Air Country Club in Los Angeles, where they were both members and occasional golfing partners.

Carroll asked Vic to give him some help getting motors from Oldsmobile or, at the very least, to put the idea to rest one way or another. By coincidence, John Rock and Vic Olesen were friends. They had worked together at Buick where John had been a sales executive and Vic had been director of McCann-Erickson, the advertising agency that served the Buick account. While John went to GM in Australia and Vic became an international executive with McCann-Erickson, they still remained friends and associates. Vic was also a friend of Knox Ramsey, Rock's marketing director at Oldsmobile.

If nothing else, Vic Olesen would be able to either help the program move along or determine that it would go nowhere. He would get answers.

That's when I became involved. Vic Olesen and I had first met and become friends in the 1960s when we were both young aspiring advertising hopefuls in Detroit, Michigan.

While we remained acquaintances for years, it wasn't until 1972, when we were both assigned to the Interpublic agency group that included McCann-Erickson, that we became fast friends. We were both in Europe. I was in Paris, working on General Motors and Opel advertising matters, and Vic was in London as a major executive involved with all GM business throughout Europe.

Our friendship grew, in part because of Vic's digestive tract. Food in France (as anyone knows) is far more interesting than English cuisine. Vic would schedule business meetings in France so we could have lunch together. At one luncheon at the Au Fin Gourmet restaurant in Neuilly, Vic ordered a big green salad of the kind that was hard to find in London. When his bowl of fresh greens arrived, he was unnerved to find a large green worm crawling around in the bowl. When he complained to the hostess, she pointed out in her imperious French fashion, "Monsieur is assured that the salad is fresh, and usually the vinegar kills them right away."

Our friendship survived the salad worm, and we hooked up again in Detroit when Vic became my boss as well as my friend. We had the unhappy assignment of trying to market gas-guzzling, 7.5-liter Buicks during the gas crunch of 1974 to 1976. Eventually, we both moved to California and enjoyed an eight-year association as partners in an advertising agency.

Vic knew of my love of auto racing and my admiration for the accomplishments of Carroll Shelby. When Carroll asked Vic for help, he immediately called me to see if I wanted to become involved with Carroll's new project.

Late in 1994, Vic Olesen and I dipped our toes into the waters of the project that eventually became known as the Shelby Series 1.

I look back now and ask: What were we thinking?

Chapter Two

Is There a Deal?

V ic's first action was to arrange a phone call to
John Rock. This was not as easy a task as one might imagine. At
that time, John's schedule was more than full with the challenge of saving Oldsmobile, and to find a time when he was available for
anything more than a how-can-we-rescue-Olds conversation was difficult. A sports car program was not near the top of his list of things to do.

Vic and I usually had coffee together a few mornings each week in a
cafe in Manhattan Beach, California, where we both lived. One particular
November morning in 1995, we discussed our pending telephone conversation with John Rock. We did not know of his feelings towards Don
Landy nor did we have any idea of the latitude he had in his job as general
manager of Oldsmobile.

In the past, general managers of General Motors divisions had been
gods. Thousands of people came under the leadership of an Oldsmobile
general manager. That person was responsible for manufacturing, purchasing, sales, marketing, and distribution. In the industrial town of
Lansing, Michigan, Oldsmobile was the major taxpayer, employer, donor,
and general benefactor of the local symphony, local charities, and other
community programs. General Motors divisional general managers were
also vice presidents of GM.

However, by the 1990s, as GM market share was decreasing, there
was a move to consolidate and to make the General Motors Corporation

more powerful, and to subordinate the divisional general managers to lesser sales and marketing assignments.

How John Rock's power was allocated was critical to how successful an Oldsmobile commitment to a Shelby sports car would be. If he had the authority to make the crucial decisions, the program could be a success. If he did not have that authority, it would be a burdensome if not impossible task. After we finished our coffee and figured out what John might have to say, we headed back to Vic's house and his telephone. John was cordial and indicated that he had some interest in the Shelby project and that he would be in Los Angeles for the auto show in early January 1996. He also said that he and Knox Ramsey, the marketing director, would meet with us there to discuss the idea.

At the show, I was able to corner John and Knox Ramsey for a few moments. I concluded that there was some interest in the project but that there were too many unknowns. Where the money was coming from to finance the operation was obviously a key item for them.

That was when John and Knox expressed their strong opinion that they could not do business with Don Landy. Landy had submitted proposals to Oldsmobile that suggested his taking over its entire motorsports program, including the World Sports Car program, its IMSA (International Motor Sports Association) program, and, potentially, the new IRL program.

"Just turn the program and the money over to me, and I will take care of everything including building the great new car" was the promise that he offered. Since, to Oldsmobile, Landy seemed overly insistent and his concept was so far afield from any method by which General Motors or its divisions could operate, the program was at a standstill. Besides, it appeared to be a proposal with no checks and balances, just a verbal "trust me."

John suggested that we contact Vic Ide and Dennis Weglarz, his performance group engineering team, to determine their level of enthusiasm and to get their views on the feasibility of the program. John said that he would arrange a conference call to make the introductions.

When that phone call took place, there seemed to be enough enthusiasm for both Vic Olesen and me to feel that Oldsmobile's cooperation might be a real possibility. We reported this back to Carroll, emphasizing that one major problem seemed to be Landy and his reception at Oldsmobile.

Carroll was having problems with Landy as well and told us to relax for a while until he figured out what to do about the management of his company, particularly his relationship with Don Landy.

Vic and I recognized that helping Carroll Shelby create a new sports car would be a lot of fun and potentially a good business venture. So we began to figure out how we could become involved *and* get paid for our efforts.

We recognized two things: first, there was value in bringing Oldsmobile and Carroll together. While under normal circumstances, Carroll Shelby would have had access to just about anyone, the current circumstances were not normal. Carroll was not sure that he really wanted to build the car, as it had been Don Landy's inspiration. Still, Oldsmobile coupled with Carroll Shelby made a lot of sense.

The second thing we saw was the obvious challenge: Carroll's kidney problem was getting worse. He was already living with a transplanted heart and, with a little luck, he would soon locate a suitable kidney donor. The strain of active involvement in a new car program would tax his limited physical resources to the utmost. Just about then, Carroll said, "I just can't deal with all them goddamn GM vice presidents anymore." Therefore, his contact with Oldsmobile had to be through someone he liked and trusted. That was Vic Olesen. Because of my friendship with Vic, I was included.

There were areas of potential income for the two of us. Maybe we could actively sell the cars; maybe we could handle the merchandising and licensing programs. There were many possibilities if Shelby American Automobiles came back to life.

Anyone who knows Carroll Shelby knows that he rarely comes out on the short end of a deal. His hardscrabble Texas upbringing seems to be part of his DNA, and sharing the wealth was not something he takes lightly.

The advice that we got from one of his friends was certainly worth a laugh. It was also worth heeding. The man said that he had been a friend of Carroll's until they went into business together. Then he said, "Carroll became tightfisted and mean."

"So," he said, "I quit doing business with him. It was far more fun to be his friend."

Being a friend of Carroll Shelby is one of life's treats. He is a man of incredible humor and a storyteller beyond belief, with a history so rich in race cars, celebrities, worldly adventures, and beautiful women that an hour with him is priceless.

However, he has a quick temper, is used to getting his own way, and doesn't like to part with a nickel of his own. While he will shop for a bargain on shoes for $12 a pair, he will toss money away on schemes so weird and strange that it boggles the mind. Bull sperm, miniature horses, vineyards, and secret new engines . . . deals, plans, and plots. Over the years, I am certain that Carroll Shelby has pissed away many fortunes.

By his admission, Carroll's business acumen is awful. He once told Vic: "There are only two things that I've ever been good at, racing cars and chasing pussy."

Don't believe it. Well, you can believe he was good at racing cars, as the world well knows, and I won't even go into his other claimed area of expertise. But don't ever believe for a minute that Carroll Shelby has no other skills, especially when it comes to business.

For all his protestations of business ignorance, Carroll Shelby is one tough and astute businessman. As a race car driver, he was able to negotiate the best rides. As a businessman, he was able to create a highly successful car company. As a race team manager, he was able to accomplish what the Ford Motor Company could not do: win Le Mans. *Twice*. None of those things would have happened if Carroll had not been up to his neck in every detail and had not had an uncanny ability to deploy the right people for the right tasks.

With Carroll's reputation in mind, Vic and I decided that, while the Oldsmobile project was merely an idea, it would be wise to create a plan that would reward us for our labors.

We knew we had to look after our own financial interests, so we met with Dick Crane, an attorney who was a friend of both Vic and Carroll. He knew Carroll's reputation and donated his time as a gesture and because he had a rich sense of humor. He knew that any attempt to pin Carroll down would be met with scorn and derision.

His advice was to make whatever agreement we could as airtight as possible and hope for the best. He would create a contract just to see Carroll's reaction.

Just as Dick Crane had predicted, at the first indication that there was an attorney involved and that we wanted a contract, Carroll exploded.

"Ah cain't give you no goddamn contract for sumpin' that I don't know is gonna happen or what it's gonna cost." So much for our contract!

The matter of the car and its potential existence was on hold for most of the year. Carroll dismissed Don Landy, and Don Rager took over as president and chief operating guy of Shelby American, Inc. He also assumed a seat on a board of directors consisting of Don, Carroll, and Neil Cummings, Carroll's attorney.

Don Rager came from California's Central Valley where his family had operated a Firestone tire store. Don had been educated as an accountant but had left corporate life to pursue interests in restaurants and movie theaters until he moved to Las Vegas. There, he moved up the business hierarchy by providing architectural services to hotels and short-term personnel to the thriving Las Vegas convention industry.

His plan was to bring Shelby American to Las Vegas where he would become the president of the largest car company in Nevada. This would bring him ever closer to his personal goal of becoming a major force on the Las Vegas civic and business scene. As a car enthusiast and, like Carroll, an organ transplant recipient, Rager was infatuated with the idea of a new Shelby sports car. Don liked to refer to himself and Carroll as collectors of spare parts. Don was also on the board of a company that was planning to build the Las Vegas Motor Speedway, which, when completed would be one of the most contemporary and complete motor racing facilities in the world. There was to be an industrial complex adjacent to the racetrack, and Don secured options on enough space to house a Shelby factory.

Bringing Shelby together with the speedway was sure to benefit both parties. With Shelby as the signature tenant, the speedway was assured a high-visibility occupant, one that could draw both publicity and other tenants who might find synergy in a relationship with the Shelby organization and the speedway.

The Las Vegas Motor Speedway was reportedly built (in Las Vegas these things are always a matter of speculation) with cash flow from Ralph Engelstad, owner of Las Vegas' Imperial Palace, and William Bennett, owner of Sahara Hotels. The general manager of the new speedway was to be Richie Clyne, Engelstad's former son-in-law and a good friend of Don Rager. In July 1995, Carroll called Vic to suggest that Vic and I meet Don Rager and discuss how we might work together. That meeting took place over lunch at the Bel-Air Country Club. Rager proved to be an affable man, full of interesting stories, but he tended to exaggerate the details of his life. He had perfected name-dropping to its highest art. His deals pending, deals in the offing, and his ability to move from one big deal operation to the next were the litany of a man obsessed with talking about his own success.

In the main, he was enthusiastic, talked sense about what he wanted to do with the Shelby operation, and was committed to go ahead with the Oldsmobile project. And best of all, he needed our help.

We collectively agreed that our next step would be to determine if Oldsmobile would be a player and if its interest was sincere. Since I had already scheduled a business meeting in Detroit, I volunteered to take an extra day and travel to Oldsmobile headquarters in Lansing, Michigan, to meet with Dennis Weglarz and Vic Ide.

That meeting took place in August of 1995. The two Oldsmobile engineers showed enthusiasm—cautious and restrained, but enthusiasm nevertheless. It was a good sign.

They needed some key information. They wanted to see a business plan that included financing arrangements, identified the principals in Shelby American, and also identified the engineering and leadership.

In turn, they showed me a book that they had been keeping that displayed all the engineering data they had collected, all the internal memos that were written, and press clippings about the car. They indicated that they were interested, and once Shelby got its act together, we could move ahead.

I assured them that we would attain all the information that they requested. I also assured them that Don Landy was no longer involved, a fact that they indicated they would pass along to John Rock.

We agreed to meet again as soon as possible and that I would contact them when I felt that we had all the necessary information in hand.

Vic and I then met with Carroll to review what had taken place and to plan the next steps. Carroll liked what we told him and directed us to Don Rager to coordinate the next all-important Oldsmobile meeting.

I called Don Rager to report on the meeting and to begin the process of assembling the information and a team to present to Oldsmobile.

Don was always in a rush. Crisis seemed to be part of his daily routine, and each day seemed to bring a new crisis that only he could solve. Messages would pile up on his desk while he complained for an hour about how busy he was. In his defense, his energy and abilities were remarkable, but his determination to be in the middle of everything only added to the pile on his desk and his woes about being overworked. His constant regime of medication only made matters worse. His liver transplant caused serious problems with his immune system, and that meant that he was more susceptible to disease than most. Additionally, he was a diabetic. The combination was deadly in terms of his physical demeanor. When he was under the influence of his medications, he was subject to severe mood swings.

When I called him and outlined the need for both information and speed, he reacted with enthusiasm, saying that he would get back to me "right away."

A week went by, and then another. I left repeated messages for him. No response. In frustration, I told Vic that working with Rager was impossible, that he didn't return phone calls. Vic said that he would talk to Carroll and try calling Don himself.

Vic succeeded in reaching him because the next phone call I got from Don was one of outrage. "Who does that son of a bitch think he is? He can't talk to me that way! I've never been talked to by anyone that way." And on and on. Finally, he calmed down long enough to apologize for venting his frustrations on me and for not calling me back. He later complained to Carroll about Vic's call. Carroll told him that if he would call people back like he was supposed to, he wouldn't get phone calls like that.

It was a telling phone call in many ways, revealing much about the true nature of Don Rager. He had told Vic in so many words that he, Vic, was not to discuss things with Carroll and that all communication with Carroll was to be through him. Being a control freak was one thing, but telling Vic that he could no longer talk to his good friend Carroll was another matter entirely. Vic did not take that too well.

It also made clear the fact that building a new Shelby sports car was to be Don Rager's project and Don Rager's alone. Carroll Shelby was only to be the name attached and not the man in command, at least as far as Don was concerned.

With the phone call storm past, I went to Las Vegas to meet with Don and to plan the Olds meeting set for November 1995, at the time of the annual SEMA convention. SEMA (Specialty Equipment Market Association) was the world's largest organization dedicated to the automotive aftermarket and related bits and pieces.

Companies from all over the world come to Las Vegas, where the vast convention center is filled to capacity with displays that range from car polish to hydraulic lifts to tires, wheels, and just about everything else related to automobiles. Everyone who has anything to do with automobiles is there to network and to see what is new.

For us, this was a perfect chance and the right atmosphere for a meeting with Oldsmobile. Dennis Weglarz and Vic Ide would already be there. We would be able to assemble all the necessary parties, including Carroll, without having the expense of a mass migration to Michigan. Also, we would be able to transport everyone to the site where bulldozers were moving the earth for the new speedway and clearing the land for the new Shelby headquarters. The whole automobile world was coming to *our* turf, and we were not about to lose the edge of that "home field" advantage.

While Vic Olesen and I prepared the meeting outline, Don worked on the requested business statistics, and Carroll began to name the people who would build the car. Obviously, the most important person would be the chief engineer. The next most important person would be the man in charge of production.

Carroll tapped Englishman Peter Bryant to be chief engineer. Peter had a long history with Carroll. When Carroll won the Le Mans 24-hour race while driving for Aston Martin, Peter was a young engineer on the race team. Carroll later helped Peter come to America, where he first worked for Mickey Thompson on Thompson's Indy 500 program. Peter had also been a key part of the Daytona Coupe racing program that had kicked Ferrari's tail in 1965.

After Shelby, Peter had continued to expand on his considerable abilities and formed a race team of his own that built and raced the powerful Ti22 cars (named after the atomic symbol for titanium) in the famed Can-Am series in the 1960s and 1970s. Peter's abilities as a successful race car engineer appeared to be ideal for the creation of the Shelby car that Carroll wanted to be "a race car for the street."

Carroll lured Peter away from a bucolic life by the central California coast to Las Vegas. Peter was a brilliant engineer but possessed an enormous ego. He was fun to be with, a great storyteller, but he could not tolerate being contradicted. Peter was usually feisty and contentious when anyone challenged him.

Tom D'Antonio became production chief. Tom had been living in Phoenix where he was recreating and selling Shelby Cobras, the car that made Carroll famous as a car builder and team manager. Part of the resurrection of Shelby Automobiles, Inc., would be the resurrection of the original Cobra.

While Carroll had taken his hiatus from the car business, companies began making replicas of the Cobra and selling them as "Shelby Cobras." In fact, the Shelby Cobra was the most copied car in the world, and Carroll wasn't making a nickel from any of it. After his heart transplant and the restructuring of his companies, Carroll determined that there was but one Shelby Cobra, and it was his. The resurrected Shelby American Car Company would recreate Cobras exactly as they were originally designed, and they would be authorized and sold by him and through dealers he appointed. He determined that D'Antonio built the best Cobra copies, so he hired him to head up production of the new Shelby Cobras and the new Oldsmobile car as well.

That was classic Carroll Shelby. Tom D'Antonio had been copying the Cobra without giving Carroll a penny, but Carroll did not get angry. On the contrary, he recognized D'Antonio's talents and hired him to give Carroll Shelby the edge he needed.

Vic Olesen and I enjoyed a rare treat. We drove to Las Vegas for the SEMA convention and the Olds meeting with Carroll. We set out in Carroll's Dodge minivan. We needed the van in order to transport Carroll's electric cart. All the walking at SEMA would be impossible, with his health as precarious as it was and his stamina so limited. The cart was to be Carroll's legs on this trip. He had the minivan prepared for the trip by replacing the transmission. Carroll claimed that the transmissions on "these goddamn things go out at 50,000 miles," and we sure as hell didn't want to be stuck in the desert with a busted transmission.

With Carroll behind the wheel, we had not cleared the city limits of Los Angeles when the new transmission began to act up. It would not shift into high gear. We discussed the options. Go back and get another car? Head to the nearest airport? Carroll needed his electric cart, so neither option was viable. As we drove along the freeway, he took out his cell phone and dialed a number. All we could hear was one side of the conversation.

It went something like: "Won't shift into high. What do I do to this goddamn thing? OK, yeah, OK, OK, we'll try that."

As soon as he hung up, he steered over to the shoulder of the freeway and turned off the engine, waited a few seconds, restarted the vehicle, and drove off again. Everything worked perfectly.

I asked, "What did you do?" He replied, "The guy told me that sometimes when you restart the engine, the computer will reset itself, and everything will be OK."

"Well, who did you call?" I asked.

"The sumbitch who makes these things. Who do you think I woulda called?"

Why didn't I think of that? Probably because I'm not Carroll Shelby.

Along the way, we discussed SEMA. Vic had never attended, so Carroll and I tried to explain to him what it was all about. We used aftermarket wheels as an example of the magnitude of the automobile parts and accessories business. Aluminum wheels, in particular, are a vast business with literally hundreds to choose from. Carroll explained that he had once been in "the aluminum wheel 'bidness' but got out because it got that anyone who could find a Mexican and a ladle could be a serious competitor."

Carroll Shelby definitely is not a racist. He is "plain spoken," that's all.

Our Oldsmobile meeting took place in the small conference room at Don Rager's Las Vegas office. The "Welcome to the Las Vegas Headquarters of Shelby American" sign outside was the perfect touch.

The small office made for a cozy meeting. Attending from Oldsmobile were Dennis Weglarz, Vic Ide, and Arlen Fadely, an Oldsmobile contract employee who worked on matters of racing. From the Shelby camp, there was Carroll, Don Rager, Tom D'Antonio, Peter Bryant, Steve Inge (Don's comptroller), and Neil Cummings. Neil was Carroll's attorney and one of the three board members of Shelby American, Inc. The other two board members were Carroll and Don Rager. Vic Olesen and I constituted the balance of the participants.

The agenda for the meeting was a presentation of the responses to the questions asked by Oldsmobile, including a preliminary description of the car. The drawing of the proposed new facility decorated one wall, and a 1/5th scale model of the car was on display.

The meeting went well and finished, as do most good business meetings, with a timetable for reconvening to push things along.

With the formal part of the day behind us, we all loaded into cars and drove out to the Nevada state men's correctional institute at Willow Springs for a look at the full-sized mock up of the new car that was being created at the prison.

While Carroll has been accuesed of using prison labor to keep costs down, that is simply not the truth. The prison program is sponsored by the State of Nevada, and the workers learn a trade, pay their living expenses, and build a nest egg. The parts they do supply to Shelby are minimal and apply only to the Cobra.

Several former inmates have been hired to work at Shelby American after their release. They are competent, reliable, and well-trained men. Carroll is not the kind of man to make a big deal of his contribution to the program. Neither is he the kind of man to back away from it. If someone wants to criticize helping inmates develop skills, Carroll doesn't care one Texas whit.

The mockup of the proposed new car was there at the prison. It was just a shell on a platform, but it was enough to whet everyone's appetite for the real thing.

On the way back to Las Vegas, we stopped at the site of the new speedway. Earthmoving equipment with wheels 20 feet high looked like little ants from our vantage point above, where the bleachers were to be located. It was an awesome sight as these monsters gouged out an arena in the Nevada desert, while USAF jets from Nellis Air Force Base, located across the highway, flew overhead.

The day concluded with cocktails at Carroll's suite in the Las Vegas Hilton and dinner at one of the hotel's restaurants. While Carroll does not readily tell stories about himself, he is quick to add corrections and highlights once he is prompted. Peter Bryant's droll wit and reminiscences of racing times past added spice to the evening, and Carroll laughed so hard that at times tears were streaming down his cheeks.

From that meeting, we were able to draft the general parameters of an agreement, which basically called for Oldsmobile to provide engines and technical support. Olds was also to make GM parts available at a fair price and to supply some money. The car was to be sold through Oldsmobile dealers, and Oldsmobile would provide assistance in establishing a dealer network.

While Vic and I had done our part by bringing Oldsmobile to the table, Carroll and Don asked us to stay involved until there was a formal agreement. So, later in November, we made another trip to Lansing to see if we could close the deal.

We went to John Rock's office at the appointed time. He was still in conference with the Oldsmobile advertising agency, Leo Burnett out of Chicago. Since Vic and I had spent our careers as advertising agency people, we had sympathy for the folks from Burnett, for we could hear John's booming voice through the richly paneled walls as he told them "they just didn't understand the problem."

When it was our turn, John assembled Dennis Weglarz and his chief engineer, Larry Lyons, and we had another rambling discussion on how this program could be accomplished. Years of experience had taught John to be a skeptic, but he felt that if Oldsmobile supplied the right kind of liaison between Shelby and Oldsmobile, the car could be built. Lyons was enthusiastic and eager for the chance to put Oldsmobile back into the performance car arena.

We had been pressing John for an answer to a key question: "How much are the engines going to cost Shelby American?" While John didn't have a specific answer, the expression he used was "I'll try to grandfather them to you." We interpreted that to mean that they would cost us very little.

Everyone at Oldsmobile was concerned about the survival of the division, and many saw the proposed sports car as having the same effect on Oldsmobile as the Viper did on Dodge. The Viper helped change Dodge's public perception from that of a company that built fusty old cars for poor people to one that built cars that were fun.

It would be the magic of Shelby at work for Oldsmobile just as it had been for Dodge.

Not everyone at Oldsmobile agreed.

Chapter Three

There are Snakes After the Rock

The New Year 1996 got off to an auspicious start. Dennis Weglarz called Don to arrange a meeting to review the bidding and to finalize the terms of the agreement. It was time to wrap up the details and start building cars.

That meeting took place at Carroll's office in Gardena, California, in early February. It was filled with surprises, especially for those who did not know Carroll Shelby. It was also a classic example of the maxim, "don't judge a book by its cover."

The building was a filthy, barnlike corrugated structure that housed Carroll's Goodyear Racing Tire distributorship and served as a repository for all kinds of strange equipment. In one shed, there was a pile of old four-cylinder Dodge engines left over from the Iacocca Dodge project.

There was the massive area where the racing tires were stored. Another area (the only clean one) was where the all-new aluminum 427-ci Carroll Shelby signature engines were being developed. There were old boats, old cars, and filth.

Carroll's quarters, though, were a world apart. He had developed a suite complete with a kitchen, a bedroom, a full bath, a living room, and his office. It was his hideaway, a place where he could escape.

Virtually every inch of wall space was covered with paintings, lithographs, photographs, plaques, and every sort of memorabilia. It was a private museum containing the highlights of an extraordinary career. If that failed to impress, the imposing pair of 8-foot elephant tusks that acted as an arch was a sure-fire attention-getter. Carroll also had a carved wooden preacher's pulpit from which he could spread the gospel of fast cars, fine whiskey, and beautiful women.

It was a perfect setting in which to wow our Oldsmobile guests with the richness of the heritage that Carroll Shelby brought to the program.

In the meeting were Vic Ide, Dennis Weglarz, and Arlen Fadely from Oldsmobile. Gary Arntson, a retired Oldsmobile engineer that Rock had put under contract to help the Shelby crew through the GM red tape, also came. Carroll, Don Rager, Peter Bryant, and I were there to listen to the proposition that they brought from John Rock.

Almost tentatively, Dennis put an offer on the table. Oldsmobile would purchase two prototypes of the new car to be presented to the public at the Detroit and Los Angeles auto shows in January 1997. They would also make an appearance at the big Oldsmobile dealer meeting in Las Vegas in April.

The big carrot was the promise that the new car would be the pace car at the 1997 Indy 500, the first IRL race that would utilize Oldsmobile-engined race cars. It would also be part of the Oldsmobile Centennial tour. An exciting new Oldsmobile-powered sports car would pace the race that would, in almost a certainty, be won by an Oldsmobile-powered race car. It was a natural, a win-win for everyone.

To top it all off, Oldsmobile promised to provide about $1,000,000 to fund the creation of the two cars.

A million dollars for all that exposure and publicity was a bargain for Oldsmobile. Chevrolet was reported to have spent $800,000 to have a V-12 engine installed in one of its vehicles for one magazine's cover story. It was chicken feed when considered as part of an overall GM advertising budget of $2.1 billion.

It wasn't chicken feed for us, though. This was a genuine high note for all of the Shelby people, so I didn't understand why Dennis presented the proposal with such reticence. I found out later that evening when I had dinner with the Oldsmobile crew at Houston's Restaurant in Manhattan Beach, California, which was on the road back to their hotel by the airport.

Oldsmobile knew that in the past Carroll Shelby had commanded vast sums from Ford, and later from Chrysler, for the miracles that he performed for them. Dennis and his crew were afraid that the "mere" million-dollar offer might insult the great man.

To the contrary, Carroll and Don were delighted. They both knew that times had changed. Lee Iacocca had been a rare find for Carroll. Iacocca had wanted excitement, first for Ford and then for Chrysler. Carroll had performed for him, and Iacocca controlled the purse strings. Carroll made sure that anyone he dealt with understood that he was acting in Iacocca's behalf. Earlier, when Carroll undertook the Le Mans project for Ford in 1966, it was under blanket orders from Henry Ford II that said, "Win." Therefore, anything that Shelby needed became a priority at Ford. Later at Chrysler, with Lee Iacocca in charge, the same rules applied to Carroll Shelby's projects. Money had always been available with few questions asked.

General Motors was a company apart. Nameless executives with no avowed passions for anything other than profit were not likely to provide Carroll with the free-spending programs that he had enjoyed previously. John Rock was as close to a believer and doer as GM could offer when it came to performance programs. Even in his position as a GM vice president and general manager of Oldsmobile, he could not commit to vast sums. Under circumstances such as those that existed at competitive car companies, Rock would have thrived. Carroll appreciated John's position and referred to GM's executives as being a "bunch of tight asses."

Carroll Shelby may have been a big name, but he was never too big for his own good. Say what you will about Carroll; still, he was the consummate realist. And when reality was "only" a million dollars, he looked it squarely in the eye and accepted it for what it was.

At last, there was a "handshake agreement" and objectives. The 1997 auto shows in Detroit and Los Angeles were less than a year away, and the effort required to have two cars ready, one for each show, would be monumental.

Peter Bryant was commissioned to begin creating the car. Carroll had some general guidelines. The first criterion for any Shelby vehicle is that it must be fast. In order to be fast, it had to be light, especially since the Olds Aurora engine was only 4.0 liters. And it had to be comfortable. Carroll was now 73 years old, and he didn't want to ride around in something that didn't have a modicum of civility.

Controversy jumped out at the very start, as the team discussed the possibility of a transaxle. A transaxle is an arrangement whereby the transmission and differential are combined into one unit at the rear of the car. They are connected by a torque tube—a super-strong tube that stops the engine and transaxle from twisting at different rates. This layout was advantageous in that it allowed the weight of the transaxle to offset the weight of the engine at the front of the car. The goal was to have 50 percent of the weight on the front wheels and 50 percent on the rear wheels. Many cars have used this arrangement. Notably the Porsche 928 and the C5 Corvette were programmed to incorporate a transaxle.

While a transaxle was not required as part of Bryant's first design, it eventually became necessary in the final design, in order to provide driver hip and leg room and enough space between the driver's head and the windshield.

Peter Bryant's first concept was to take the entire Aurora drivetrain and put it in the rear of the car. This would have created a transverse mounted mid-engine car and utilized the GM automatic transmission. The second proposed configuration was a traditional front-engine, rear-wheel-drive car with a Richmond six-speed transmission mounted directly behind the engine. This car would utilize a mild steel square tube chassis with carbon/Nomex/honeycomb panels.

This second configuration was chosen and executed for the Detroit and Los Angeles auto shows. Later, criticism of the extremely cramped cockpit made the Series 1 designers rethink the chassis layout.

Trouble was imminent because Peter was opposed to an all-aluminum chassis, and the Oldsmobile group was adamantly opposed to utilizing the transaxle. It knew about Chevrolet's difficulties in engineering the Corvette unit. It did not see how the small Shelby outfit could manage the task. Carroll ultimately decided on an aluminum chassis although Peter was adamant that his final production design would reduce the weight to 250 pounds.

In the middle of February 1996, an article appeared in *Automotive News* about the restructuring of General Motors. General Motors had been restructured many times in the past. Each restructuring had created an even more bureaucratic operation than the structure that it replaced.

But this latest "restructuring" was more like a dismantling. Following a boardroom revolt in 1992, Robert Stempel was ousted as chairman of

GM and replaced by John Smale, a board member and former chairman of Procter & Gamble (P&G). General Motors was a manufacturing company that marketed cars to its dealers, who then sold them to consumers. P&G was a package goods company that marketed directly to consumers through supermarkets.

The GM board felt that an infusion of consumer marketing would change the culture of GM and help stop the market share slide that had been taking place over the past 15 years.

One of Smale's first acts was to go outside GM to find a marketing person who could change the culture and bring marketing discipline to GM. An exhaustive search brought forth a candidate who knew nothing about the automobile business and its complexities. But he was empowered by the chairman and supported by the president, John Smith, to go forth and market GM back into prominence, even if it meant severely rocking the boat.

The new man was Ron Zarella, the recently deposed president of Bausch & Lomb, the optical giant. It was a big step into a new arena for Zarella, but with backing from the top, it was the chance to make a mark by turning around the staid and leaky ship of General Motors.

One of the biggest obstacles to cohesion that Zarella saw was the traditional division structure that had been created by longtime GM president and CEO Alfred P. Sloan. Sloan's vision was that each of the divisions was a stepping-stone to the next division. Chevrolet was the entry-level division with low-priced cars for everyone. Pontiac was a step up from Chevrolet; Buick and Olds were for the next aspiration level. Cadillac was for those who reached the top.

Over the years, the concept had faded through corporate greed and myopia. The levels and the divisional identities became completely blurred as Chevrolet offered such wide-ranging cars, from the cheap and lowly Chevette to the expensive and sporty Corvette.

There was product and price overlap at every division, and Cadillac created the greatest sin of all by putting leather seats in a Chevrolet Cavalier and calling it a Cimarron. To top it all off, quality fell by the wayside as the accountants did their best to squeeze every last nickel out of each product.

In the late 1980s, there were paint jobs on GM cars that flaked so badly that the chips could be washed off with a garden hose. In the face of Japanese quality and confused marketing programs, GM had to take some drastic steps, and Zarella's program was deemed necessary for survival.

The impact on the Shelby program was both immediate and enormous. John Rock, who had been the king of Oldsmobile, was now not just a king without a throne, he was—even worse for the Shelby project—a man without a checkbook. Marketing took the responsibility of assigning a marketing manager who had brand managers reporting to him and of assigning platform managers who oversaw the creation of new cars. General managers were now excess baggage in a program that would, within two years, reduce each car division, currently staffed by hundreds, to marketing and sales support staffs of about 30 people.

Each of GM's divisions—once giant independent car companies—would soon be downsized to a suite of offices in the RenCen, a building on Detroit's riverfront that GM had bought from under the nose of Ford. General managers became general marketing managers with a fraction of the authority that their former title had carried in the good old days.

Since creating a car for GM outside its strictures was tricky at best, John Rock in his new reduced role was caught in the middle. While there was not yet a contract signed between Shelby and Oldsmobile, there was a gentleman's agreement, and Shelby was now spending money on the car's development.

The man who now controlled the marketing purse strings at Oldsmobile was Steve Shannon. Steve had recently come to Oldsmobile to replace Knox Ramsey as marketing manager. His previous assignment had been at Saturn, where marketing had taken precedence over product and had given GM a costly but highly visible indication of change. Shannon was also the son-in-law of William Hoagland, the vice chairman of GM.

Now, rather than move ahead with John Rock as the spiritual creator and advocate for the Shelby program, the game had to begin all over again. The Shelby program was without a sponsor. If Shannon didn't think it was a good idea and a valuable program, John Rock would look like a powerless fool. Even worse, the Shelby people would look like total idiots for beginning to spend money they did not have.

We had to get Steve Shannon into our corner by whatever means it took.

For his part, Shannon was supposed to represent all that was new about GM. The idea of continuing a project that John Rock had started was an obvious problem. Since it was clear that divisional general managers were now obsolete and "marketing" was the wave of the future, there was little incentive for Steve Shannon to be an enthusiastic supporter of John Rock's program.

In an effort to keep the ball rolling and the car heading toward reality, Eric Dahlquist arranged a meeting in March, 1996, with Shelby, Rager, Bryant, and myself from Shelby, and with Rock, Shannon, and Weglarz from Oldsmobile. Dahlquist was president of the Vista Group, a company in Burbank, California, that serviced press cars and performed a number of promotional services for Oldsmobile. Dahlquist had also become a good friend of John Rock and was a long-time friend of Carroll Shelby. He was the logical go-between who, we thought, could make good things happen.

It was the first face-to-face meeting between Carroll and John Rock. It was only natural that they would find common ground. Both were hunters and adventurers and had many friends in common. The two bigger-than-life characters were instantly compatible. At any other time and under any other circumstances, a John Rock/Carroll Shelby combination would have been dynamite, with the resulting sports car becoming a world-beater. Of course, getting Carroll Shelby and John Rock together was not the problem. The problem was Steve Shannon.

A small patch of a common ground presented itself. Steve Shannon was about to donate a kidney to his ailing son, and both Carroll and Don Rager were not only organ donor recipients but also active in organ donor organizations. They were able to offer firsthand reassurances to Steve about the upcoming procedure. But they did not seem to be able to convince him that the Series 1 program was a viable activity. In fact, Dahlquist drove Shannon back to the airport after dinner and, while the trip was brief, Shannon spent the entire time railing about what a stupid program it was and how useless it would be to Oldsmobile. Perhaps the greatest miracle of all is that somehow, even with all of his negative views, the program remained on the active list.

On this evening, Carroll enjoyed his first night out with his new kidney. After a year or more of searching for a proper donor, Carroll's son, Michael, had come forward to help his father. It is hard to believe, but Carroll had been recovering at home only days before. Only if you do not know about Carroll Shelby should this surprise you.

Now Carroll had both a new heart and a new kidney, and he was ready at the drop of a hat to support any person and any program that improved the cause of organ donor programs. The few months prior to

Carroll's kidney transplant were tough to watch. He was obviously failing. His color was poor and his energy limited. As much as he tried to put a good face on his physical problems, there was always the lurking fear that he might not make it.

Someone remarked that Carroll couldn't possibly die because he had too much left to do.

The Shannon meeting had been a faltering "next step," and there was still some heavy-duty convincing that had to be done in order to get a contract worked out. The biggest and most frustrating problem was that in the convoluted new system at GM, responsibilities were hard to pin down. There was another difficulty: Carroll had always been a controversial character. Many felt that no good could ever come from any association with him.

While Shannon was the man in charge of marketing, brand managers made budget allocations. These people were responsible for each brand that GM offered. In this case, John Gatt was the brand manager for Aurora. His bonus and his future were directly tied to how well his brand fared in the marketplace. Brand managers outlined their needs and the attendant estimated costs. Budgets were then submitted to the marketing manager, who synthesized them into a divisional budget that was then sent to the General Motors corporate staff for approval.

Gatt's first reaction to the Shelby proposal was negative. He did not think that the people who purchased Aurora sedans had anything in common with people wanting high-performance sports cars.

He may or may not have been right. Oldsmobile needed to be in touch with those who would consider a high-performance sports car, and they certainly would have welcomed them into Oldsmobile showrooms, but somehow there was no ability to link excitement and enthusiasm with Oldsmobile.

The other matter was the budget. Since the proposed sports car used an Aurora engine, the money would have to be taken from Gatt's budget. While it would not be a lot in terms of the general size of automobile marketing budgets, Gatt would have to justify the expense in terms of public exposure and in terms of creating desire for an Aurora. He was not sure that he could do it.

One school of thought was that Oldsmobile might be too far gone to save. Certainly Rock didn't think so, and neither did Dennis Weglarz and

Vic Ide. They were busy helping propel Oldsmobile to the World Sports Car championship as well as pushing them to the IMSA sedan championship. Those programs and the Shelby program required belief in Oldsmobile and its future as well as dedication and enthusiasm from GM. From their standpoint, Oldsmobile was not about to fade away. At least, if it did, it would be with racing championships under its belt. Gatt's view of all the racing programs was that the Aurora engine racing programs should be separate from anything to do with the car.

At this juncture it was clear that General Motors had changed. While the GM of old had been arrogant and shortsighted, it was firmly entrenched in the automobile business and had been under the leadership of engineers as presidents with board chairmen from finance to watch the purse strings. Now GM appeared to be in the hands of those who had little love of automobiles and intended to market them as one would market soap or refrigerators. The new GM was just as arrogant as the old GM, just in a different way. And it was not in a way that favored a project dedicated to creating a masterpiece for the roadways.

The next meeting on the subjects of budget and contract was held in Phoenix, Arizona, later in 1996. The inaugural race of the IRL was taking place at the Phoenix International Raceway. The pertinent Oldsmobile crew would be there: Weglarz, Ide, and Fadely, who were there to observe how the new series would commence, along with John Rock and Steve Shannon, who were there to get a feel of what was to come with the Olds/IRL program. It also gave us an opportunity to try to put closure to the contract terms.

Weglarz had asked Don Rager and me to meet with him, Vic Ide, and Arlen Fadely on Saturday afternoon. Don and I went, expecting to sit and resolve issues on that day. Instead, we met with them only to discuss the next meeting that we were to have the following morning with the three of them plus Rock and Shannon. How to sell Shannon on the program was the big question. Steve Shannon was just not a believer, and it appeared that he did not want to go along with John Rock's program, whatever it was. Even though John was, on paper, his boss, Shannon appeared to relish the opportunity to show his independence. Don and I now saw a revised deal that included less money and less technical support. The promise of becoming the pace car for the Indy 500 also came off the table. Because the 1997 Indy 500 was a big Oldsmobile Centennial event, Gatt wanted the race to be paced by an Aurora, a car that Oldsmobile actually sold. In fact, the Aurora V-8 was expected to power the Indy 500 winner.

With the knowledge of what was facing us the next morning, Don and I headed to the airport. He had to fly back to his home in Las Vegas and I was returning to Manhattan Beach. We met for a couple of hours at the airport before departure. Don had to figure out whether or not the program was still viable, and I had to write a new presentation. If nothing else, while we were on short notice, we at least had some indication of the new rules and would not be in the situation of trying to figure out our position while in the meeting and at the bargaining table.

It was back to Phoenix in the morning and toward the hotel where the meeting was to take place. Sadly, the meeting was an embarrassment to John Rock. All his promises were off the table, and a person, whose agenda seemed to focus on embarrassing him, took over the show. Roadblock after roadblock was erected, but fortunately, Dennis and crew had prepped us thoroughly and with enough time so that we were prepared to respond.

While Don stuck to his guns on every point, in the end it came down this: did we or did we not want to proceed with the car under the new terms, which meant no cash and leaner conditions? Don bit the bullet and decided to go ahead. He was confident that we could at least get the prototypes built in time for the Detroit and Los Angeles auto shows. I was happy that I didn't have to make that decision. It appeared to be financial suicide for Shelby American, but Don felt that he had to make it happen.

Although battered and bruised financially, we were still in the game, and it looked like we could build the car. Backing out at this time would probably have been the wisest thing to do. But having a new Shelby sports car on the road was vital to the future of the revived Shelby American car company. Besides, after all the publicity that had been generated, it would have been a slap in the face for Carroll to be turned down by Oldsmobile, a car company in trouble. Don Rager was acutely aware that it was the image of Carroll Shelby and his accomplishments that would ensure the company's future and his own stature in Las Vegas. There was no room for failure. The word had never been part of Carroll Shelby's vocabulary, and we could not let it be part of ours.

By this time, Don had moved the company into a temporary facility on Valley View Boulevard in Las Vegas. The space was in an industrial park that offered room for the start of manufacturing Cobra cars and some office space. It wasn't much, but at least it was a dedicated facility, and Cobra production was up and running. By then, Bob Marsh had joined the staff. Carroll felt that it was time to get a professional on the staff to oversee Series 1 production, and that man was Bob. While Tom D'Antonio was an incredible fabricator and had been brought in to supervise the Cobra program, it soon consumed all of his time. Besides, overseeing semi-mass production was beyond his area of expertise.

Marsh had previous experience with Carroll. He had been in charge of producing the Shelby Dodge cars of the early 1980s. Since that time, Bob had moved on to another company that produced farm equipment and school busses. Bob Marsh was an experienced production expert, and his expertise would be necessary to take the Shelby Series 1 from prototype to reality.

Anyone visiting either the Las Vegas facility or Carroll's rundown operation in Gardena—both grimy, cramped, ugly, and inefficient beyond belief—with an eye toward investing would surely have turned tail and purchased stock in DeLorean. I have no idea what John Rock's thoughts were when he made his first visit to the Las Vegas location, but he held his tongue. The subject of his visit was how to organize the program. What should the facility be like? How might the Olds dealers be involved both as dealers and as financial partners? Finances were more important than ever now. Without Oldsmobile's financial backing, funds had to come from somewhere to get the program off the ground.

John suggested that we turn to Oldsmobile dealers for financing.

As part of the agreement with Oldsmobile, the new cars were to be sold through Oldsmobile dealers. In the area of finance, John was extremely creative. He had visions of Olds dealers investing in the new building planned for the Las Vegas Motor Speedway complex and utilizing part of it as a showroom. He also suggested that we consider creating an Olds dealer corporation to fund the program. His ideas piqued our interest, and we agreed to meet again to further refine them.

We also discussed the retail price of the car. Carroll had stated in the press that his new car would cost about $75,000. Everyone involved knew that Carroll was just making noise—noise that would keep the engineer's eyes on a reasonable bottom line cost. John Rock suggested that the car should cost no more than $100,000. He felt that $100,000 was about the squeeze point at which buyers would look at other options. His simple formula was that Shelby should build it for $60,000, sell it to the dealers for $80,000, and the dealers would sell it to the public for $100,000. That is how $100,000 was set as the arbitrary target retail price. This was neither an order nor a recommendation; it was a suggestion that, if feasible, seemed appropriate to John.

Another subject of the meeting was to pin down details of the Oldsmobile/Shelby agreement. This part had to do with parts availability, the cost of parts, engines, and other necessities.

These issues would not be resolved for a number of months, but none of it would matter if we could not raise the funds to build the prototype. That was the subject of the next meeting, with John Rock and members of the new marketing staff, including John Gatt, in East Lansing, Michigan.

Part of the discussion was about how Oldsmobile would be able to capitalize on the existence of the car. This discussion was, in part, an attempt to show John Gatt how and why the car would be advantageous to his Aurora program. He would not commit, and that part of the meeting ended with no resolution.

No matter, because for us the biggest item on the agenda was how to raise money.

John Rock had another suggestion. This new idea was to approach one or two key Oldsmobile dealers and offer to let them become full-equity partners in the program. They would fund the start-up, and they would be repaid out of advance dealer orders. Once again, we had a good idea from John, but one totally removed from the last proposal. We needed to have closure and a plan from him that he would endorse and support. So far, plenty of smoke but no fire. With each new meeting with John, it was as though the last meeting never took place. He would start each meeting with, "I had some thoughts on how to get this done." Meanwhile, the rest of us had come prepared to move ahead with his recommendation from the previous meeting

To make matters worse, after the meeting, John reported in side discussions that things at General Motors were going from bad to worse, at least in the political arena. He and Ron Zarella were clashing on just about everything. John was not certain about how much longer he would be on the payroll; until the end of the year was his most optimistic estimate. The pressure was on. Without John's assistance, we would have little to no chance in gaining dealer support and financing.

This last idea of John's was a viable one, but we needed to have a key dealer to work with. This dealer had to be someone the other dealers respected and had enough money to start the financial ball rolling.

One of my good friends is Rick Fischer, who comes from a family of General Motors automobile dealers. Rick is, himself, a GM dealer in Ypsilanti, Michigan. I called him for advice. I needed to try out the idea on a dealer and to see if it made any sense.

Rick Fischer is an exteme car enthusiast, and his only regret was that he was not an Oldsmobile dealer so that he could participate in the Shelby program. Not only did he think that John's concept was workable, but he also recommended that we contact his brother, David Fischer. I was a bit surprised that Rick would suggest his brother. I had always respected David as an extremely astute businessman and outstanding car dealer. Yet, I had always thought that he was extremely conservative and certainly not the kind of risk taker who would consider participating in John Rock's idea.

David Fischer owned Suburban Oldsmobile in Troy, Michigan, and held many other auto franchises, including Cadillac, Nissan, Saturn, Chrysler, Volvo, and Buick. Dave was not only one of the country's leading Olds dealers but is also widely respected, influential, and affluent. A third brother was also in the retail car business: Bill Fischer had a dealership in Stuart, Florida, where he sold Oldsmobiles, Cadillacs, and Mazdas.

I called Dave Fischer and arranged a meeting in Troy. I had told him that I was bringing the president of Shelby American to meet with him, which I think he interpreted to mean that Carroll Shelby was joining us for lunch. In anticipation of this, he brought his son David to meet the legend.

He appeared to be taken aback when I introduced him to the president of Shelby American, Don Rager. However, he recovered quickly and was open and receptive to the concept of financing the Series 1 program. He thought that the car would be good for Oldsmobile, and given the right set of circumstances, he would consider our idea.

What surprised both Don and me was the fact that David Fischer, one of the biggest Olds dealers in the county, had no idea that the Aurora engine had so much potential. He did not know that the Oldsmobile Aurora-powered race cars were achieving such success on the racetracks. In the past few months, Aurora-powered cars had achieved overwhelming success at Daytona and at Sebring. These were major achievements for Oldsmobile and would surely have generated enthusiasm among the dealers and prospects, had they been informed.

Why do it if you can't brag about it? Apparently the new brand management system didn't necessarily put the people with enthusiasm into the position of making such decisions.

David Fischer told us that he was interested but would like to discuss it with John Rock. He wanted assurances that John and the full weight of his office were behind the program before he committed himself to the cause. This message was passed on to John Rock, who said that he would call David and go over the details. John never called David, and a potential opportunity for future financing died on the vine.

While all of the fundraising activities were being evaluated, Don was discussing the program with potential suppliers. Who could make the carbon fiber body? Where would we go for seats, interiors, wheels, and other equipment?

At least tires were not an issue. Carroll Shelby is a Goodyear Racing Tire distributor, and his loyalties to Goodyear go back a long way. Goodyear provided help with both tires and money when Carroll launched his initial Cobra racing program, and Goodyear and Carroll grew up in racing together. Carroll was rewarded with a Goodyear Racing Tire distributorship; Goodyear was rewarded with passionate loyalty from Carroll.

As part of the exploratory program with Oldsmobile, Rock assigned Gary Arntson to help Shelby along. A retired Oldsmobile engineer, Gary had been involved in creating prototypes, show cars, and special vehicles. He also knew how to get things done within the GM system. He knew suppliers, he knew parts, he knew design problems, and he was determined. He had to be in order to cross all the disciplines and interdepartmental political lines in GM. Along with his skills and knowledge, Gary had a disposition well suited to the Shelby project. He was patient and knew exactly how to accomplish the team's goals without bruising egos.

Being the only person who knew exactly what needed to be done to complete a car, Gary Arntson was a major asset to the program from the beginning. He was familiar with every detail, from door seals to all aspects of certification. Everyone else at Shelby was learning on the job.

One issue that had to be resolved was the name of the car. The obvious choice was "Cobra." Carroll had sold the name to the Ford Motor Company for $1.00, a move that he later regretted. In addition, Carroll and Edsel Ford were at odds. After Iacocca left Ford—was fired by Henry

Ford II to be more precise—Carroll had spoken out about the injustice of it. That, plus issues surrounding just who owned "Cobra," made the Shelby/Ford relationship rancorous.

Ford did own "Cobra," although Carroll's cars were Shelby Cobras. In addition, there were car builders making knockoff Cobras and calling them Shelby Cobras. This licensing mess is still being unraveled.

Fortunately, Keith Crain, publisher of *Automotive News,* was a friend of both Carroll and Edsel Ford. Keith became the peacemaker, and a renewed relationship with Ford led to a settlement about the Cobra name. Ford would go after anyone who used the name without license, and Carroll could carry on calling his continuation versions of the original Cobra, "Shelby Cobras."

Everyone was happy, except it took away the potential use of the most exciting name in American auto history for the newest Shelby. Everyone involved went through a litany of possible names. Most were snake related. Shelby's cars were named after snakes. Cobra. Viper.

Carroll's view was simple. "Who gives a shit what you call it. The name will mean something if the car is great." He went on to relate how the Mustang GT350 was named. The number *350* didn't mean anything. It was a name that Carroll came up with in frustration after hearing the Ford marketing people and his own people argue about what to call the hot new Shelby Mustang version for 1965.

Legend has it that Carroll walked over and said, "Enough of this bullshit. How far is it to that building over there?" The reply was, "About 350 feet."

"Good," said Carroll. "It's settled. We'll call the sumbitch the GT350."

And, he was right. The Ford Mustang GT350 became a legendary car, and the name didn't have a thing to do with it.

The best potential car names were still snake names, and the best of the snake names were relatives of the cobra. When Carroll learned that one of the preferred names was a cobra species he exploded.

"Don't you all understand that ah cain't name anything that has anything to do with Cobra. Ford won't let me." The agreement with Ford prohibited even the use of names of cobra relatives. Carroll was not bitter; he knew there were plenty of opportunities ahead, and they did not depend on anything so trite as a clever name.

Peter Bryant came through with a simple solution. John Rock had mentioned that if this first Shelby/Oldsmobile program was successful, there was no reason why a second car could not be considered. Since building for the future fit right into the Shelby plan, Peter suggested that we call the car the "Series 1," with the clear implication being that a second car, the "Series 2," was to follow. Peter went on to create a badge for the car that had a snake eye blended into a checkered pattern that signified the checkered flag denoting a race winner.

The name was acceptable to everyone. Especially since, as Carroll said, "the name don't mean shit." In fact, the magic of the car was not the brand name—Series 1, Cobra, or whatever. It was the name "Carroll Shelby" that made the difference.

Coming up with a name was fine, but we were running out of time. It was clear that John Rock would not be around much longer. His timetable for retirement was now the end of 1996. It was late summer, the contract was still not signed, and we still did not have a firmed-up program for signing dealers and raising money.

Just about all the contract details had been worked out between Don, Dennis Weglarz, and the GM legal staff. The contract terms were nowhere near what we had discussed going in a year ago, but Don felt that they were livable and that the car could be built.

In spite of the lack of a formal contract signing, the preliminary work on the car had to move ahead. We assumed that the auto shows in Los Angeles and Detroit would be the first public showing of the new cars and a featured part of the Oldsmobile exhibit.

Michael Mate, an illustrator from Colorado, had created the original body shape. However, in the years that passed since that shape was first created, other cars appeared on the scene that were similar in nature, especially the new Jaguar XK coupe. Don, Carroll, and Peter all wanted the shape of the car to bear some resemblance to the original Cobra. Aggressive and powerful-looking with a bit of retro Cobra thrown in for good measure were the styling objectives.

To accomplish a new look, Peter engaged the services of the team of Lavin Cuddihee, Don Vena, and Alec Tam, three very talented automobile designers. They worked on revising the shapes for both a roadster and a coupe. They even worked up a removable hardtop that blended the top and the bottom of the car together in a graceful manner.

In addition, Peter brought in some sorely needed engineering help. He had been struggling with the enormous complexities of designing a car from the ground up by himself. In order to be light, it had to be small, which meant it had to have a short wheelbase. In order to be balanced, it had to have the engine set back in the frame. There had to be room for a radiator, a battery, suspension components, and, of course, passengers.

While the engine was aluminum with all the specifications of a racing engine, converting it to the new car was a major undertaking. In the first place, the V-8 engine in the Aurora was mounted sideways and used with front-wheel drive. It was hooked to an automatic transmission, and all the accessories such as the starter, generator, water pump, and fuel pump were accessible for the transverse mounting arrangement.

The new sports car would be rear-wheel drive, use a manual transmission, and had to be packaged in such a way that the accessories could be reached in the fore-and-aft engine installation. The engine had to be revised to take a clutch. A bell housing to cover the clutch and handle the addition of the manual transmission had to be designed and fabricated.

To help him in this task, Peter had brought in Mark Visconti. Mark was in his late 20s and a graduate of the University of Colorado. Mark had aspirations of becoming a football player until he ruptured his lower back during summer training. His first Shelby assignment was the development of the rear chassis and suspension components. Welcome to the world of high-pressure automobile design, Mark.

Peter and Mark had previously worked together on an automotive project, the Vector program. The Vector had been the dream of one man, Jerry Weigert, who had wanted to build the ultimate sports car. It had been an ongoing project for years. It had become an automotive joke because there were too many years of unfulfilled promises.

The Vector was sleek, low, powerful, and full of innovations. However, the price was astronomical, and there was never a prototype car that would function. Each time the car was turned over to the automotive press for tests and evaluation, there would be a serious malfunction. Weigert's adventures in gaining financing were legendary, including turning to the Far East for capital. His association with Vector came to an end when he was locked out of his own plant, and the whole operation moved to Florida under new management and new ownership. The few Vectors that eventually made it into customer's hands appeared to be fine automobiles.

Not only did Mark bring some specific abilities in creating supercars, but he brought considerable experience in aerospace, including his involvement on extremely sophisticated space-related programs while he was employed at TRW. He knew composites and adhesives, two important elements in creating a lightweight sports car. While involved in aerospace, he had created aluminum extrusion/aluminum honeycomb structures as well as some composite structures for a top-secret "black" program.

Carroll was impressed. He had always been obsessed with technology and was widely read on many technical subjects. His office was always piled with technical journals that he read and seemed to understand thoroughly.

In one way, this interest was great, because as the spiritual leader, he needed to be ahead of his designers and engineers. He had to be able to point out new methods and new materials. He also liked to be able to stick it to his troops. In another way, it wasn't so great. Shelby would read something that he felt had application to his car. He would then inform the world that this new feature or new material would be incorporated into the car. Often it was a material or a process that was yet to come or so outrageously expensive that it would be impractical. It would then be up to the engineers to stop everything, research his idea, and go back to him with the reasons why it would not work. This was a time-consuming proposition, and the engineering staff quickly became adept at heading elsewhere when Carroll showed up with a magazine article in hand.

The third key member of the team was Kirk Harkins. Kirk was one of those rare people who could look at a design, conceive how it would work, and create pieces out of steel and aluminum that would accomplish the job. Kirk is what is known as a "fabricator." He had been with Carroll Shelby for some time and had done much of the design and engineering for a race car that Carroll had conceived for amateur racing.

Kirk was a large and imposing man, possessing of all the charm and finesse of a drill sergeant. He was used to getting his way, which in terms of building cars meant that anyone who wanted to do something stupid or impractical or that he felt would not function properly got an in-your-face argument. Kirk was usually right about things mechanical and was forceful enough to keep progress heading in the right direction with a minimum of bullshit.

The previous Shelby car that Kirk manufactured was called the "Shelby Can-Am" car. It was created for a Shelby Can-Am series that utilized one make of purpose-built cars that were all-out single-seat race cars with full bodywork. The cars used Dodge V-6 engines. The Shelby Can-

Am series was designed as a specific formula. All cars were the same, and all engines were tuned to the same specifications. All cars were equal, and it was the driver who made the difference. The series was sanctioned by the Sports Car Club of America (SCCA).

Jim Harkins, Kirk's father, and Eric Barnett also joined the fabrication team. Jim Harkins was a machinist, a man who could create precision parts from pieces of raw material. Kirk, Jim, and Eric formed the team that would now begin to work around the clock to create the components necessary to put the show cars together. The site of their labors was the barnlike structure of Carroll's Gardena facility.

They resurrected old lathes, an ancient iron bedplate, milling machines, and metal shears and added new equipment as needed. In the main, it hardly looked like the kind of place where a sophisticated, high-performance sports car would be birthed. The floor was pitted concrete, the walls were gray and dirty, and the lighting was sparse. In the middle of it all, on the old iron bedplate, were the beginnings of the Shelby Series 1.

Originally, the prototype would have been built in Las Vegas with Tom D'Antonio doing the fabrication. The new setup, with Mark and Kirk in Gardena, California, just outside the door to Carroll's office, put Peter Bryant at a terrible disadvantage. He was discussing the project with Don in Las Vegas, while Mark and Kirk were actually doing the building and consulting with Carroll. It became a two-headed monster and was impossible to control.

The September 23, 1996 edition of *AutoWeek* carried a story announcing that the paperwork had been signed on September 11 that would put the Olds 4.0-liter 32-valve motor tuned to 350 horse power into "Shelby's modern interpretation of the Cobra."

"'Certainly it will have Shelby, Oldsmobile, and Aurora in it,' Shelby says. 'But it might not be called a Cobra. . . . It's going to be a little ass-kicker,' he says and it is 'not going to be a tin can.'"

The article further indicated that there would be both a coupe and a roadster and the goal was to keep the car at less than 2,400 pounds. The quoted price was the same $75,000 that Carroll had mentioned previously. There was an illustration of the car that resembled the Viper more than what was planned for the Series 1.

The next big Shelby event in September 1996 was the inaugural race at the Las Vegas Motor Speedway. While the Olds Aurora-engined cars were not yet in the picture, Oldsmobile was there as a major participant in this Indy Racing League event. A press conference was planned in which John Rock and Carroll Shelby would jointly announce the signing of the Shelby/Olds agreement. It would be held in a huge Oldsmobile hospitality tent in the exposition area just outside the grandstands. Olds passenger cars as well as an actual Aurora-powered race car would be on display.

A near disaster occurred on the Thursday before the Sunday press conference. Ron Zarella had issued strict orders to John Rock to not publicly say anything at all about the Shelby/Oldsmobile alliance.

Zarella knew that the deal was done, but for some reason he didn't want it publicly acknowledged. He probably hoped that the project would just fade away with John or that he would heap the final insult on John by keeping him from the press.

When Sunday came, there was plenty of food, soft drinks, and coffee at the Olds hospitality tent. As for the press conference, there wasn't one. At least there wasn't one that anybody noticed. There were instead just a few words each from John and Carroll that had nothing to do with any possible deal between Olds and Shelby. The lack of confirmation created more news. "What in hell is going on?" was the press takeaway from the event.

The real significance of the day was what took place when John and Carroll had a few brief moments together. It was only their second time together, and the conversation and its ramifications stunned John Rock like a bolt from the blue.

Carroll said to John, "I know that you are retiring. When you do I would like you to become president of Shelby American and run my company."

John was completely taken by surprise. He had contemplated nothing like this. His focus was on wrapping things up at Oldsmobile, and he had not given much time to life after GM. And he hardly knew Carroll, what his companies were, or anything else. John couldn't respond, except to say, "I'm flattered, and we'll talk later."

A startled Rock took Vic Olesen aside and told him what had happened. Vic was bemused. He had known that Carroll would take a liking to John. Their personal styles were very much alike. They were both quotable, and while Carroll was an absolute darling of the press, John had developed a lesser but similar reputation with them for speaking his mind and using profanity with impunity. A John Rock interview was always a lot of laughs, filled with usable quotes mixed in with the message. A John Rock interview, then, had an eerie resemblance to a Carroll Shelby interview. No wonder they found each other.

Vic's advice to John was to sit tight, that Carroll was apt to make off-the-wall remarks like that, especially if he felt comfortable with the person or if he felt that someone would be a help to him. Obviously, Carroll was looking for a successor, and while Don Rager was the president and CEO, he was not a public figure who could command a presence with the press. John Rock seemed the perfect person to carry on the Shelby legacy.

He was automotive smart, knew his way around, could open doors, and loved to let it all hang out when it came to interviews. He wasn't an ex-racer, but he was still a famous car guy.

All well and good, but with the Shelby/Oldsmobile agreement finally signed there were just 90 days in which to complete cars for the auto shows.

Peter Bryant created an unusual suspension system that would give the car increased ability to corner quickly. The target was a car that would exceed 1g in lateral acceleration—in layman's language, that meant a car that cornered like a race car. While the subject of a transaxle had been explored, the show car was to have a six-speed transmission mounted directly behind the engine.

The use of aluminum for the chassis was important because of the resulting weight savings, but for purposes of getting something done that had four wheels and would support an engine, a steel armature was created. This armature would cradle the engine, provide support for the transmission and differential, and hold the body and windshield in place.

It was at this point when the serious arguments began over the use of aluminum versus steel for the chassis, with Mark and Kirk on one side and Peter on the other. Peter felt that steel was a better choice, that it would be cheaper to manufacture, and that his proposed design would be just as light as aluminum. Mark and Kirk were convinced that the use of aluminum would make a lighter and stronger chassis. Carroll resolved the argument, and aluminum became the metal of choice.

The show cars were intended to showcase the styling and the size. They were also to be used to gauge public and dealer opinion. Was it a good enough concept to command about $100,000, more than twice the amount of a new Corvette, and considerably more than most Porsche models?

SNAKE BIT

In late October 1996, the project moved from the dingy surroundings of Gardena to Leonard Dodd's shop in Irvine, California. Dodd was an ex-Detroiter who moved to California, opened his own studio, and built prototype automobiles there. His firm, Automotive Engineering and Design, had the expertise necessary to take the new design and turn it into an automobile, or at least something as close as possible to the final product.

At this point, there was still no final decision as to whether the car would be a roadster or a coupe. With vacillation becoming a problem compounded by the timeframe, a removable hardtop was created. After looking at all options, Don Rager settled on the roadster design but with a convertible soft top. The original Cobras had been roadsters, and even though the most famous Shelby car ever was his Daytona Coupe, Don felt that a roadster should be the next incarnation of the best of Shelby.

Later, the convertible top proved to be one of the most difficult pieces of the car.

The issue of a removable hardtop versus a convertible top had other significance. The so-called race car for the street suffered its first compromise when the heavier and permanently attached convertible top was selected over the lighter car with a removable hard top.

While the crew worked around the clock to get the cars ready to ship to the shows, Vic Olesen and I were putting a full court press on John Rock to head us toward the right dealers before his retirement at the end of the year. We still needed to nail down the financing.

Our final plea for dealer location assistance came in a last John Rock/Oldsmobile meeting at the Valley View office of Shelby American in early November 1996, when John came to town for the SEMA show. John celebrated his last official attendance as the Oldsmobile executive by hosting a small dinner party at Ruth's Chris Steak House in Las Vegas. It was his farewell to Dennis Weglarz, Vic Ide, and others who had done so much to create Oldsmobile's success in international racing competitions.

Later in November, John held his last meeting with the Oldsmobile Board of Governance, a committee that he had formed when he came to Oldsmobile to help him steer the troubled division in the right direction. It comprised a variety of dealers of all sizes and of all locations. At this last meeting, John Rock raised the subject of the Shelby project. He said, "Many of you may have heard of a possible project with Carroll Shelby. It may or may not happen. If you are interested, give me your name and I will pass it along to them." It was hardly a ringing endorsement, but at least it was now out of the box. Indeed, many dealers had heard of the project and expressed interest. From that meeting, John sent us a list of dealers to contact.

We had prepared a brief prospectus that contained outlines of the program. It gave a brief technical description, a schedule of when it might be built, named the individuals involved, and asked for an up-front commitment of $50,000 to be part of the team and participate in the program. It also stated that there would be no more than 50 dealers involved, and that the $50,000 was a guarantee that at least five cars would be available to each participant.

The prospectus gave some target specifications for the car. It was originally to have a 95-inch wheelbase, weigh 2,400 pounds, and have 350 horsepower. The target price to the dealer was $75,000, and production was estimated to begin in October 1997.

Each dealer's $50,000 investment was to be secured by a promissory note that would pay interest at two points over prime. The notes, signed by Don Rager, were secured by the value of the prototype that was estimated to have a collector car value of $1,000,000.

The plan was to build a total of 500 cars. A limited run of 500 cars would ensure exclusivity and provide a clear beginning and end to the program. Since franchising a group of dealers to sell only 500 cars was both costly and time consuming, Rager decided that the Olds dealers would be sales agents. They would do the prospecting, and they would find the customers, but Shelby American would actually make the sales. By approaching the problem on the basis of sales agent versus dealer, there were advantages to both parties. If the Olds dealers were to be Series 1 dealers in the traditional sense, a franchise arrangement would need to be created. Since the franchise laws vary from state to state, the time and money required to establish them would break Shelby American. Instead, we created an arrangement that made Shelby American the dealer and the guardian of all finances. All car payments were to be made to and all sales contracts were to be signed by Shelby American. The Oldsmobile dealers were to sell the cars and forward the deposits to Shelby American. The dealers were to be paid their sales com-missions—$20,000 per car—when the car was actually delivered and the customer's money was safely deposited into the coffers of Shelby

American. This was good for the dealers since it placed liability for the funds with Shelby American.

Since we were fast running out of time, Vic Olesen and I divided the list in half and began making phone calls. Anyone who took the call was sent a prospectus and then received a follow-up phone call.

It was like selling a bag of smoke. There was nothing concrete, no photos of the car or the factory, just a name and the promise of something great to come.

While there was interest by some dealers, there was skepticism by many. Some were curious but had no inclination. Others had the inclination but no money. From the enthused but unable, we were given leads to other dealers. We had set a goal of no more than 50 dealers, yet it looked like 50 was going to be hard to achieve. We also promised that we would not appoint two dealers in any single market area. There was no need to set up competition in a market for a car that would see only 500 built over an 18-month period.

There were a few complications. John Rock's friend, Leo Jerome, an Oldsmobile dealer in Lansing, Michigan, was promised that he could become a dealer. However, Jerome said, "Yes," but never sent a check. He had given his word to John to be part of the program, but his heart was not in it. In the meantime, we had previously discussed the possibility with David Fischer in the affluent Detroit suburb of Troy. Fischer's Suburban Oldsmobile covered the wealthy north suburbs of Detroit, including Bloomfield Hills, where many auto executives lived. It was far better for Shelby to be represented in that part of the state than in remote Lansing.

To solve the problem, we approached Bill Fischer, David's younger brother who had an Oldsmobile dealership in Stuart, Florida. We figured that the brothers could share the opportunity. As it turned out, Leo Jerome decided against participation, and both David and Bill Fischer became authorized sales agents for the Shelby Series 1. Of the three brothers, the one with the greatest enthusiasm for the project was Rick Fischer, whose GM dealership included Pontiac, Buick, and GMC, but not Oldsmobile.

By the end of 1996, we had located 16 Oldsmobile dealers who sent in checks for $50,000 each. We had $800,000 in the bank. We still had a long way to go, but the beginnings were heartening.

There has been much talk in the auto industry about "brands" and "brand management." We showed the world the real power and true meaning of branding. We raised nearly a million dollars with nothing more than a home-produced brochure that promised to build a car that did not even exist on paper but would carry the name of Carroll Shelby.

We hitched our wagon to a star and convinced others to join the wagon train.

Chapter Four

The Invasion of the Soap Salesmen

In 1895, Ranson Eli Olds teamed up with Frank Clark to produce a self-contained gasoline-powered carriage. Two years later, Olds and a group of Lansing businessmen formed the Olds Motor Vehicle Company. Within 10 years, America was singing—literally—the praises of the Oldsmobile:

> *Come away with me Lucille in my Merry Oldsmobile*
> *Down the road of life we'll fly automo-bubbling you and I.*
> *To the church we'll swiftly steal, then our wedding bells will peal,*
> *You can go as far you like with me, in my merry Oldsmobile.*
> *In My Merry Oldsmobile*
> —Words by Vincent Bryan
> Music by John Edwards, 1905

The Oldsmobile etched its name and the name of its often-forgotten founder into the pages of automotive history. Oldsmobile is credited with the first automotive assembly line, begun in 1901. Two Oldsmobiles finished the first transcontinental race—from New York to Portland, Oregon—in 1905, taking only 45 days. In 1926, Oldsmobile was the first carmaker to sport chrome-plated trim. The 1940 models, with "Hydra-Matic Drive," were the first with fully automatic transmission.

Oldsmobile advertising slogans were legendary. "The car that has everything" (1935). "A beauty in armor" (1937). "Make a date with the 88" (1949). "Pick the Rocket to fit your pocket!" (1965). "Oldsmobiles— always a step ahead" (1971).

So much for the proud history.

John Rock's departure from Oldsmobile and GM was a watershed event for the company. It was combined with the departure of the general managers of other GM divisions, including Jim Perkins, who had been the last genuine Chevrolet general manager. It wiped the slate clean of those who believed that each GM division was an entity unto itself and that product was king.

Rock, Perkins, and others were put out to pasture because they were the antithesis of the new direction in which Ron Zarella wanted to take General Motors. These men, like others of the "old guard," fought valiantly for the brands they represented.

To Rock, the brand was *Oldsmobile*; to Perkins it was *Chevrolet*. These were not just "brands," they were car companies with traditions and distinct personalities worth fighting for and preserving. The new view was that marketers had to be dispassionate and view the cars as commodities. (Later, some pundits referred to GM as "Generic Motors.")

The new GM philosophy was that everything they sold was a brand. A Chevy Cavalier was a brand, and as a brand, it was to be more important than the name Chevrolet. Seville was a brand, as was Grand Am. To be sure, people needed to know where to buy a Cavalier, Seville, or Grand Am, but Chevrolet, Buick, Cadillac, and other divisions were now submerged and subservient in importance to the individual car names.

Not only was this confusing, but an entire new class of people joined the fray. These were brand managers who were supposed to be in charge of the care and feeding of the many brands. The idea was to go outside the auto industry to harvest these people, because the new management felt that there was too much inbreeding within the auto industry. They felt that car people didn't understand or know what consumers really wanted. They only knew about cars. The new people came from other disciplines. People from the soft drink, fast food, and other unrelated industries were now in charge of the car business, and their orders were to create marketing programs that would make prospects differentiate the many car lines that GM offered, even though many were virtually identical under the skin.

Not only did this add an additional layer of management, but this new layer also had no idea of the history of what they were selling, the needs of the dealer body, or the mechanics of the product. These brand managers were woefully underfunded to do what they should have been doing. Instead of having a mighty budget to sell Chevrolet, there were now about 20 different small pools of money to be used to sell each Chevrolet brand. The brand managers quickly learned that in order to succeed there had to be larger budgets. Since the overall pot was no bigger, the only way to obtain more money was to lobby for it, to obtain additional dollars from someone else's budget. It was a political, impractical, and unholy mess.

The blue oval that signifies Ford and the Chevrolet bow tie are arguably the best known and most widely recognized symbols in the automobile industry, perhaps in the world. Under the new system, the valued bow-tie symbol was virtually ignored.

Jim Perkins had put his career on the line to save the Corvette from elimination by corporate bean counters. Corvette was the most loved and most respected car in Chevrolet (and General Motors). Corvette represented something special. It was the best and most positive statement about Chevrolet and its heritage. Jim was a believer. He knew he was right, and history proved this so when the next-generation Corvette (the one he saved) arrived for 1997 and became a world-beater. Burying the Chevrolet bow-tie symbol in the background was an insult and downright stupid. The Corvette was an integral part of the Chevrolet name and heritage, and the bow tie was important because of the statement that it made about Chevrolet. The brand management system wanted to kill off the Corvette because it was too costly, but Perkins knew better. The bigger costs in the long run would be the loss of face, enthusiasm, and customer support.

John Rock fought to bring the Aurora and the Aurora V-8 to Oldsmobile because he needed a flagship automobile to highlight the resurgence of Oldsmobile. He wanted the Olds Aurora V-8 to be a performance symbol and to recreate the Oldsmobile image generated by the Olds Rocket 88 in the late 1940s.

But when the Aurora was announced, it carried no Oldsmobile identification. The feeling was that perhaps there was too much bad baggage associated with the Oldsmobile name, and the Aurora would constitute a fresh start. However, without any Oldsmobile identification, its luster could hardly be expected rub off on any of the other cars.

A basic rule of thumb in automobile advertising is that a minimum of $100,000,000 (yes, that's one hundred *million* dollars) worth of advertising is needed to launch a new brand. The Aurora got a fraction of that amount, and the advertising had to carry the extra burden of explaining what it really was. (There was an Oldsmobile hiding in there someplace.) People had to be educated that the Aurora was a brand-new car and that it was available at Oldsmobile dealerships even though it did not carry the Oldsmobile name.

The Aurora marketing program was a stretch of the consumer's imagination, and the Aurora, even though it was a decent car by GM standards, never achieved the breakthrough that Oldsmobile needed.

One widely held school of thought is that by utilizing strong central brands, such as Chevrolet and Oldsmobile, the communication's task is made easier and less costly. If people think highly of Chevrolet, when a Chevrolet Cavalier or Chevy truck is introduced, people will automatically ascribe the virtues of Chevrolet to it.

Under Ron Zarella's new GM system, each car was to become its own strong brand, and a brand manager was assigned a car to develop and promote. This is basically the way Procter & Gamble markets its hundreds of brands, from Ivory soap to Tide. In the case of a soap product from P&G, the price to the consumer represents about 20 percent product and 80 percent marketing expense. With automobiles, the reverse is closer to the truth. Unfortunately the advertising and marketing budgets required to support such a program and to make it effective would far exceed the reported two billion dollars that GM had already spent on advertising.

The real problem that GM faced was that they were trying to mask mediocre cars behind marketing schemes. The real "car guys" like Perkins and Rock knew this and were not easily convinced that the new way of thinking would work.

Bill Bernbach was the man whose advertising agency, Doyle, Dane, Bernbach, created the famous ad campaign for the original VW Beetle and that led the advertising revolution of the 1960s and 1970s. He claimed that people would always find a good product; it just takes time. Good advertising will kill a bad product faster than bad advertising because more people will be disappointed faster. Bad advertising will only slow the public acceptance of a good product. Good advertising only gets customers to good products faster.

Carroll Shelby said the same thing in more basic terms. "If it ain't worth a shit, people won't buy it, and it don't matter how much you spend on the ads!"

The impact of the new GM philosophy on an outside-the-box program like the Series 1 program was enormous. It just didn't fit, and it was a distraction. It wasn't a brand, and it wasn't brand marketing. And, all the "car guys" had been silenced.

This latest shift to brand management was just another of the many rethinks that had caused GM to falter. The first step backward was when the accountants took over.

A wise old sage from the GM of many years ago told me once, in dead serious tones, that it was the phenomenon of "common doors" that was killing GM. I laughed, but he went on to explain that since car doors were incredibly expensive to develop and produce, all GM cars would utilize the same basic doors. This meant the main part of the automobile, the central body, had to be the same for each car. Hence, a large part of the individual car identity was gone. The length of the wheelbase did not change the door, so the divisions now had to fight over bumpers, hoods, and trunk lids. The difference between a Pontiac and a Buick was a matter of appearance rather than fact.

That General Motors was shortsighted and cynical about the differences between the various cars became embarrassingly evident when, because of problems in an engine plant, GM had to substitute Chevrolet engines for the famous Oldsmobile Rocket engine.

Oldsmobile had risen to fame on the strength of the Rocket 88, an engine similar to one used in the Cadillac, representing the first new generation of modern V-8 engines in American cars after World War II. The Rocket 88 Oldsmobiles were fast, and people wanted them. Switching a Chevy engine for an Olds Rocket engine, especially without telling the consumer, shouldn't have been thought of, let alone executed.

When consumers discovered that they had been duped and instigated class-action suits, Pete Estes, the then-president of GM was heard to say, "What the heck, everyone knows that all our engines are the same." Needless to say, the backlash was terrible, Oldsmobile lost considerable face, and sales suffered accordingly when it was publicly and positively proved that an Oldsmobile was a glorified Chevrolet. It was also a sad commentary on the General Motors view of marketing.

The other side of the coin was that with each GM division being a fiefdom, the rivalries forced general managers into becoming political animals. The corporate good was subverted to the opportunity to obtain a better grille, more horsepower, or better seats than the sister division. Nothing outside the realm of the corporation mattered, and all the focus was inward. Ford and Chrysler were, at the time, relatively weak sisters and the fight for sales was a GM family affair.

While these internal battles were going on, the imports slipped in under the radar screen and became more than viable contenders. Their strengths did not manifest themselves until the onset of the Arab/Israeli conflict that erupted in the fall of 1973. With long lines at the gas pumps, 450-cubic-inch gas guzzlers were no longer the cars of choice for most Americans.

Hastily cobbled together vehicles, such as the Chevrolet Chevette (which was an American version of a car already being built by GM in Brazil, Germany, and England), were no competition for Toyota, Volkswagen, or Datsun (Nissan). Nor were the Dodge Omni, Plymouth Horizon, or Ford Fiesta—also amalgamations of European parts and technology—any match for the Japanese competitors.

Those small domestic cars helped stem the import tide for a short while. When the first gas crunch passed, vehicle-storage lots around Los Angeles filled up with unsold Japanese cars. When the next Middle East crisis arose in the late 1970s, the lines returned to the gas stations, and what had been surpluses of Japanese economy cars turned into shortages and a bonanza for the import car dealers.

During the time between the gas crunches and while the domestic auto industry was paying little attention, the Japanese carmakers improved the quality, performance, and content of their vehicles. Americans who had been forced to make a choice between fuel economy and quality features were so pleasantly surprised at what they found in their Toyotas that they never looked back. The domestic auto industry has been trying to catch up ever since.

The GM response to the product gap was to begin the era of brand marketing under the leadership of Ron Zarella. Brought in by ex-P&G chairman John Smale to lead this new revolution, Zarella thought that cars could be sold like soap, toasters, brooms, and other household products. A car was just another commodity, and if car designers would just listen to customers, the manufacturing might of GM could make a car for every purpose and every lifestyle.

The voice of the "car guy" was gone, and committees designed cars according to what consumer polls and focus groups indicated customers wanted. The ultimate manifestation of this philosophy was the Pontiac Aztek. It was a General Motors camel, a horse created by a committee. Not just any committee, mind you: a committee without any sense of automotive style, history, or intelligence.

It seemed to waken the giant GM to the fact that things were not right. Zarella left not too many months later. In the meantime, adventurous ideas like an Oldsmobile-powered Shelby sports car suffered. John Rock later explained how the damage was done:

"The rumors of Oldsmobile's demise had all but subsided in the press. However, we were still perceived as "your father's Oldsmobile". I thought we could reach back into Oldsmobile's rich heritage of innovation and performance to put a halo over the brand. What better way to accomplish this than a Carroll Shelby two-seater powered and sold by Oldsmobile, in the Ford Cobra tradition!

"The only problem was, I had all of Oldsmobile's new product budget committed to the yet-to-be-announced Intrigue, Alero, and "Shortstar" V-6 engine. Carroll already had the car in his head but not quite enough money in his "ass back pocket".

"My advertising manager was young with a good career in front of him. He had no appetite for an "under-the-covers" car program without corporate approval that was bound to get extensive publicity. He drifted over to my bosses' "corporate bedroom." The politics got tough and I took the "golden handshake."

"I felt that I had let Carroll down. In hindsight I should have taken the job he offered me to finish the car."

Chapter Five

The Beginning of the Snake Dance

B oth cars made it to their appointed auto shows. A Series 1 decorated with an orange paint stripe over its silver body was presented at the Oldsmobile exhibit at the Los Angeles show in January 1997, and a silver car with a blue stripe was unveiled at the Olds exhibit at the Detroit show a week later.

It was the first look for the world, and first impressions are important. If the car received lukewarm reception by the dealers, the press, and the public, the Series 1 would be a disaster.

There was a good turnout for the Los Angeles show. Two Series 1 dealers were in attendance: Kent Browning from Browning Oldsmobile in nearby Cerritos and Avery Greene from Vallejo, California. These two men, representing Southern and Northern California, had the Golden State covered.

John Rock's replacement as general manager of Oldsmobile was also present. The new man was Darwin Clark, who had worked with John at the Buick division. Darwin's most recent assignment had been director of sales and marketing for GM of Europe. He had been headquartered in Geneva, Switzerland. Unlike most automobile executives, Darwin Clark was an automobile enthusiast and had purchased a Lotus while he lived in Europe and had maintained a love affair with Corvettes over the years.

Darwin, who had a marketing as well as a sales background, was representative of the new face of GM: marketing orientation. Both Vic

Olesen and I had met Darwin on previous occasions, but neither of us, nor anyone else at Shelby, had any idea where the Shelby project stood on his list of priorities. Vic cornered Darwin for a brief moment at the show. Darwin said that he hoped the project would go forward and that if the car was to be built, Carroll Shelby was certainly the man to do it. He also indicated that Vic should feel free to call him at any time regarding the project. While the godfather of the project, John Rock, was no longer involved, his successor appeared to be inclined to make the most of the opportunity.

For all of us on the project, this was an unexpected piece of good news. At least it wasn't another blast of bad news.

Following the Los Angeles show, *AutoWeek* featured the Series 1 on the cover of the January 27, 1997, issue. The four-page story by Mark Vaughn reiterated the details, including the target price of $75,000.

As reported by Vaughn, Carroll also announced his reasons for recreating the Cobra: "'I'm tired of imitations,' he told us three years ago when he announced the car. 'Folks have put the Cobra name on all sorts of stuff over the years but none of them were *Shelby* Cobras. Before they throw the last shovel of dirt on me, I want to take one last shot at an honest-to-goodness Cobra.'"

Don Rager represented Shelby at the Detroit show. The blue-striped car made its debut. (All cars were to be painted a special silver that was created by PPG for Oldsmobile and called Centennial Silver.) To add the Shelby touch, Don wore a black cowboy hat, which resulted in a few snide comments in the formal atmosphere of the gala premiere at the Detroit show.

We learned a great deal at the shows. First, there was genuine enthusiasm for the car. While it was not radical looking, it looked fierce. It looked gutsy. Dealers who saw the car liked it, and a number of prospective dealers went away satisfied and ready to become involved.

Second, we learned some things about the car's styling. We figured out that the little winglet on the deck behind the cockpit was superfluous and gimmicky. Third, we learned something about the interior space. It was evident that there was just not enough room in the car. The way that it was set up, with a six-speed transmission located right behind the engine, was neither contemporary enough nor would it allow enough room in the interior. To enable enough room for a driver, the transmission would have to be moved to the rear as a transaxle.

The March 1997 issue of *Motor Trend* also carried a cover story about the car. The four-page editorial was accompanied by dazzling color illustrations of the car and raves about the carbon fiber body. The piece also touted the fact that it was to be the first American production car to be so equipped and pegged the price to be somewhere around $80,000 to $90,000. *Motor Trend* estimated the weight at 2,300 pounds, the horsepower at 350, and the acceleration time as 4.5 seconds from 0 to 60 miles per hour.

The rush to finish the two cars for the auto shows also created some problems. It was the youth and exuberance of Kirk and Mark versus the age and (some believed) stubbornness of Peter Bryant. There was considerable friction over the design of the car. The argument about steel versus aluminum for the chassis was only the beginning. Peter also had an imperious attitude when it came to democratic discussions about the design.

This was exacerbated when another member joined the engineering team. With dealer funding coming in and the project moving along, the team needed more engineering help. Mike Edwards, who had worked with Peter and Mark on the Vector project, was Mark Visconti's close friend, and had been the best man at Mark's wedding, also signed on.

Like Mark, Mike's credentials were impressive. He, too, had worked in aerospace and had worked on the B-2 bomber and the YF-22 fighter programs while at Northrop. He had worked with Mark on various space-related programs, and his most recent assignment was working with Swift Engineering, where he helped build the Swift Champ car that Michael Andretti drove to victory in its very first race.

It was like having three hungry young tigers who Peter had to manage if he wanted to maintain control of the project, especially since he was in Las Vegas and the car was in California. The arguments grew fierce, and Don Rager was called in all too often to mediate. At one point, Don suggested to Peter that rather than have screaming matches with Kirk, it might be best if they quietly left the room together to discuss the matter outside, beyond the earshot of the rest.

Predictably, the next meeting of the engineering staff erupted into a shouting match, in part because Mark, Kirk, and Mike had worked all through the night while Peter (for once) went home to his motel to sleep, shower, and refresh himself. This infuriated Kirk. Peter, following Don's advice, suggested "we go outside and discuss the matter." Kirk Harkins stands around 6 feet 1 inch and weighs at least 275 pounds. Peter Bryant was about 60 years old, standing at probably 5 foot 8 inches and weighing in at 180 pounds. He had no idea that he was inviting Kirk outside to duke it out. He was merely following Don's suggestion that they try not to disrupt the entire company with their yelling matches.

When Kirk strode out the door and began to roll up his sleeves while saying, "OK dude, let's get it on," Peter came to the realization of how Kirk had interpreted his request.

"Hey, mate," he said. "I want to 'discuss' it. You think I'm bloody nuts?"

Don Rager's involvement in the product decisions was not necessarily helpful. While someone had to resolve the technical and philosophical differences within the engineering group, Don was not an engineer. He held opinions, but they were not always technically supported, and some decisions that were made in the name of compromise between the two factions resulted in compromise to the car's integrity as a "race car for the street."

Now that John Rock was out of Oldsmobile officially, Carroll wanted to follow up on the offer that he made to John at the race in October. He asked that Vic Olesen arrange a lunch that he would host. Carroll wanted to meet face to face with John to see if there was any common ground or reason for further discussion. He specifically asked that Rager not be included in or advised of the meeting.

This placed Vic and me in a difficult position. After all, we were sort of working for Don Rager, who was officially in charge of the car program, but we were there at the behest of Carroll. Of course, John was our friend who we had encouraged to bring Oldsmobile's support to the project.

Despite the conflict of loyalties, we decided that we had no choice but to arrange the meeting and not tell Don. Circumstances beyond our control made the task easier. John, who still lived in Lansing, Michigan, where he was now the president of the chamber of commerce, was scheduled to speak at a banking convention in San Diego. He said that he would be happy to come to Los Angeles, meet with Carroll, and then go on to San Diego for his speech. He suggested that Vic and I accompany him, and we obliged.

The lunch meeting was interesting (as is every meeting with Carroll Shelby), but it accomplished nothing. Carroll repeated that he wanted John to take over his companies, but he was not specific in terms of the structure, the projects, the range of Shelby projects, or of the Shelby companies involved. Naturally, John was concerned about Don Rager and his position in the company. Don would not take kindly to the idea of John Rock taking over his projects or of having to report to John. In John's vision, there was nothing but trouble brewing, and Carroll had not given him any upside potential. Furthermore, while John would probably end his residence in Lansing, he was certainly not inclined to move to Las Vegas.

The first stop after lunch was at the Shelby shop in Gardena. John although he had visited the similarly drab Shelby facility in Las Vegas, was used to the might and grandeur of General Motors. He was taken aback when he walked in to the dreary presence of Shelby American in Gardena.

There, in a corner of the dirty old barnlike facility, were the beginnings of the Series 1. The entire operation appeared to be so small, so insignificant, and so impossible that John almost gasped. He had not met Mark, Mike, and Kirk before, but he did know of their credentials. That was about all that gave him some comfort.

His comment when we left was, "Jesus Christ, three kids and a Shelby 'wannabe' [Rager] in a dirty old building. Just what in hell have I done? If any dealer who put up any money for this program ever saw this, they would come after me with a club." While right then and there it looked like an impossible proposition, it was a serious project that was underway. Or so we thought.

John, Vic, and I went to San Diego and to Vic's home where we gathered John's suggestions on more dealers to contact and to discuss what might come from Carroll's interest in John. We concluded that John could not become president of Shelby American. There were too many negatives, including the fact that Don Rager was there and in command. Having John come aboard in just about any capacity would only upset Don. However, John was interested in discussing other avenues with Shelby, with Vic and myself as associates.

We took the opportunity to press John for the names of more dealers who might be willing participants in the Series 1 program. We were still a long way from our maximum goal of 50 dealers, and a recommendation from John was still a good entry to most Oldsmobile dealers.

John suggested that we fly down to his place in Mazatlán, Mexico, for a couple of days the next month (March) to explore some additional business possibilities. We agreed, and the next day Vic and I accompanied John to his rendezvous with the banking community and listened while he gave advice to the bankers about how to do better business with auto dealers. As usual, John was funny, profane, and insightful while he delivered his message.

Obviously our clandestine meeting with John Rock did not sit well with Rager. (Carroll had made sure that he learned about it.) Rager was furious. He was like a mother lion protecting her cubs. We were seen as invading his turf. The resurrected Shelby American automobile company was Don's. His accusation was that we were disloyal and that anything to do with Carroll Shelby and Shelby American had to be cleared by him. "Carroll just fucks things up," was his comment, along with words to the effect that goddamn John Rock was nothing but a pain in the ass and that he, Don Rager, would forevermore be president and in charge of Shelby American.

Clearly Don had reason for anger, but it was certainly not a situation that we could control. I would dare anyone to try to control Carroll Shelby, and it was certainly not in the province of Vic or me to try to tell Carroll who he should meet with and about what.

Eventually Don recognized this, and our relationship went back to civility. Situations like this amused Carroll. Once, at Bel-Air Country Club, Carroll was presented with a giant swizzle stick in recognition of the fact that he was a giant "shit stirrer." Carroll knew how excitable Don was, which was good enough reason to tweak him a bit just for the fun of watching him get hot.

Whether or not he did it to keep Don Rager on edge is a matter of speculation, but Carroll constantly needled Don. Carroll described Don as a man who "was always trying to put 10 pounds of shit in a 5 pound bag." Carroll never let Don go on for too long without reminding him that it was, in fact, Carroll who was in charge, and not him.

In March 1997, Vic and I flew to Mazatlán for a couple of days with John and his wife, Bonnie. Their winter retreat could best be described as a palace by the sea. While we had a grand time and enjoyed the Rocks' hospitality, we came to no conclusions about future projects. I think John's last years at GM used him up, and his job until December was to finish his term as president of the Lansing chamber of commerce.

Don Rager next asked Vic and me to help present the Series 1 at an Oldsmobile dealer meeting. Oldsmobile had planned a major "come to Jesus" revival meeting in Las Vegas in April 1997. We all agreed that it would be a great opportunity to show the car to the dealers, hopefully sign up a few more, and get feedback from them on how to best run the sales program.

The Olds dealer meeting was important. Oldsmobile, which had been teetering on the brink of disaster, had new products and programs to reveal to an anxious dealer group. As is typical with all the major car companies, the event was absolutely first class. The fabulous MGM Grand Hotel was almost exclusively turned over to Oldsmobile. There were receptions, grand feasts, product shows, and a very upbeat presentation about the future of the Oldsmobile division by Darwin Clark.

The Shelby meeting was held in a race car garage in the infield of the Las Vegas Motor Speedway. The racing atmosphere was perfect for Shelby. Shelby cars were fast, and Carroll's legend originated on racetracks. By this time, we had about 18 dealers enrolled, and they were all invited.

For me, it was the first time I would get to meet many of them face to face. I recall these people in attendance: Mike Juneau from Milwaukee; Tom Emich from Tucson; Greg Ryan from Billings, Montana; George Berejik from Needham, Massachusetts; David Butler from Troy, Michigan; Lisa Schomp from Littleton, Colorado; Walt Otto from Albany, New York; and Cliff Findlay from Las Vegas. These names may not mean much to automotive enthusiasts, but they represented our opportunity for success.

Cliff Findlay was unforgettable. He was at least 6 feet 8 inches tall, and I couldn't help but wonder how he could fit into a car. Don Rager had told him that professional athletes were a "prime marketing target," so he need not worry about the car's legroom. George Berejik was the owner of a small dealership, but he was a rabid Oldsmobile fan. Not only did he own a big collection of significant Oldsmobile cars, but he had also been involved with the Smothers Brothers when they ran Oldsmobile drag racing cars.

A chartered bus picked the group up at the MGM and transported them to the track. En route we passed the site where the new Shelby facility was to be constructed. The speedway complex was impressive, and our meeting was one of enthusiasm and optimism. The Las Vegas dealer, Cliff Findlay, reported that he had sold four cars to one man who had made a $50,000 deposit on each car.

While the group was impressed, it was agreed that the initial deposit was to be $25,000, with $10,000 paid to get on the waiting list to buy a car. The remaining $15,000 was to be paid when Shelby was ready to assign a serial number to the car. After that, initial deposits would be 25 percent. When the car was ready to go into production, there would be a second deposit of 25 percent, and the 50 percent balance, plus any applicable taxes, would be due at delivery. After the customer made the final payment, the sales commission of $20,000 would be paid back to the dealer.

The distinction between deposit percentages and the dealer's $20,000 became important later when the price was increased and the sales commission remained the same.

This meeting was also an opportunity for Don Rager to articulate the totality of the program. Don's vision was that by taking part in the program as either a dealer or a customer, you became part of the Shelby brotherhood. The Shelby American Automobile Club (SAAC) had been in existence and a driving force for over 20 years. It was SAAC and its 5,500 members that kept the Shelby legend alive with their meetings, newsletters, and club registry of owners.

Each member of the Shelby group involved with the Series 1 made a brief presentation, which was basically an introduction and a description of what each individual did so that the dealers would know where to direct questions. Tom D'Antonio remained as head of production, and Wayne Stoker was introduced as the new head of financial operations. Wayne had been a partner in the accounting firm of DeloitteTouche. Steve Temple was introduced as head of PR and marketing. Peter Bryant described the details of the car.

Steve Temple had been hired by Carroll and Don to take over the Cobra sales program and to become involved in all Shelby American marketing activities. He had been the editor of *Kit Car* magazine, one of the many Petersen publications, and as such, he knew his way around the kit car industry.

Series 1 owners would be part of the Shelby legacy, and when a buyer came to Shelby American to take delivery of his or her car, the buyer would be handled with deference and treated to a genuine Shelby experience. That experience would include a tour of the facility to watch cars being assembled and a full orientation program, where the intricacies of the car were spelled out and revealed. The capper was to be track time. First, with a professional driver to demonstrate the full capabilities of the car, and then with the pro in the passenger seat giving instruction while the customer drove some hot laps. A personalized gift for each buyer would be included. The actual delivery of the car would be made to the buyer's home in a special Shelby enclosed car hauler. Shelby would foot the bill for the buyer's airfare and a first-class hotel room as part of the deal. Davey

Hamilton, who had performed well in the CART racing series and who was now a top-rated IRL driver, had been recruited to be the resident provider of demonstration drives.

It was a great concept. One dealer, Lisa Schomp from Littleton, Colorado, expressed it best when she said, "Oh, we are selling an American automobile experience."

We also questioned the group about the number of dealers that would be appropriate for proper distribution of the car. Originally, we had thought that a maximum of 50 would be about right. Fifty dealers would enable us to cover all the major markets in the United States, and it would also provide a good geographic distribution for the purposes of service. However, the dealers strongly recommended that we limit the number to 25. Obviously, the fewer slices of the pie, the greater the opportunity for profit. Fifty dealers would have meant an average of 10 cars per dealership. With only 25, the number available for sale would go up to 20 units. Twenty cars with a gross profit of $20,000 each would be a nice reward for a $50,000 investment.

The highlight of the meeting came when Don opened a garage door and John Rock drove the first running Shelby Series 1 into the garage and into the center of the meeting. His passenger was none other than Carroll Shelby.

Once again, *AutoWeek* covered the event and also reported that Alcoa was working on a more conventional aluminum chassis to replace the tubular steel design used on the prototype.

In the months after the Los Angeles and Detroit auto shows, the engineering staff had been hard at work developing the car. In effect, they started all over again. The chassis was now aluminum, as the team had chosen, replacing the steel chassis that had been seen in L.A. and Detroit. While working with the Olds team (Gary Arentson, Dennis Weglarz, and Vic Ide), Mark Visconti, Mike Edwards, and Peter Bryant had been poring over the GM parts books to learn which standard GM parts could be adapted for Series 1 use.

The cost of engineering and manufacturing the necessary door hinges, electrical components, brackets, suspension components, and other items would have been more than prohibitive. As it was, the team had estimated the cost of materials for Bryant's original design to be about $73,000. This amount would not allow for the $100,000 retail price that Don had been aiming for. And from the very beginning, Carroll had said, "There weren't no goddamn way that you could sell a sports car for $100,000."

John Rock had once commented that nobody ever got rich by trying to build 500 sports cars for $100,000 each.

If only we had listened to him!

Peter's cost analysis was set aside. However, Don and Peter were getting to the point of zero communication, and if Peter had said the car had $2.00 worth of parts, Don would have either ignored him or yelled at him.

The planning sessions with Oldsmobile brought out more difficulties. The Shelby engineering team wanted to go with a transaxle. The Oldsmobile response was a resounding "No." The soon-to-be-introduced new Corvette was to use a transaxle, and GM's Corvette team did not want its introduction diminished by the fact that the Shelby Series 1 had it too.

GM's Corvette team had another problem with Shelby using a transaxle. Since it had taken Corvette years to develop a transaxle, there was no reason to expect that the small team from Shelby could accomplish a transaxle program in such short order.

As an alternative to finding a different transmission, Mark Visconti discussed using the new Corvette unit that was built by Borg Warner. Corvette denied the request for two reasons. The first was the need for Corvette exclusivity, and the other was that Borg-Warner did not have the ability to build enough to meet initial Corvette demands, let alone do a special project for Shelby.

At the insistence of Oldsmobile, the Shelby engineers publicly abandoned the transaxle concept but quietly kept looking for a suitable unit and working as though the transaxle was a done deal. The choice of transaxles was limited. The Shelby quantity of 500 eliminated the German Getrag unit, for it was too small an order. The only other unit that was adaptable was the ZF gearbox that had originally been used in a variety of cars, including the De Tomaso Pantera.

Because it was now only available for limited use, ZF had issued a license to Roy Butfoy of Dallas, who was building and selling the unit in limited quantities for specialty cars. The ZF, as Butfoy offered it, was a five-speed unit, and the small-displacement Oldsmobile Aurora engine required a six-speed unit to maximize the engine's performance. Butfoy agreed to re-engineer his transmission so that another gear selection could be added, and work went on clandestinely.

The suspension design caused even more friction within the engineering staff. Peter, who had created many racing cars, wanted to move ahead with his new design that he believed would give the car added cornering capacity. He was fierce in his insistence that his was the way to go.

The others felt that what Peter was proposing would be too expensive and that equal results could be obtained by using components from the Corvette and adapting them to Shelby specifications. This argument and the constant friction between Peter, as the old guard, and Mark, Mike, and Kirk, as the new, kept Don Rager busier settling family arguments than he wanted to be. Peter's expertise and knowledge were of incredible value, but the blend of personalities could not coexist under the same roof. So, Don asked Peter to turn the remainder of the design program over to Mark and his crew. It was a bitter pill for Peter to swallow, but his loyalty to Carroll and his enthusiasm for the project kept him involved in readying the car for production.

The next problem after the transaxle was the availability of suspension parts. Dealing with General Motors and the new regime was not easy. The engineers were originally told that Shelby could purchase any necessary parts from GM. This was not quite true. The new suspension was designed to use components from the C5 Corvette.

Accompanied by Gary Arntson, Mark approached Dave Hill, chief engineer for the Corvette, to discuss the use of C5 suspension components. Hill was polite but demurred because he could not release the components of the new car for use on a competing vehicle. Mark's reaction was immediate: he called Hao Wang of Multimatic with the news that C4 parts rather than C5 would be used and that he wanted the Series 1 to "stomp the shit out of the C5 in handling." Multimatic was a design and manufacturing company that specialized in race car suspension components and was a prime supplier to Shelby.

This was one case in which the Series 1 was better off with older designs. The parts that were needed were the upper and lower A-arms that constitute the independent suspension. The Series 1 was to use the same components, front and rear, modified to fit the Shelby design. As it turned out, the new C5 Corvette parts were of cast aluminum, while the older C4 parts were forged aluminum. The forged aluminum parts were superior to the new parts and were more easily adapted to the Shelby design.

In keeping with Carroll's instructions to build a "race car for the street," the front and rear suspension systems came straight from the racetrack. Instead of using a system where the coil springs were mounted on the outside of the chassis and acted directly on the lower A-arm of the suspension, the Shelby system put the springs and the shock absorbers inboard of the chassis side rails and were operated by a pushrod and rocker system.

This enabled the unsprung weight of the car to be reduced, thereby providing a greater opportunity for the shock absorbers to function predictably. Less mass to bounce gave the shock absorbers and springs a better chance of keeping the wheels firmly planted on the ground.

The chassis was designed to utilize square aluminum tubing bent into specific lengths and welded together in a jig. After the welding, the chassis was taken to be heat-treated so that all the temperatures were equalized and the chassis metal stabilized. After the heat-treating process, aluminum honeycomb panels were to be glued into place in key areas, such as the floor and bulkheads. The concept followed aircraft design principlesfor stiffness and light weight. In concept, it was ideal.

While John Rock had shuddered at the sight of "three kids" developing the car in an old garage, what was actually happening there was quite remarkable. Whether it would prove to be financially viable was, of course, another story. But the business plan, as it developed, was brilliant.

The concept was that the vendors would foot the bill for development, and they would be rewarded by the fact that Shelby would purchase their specifically designed parts at a price that would cover most, if not all, of their costs. It was just a different twist on how things are done. Normally, the manufacturer develops the parts and pieces and bids them out for production. The cost of development is carried by the manufacturer. In the end, the consumer pays because the costs are included in the purchase price. This program enabled Shelby to draw on the abilities of some of the best expertise in the automobile industry with no up-front cash. Vendors would be paid as deposits were received from customers.

Mark Visconti's wife, Lara, then came up with "Team Shelby" as the designation for the operation. It was more than the name for a team effort. It was also a way of generating enthusiasm and support. Joining Team Shelby had a lot more appeal than asking vendors to kick in on spec. Steve Temple expanded the concept to the press, and soon the team included everyone involved, and they were now wearing caps, jackets, and T-shirts emblazoned with "Team Shelby."

What a brilliant way to market the brand! Or were we beginning to think like those faceless marketing men at GM? No matter, we were marketing to raise money to bring this project back to life.

The next GM problem that arose was with the engine. The Aurora V-8 was the bastard stepchild of the Cadillac Northstar engine. It existed only because John Rock had made a strong enough case that Oldsmobile needed it to survive. GM Powertrain, the GM division responsible for the engine, had no desire for the engine to be used outside of GM. They did not want to sell it to Shelby, and they did not want to have any part in its modification.

In its base form, the Aurora V-8 developed 240 horsepower. The Olds engineers felt that 345 horsepower was obtainable with a good margin of reliability. Since GM Powertrain did not want to cooperate in the development of more horsepower, the Olds engineers, always on our side, were forced to go to outside sources for help.

In today's engines, it is far more difficult to boost horsepower than in the days when mechanics could easily modify them with basic hand tools. The Chevrolet V-8 has been changed, altered, and modified for hundreds of different applications, from cars to boats. VW engines have been used in everything from dune buggies to airplanes.

In order to be able to run on the street, today's automobile engines must pass strict EPA emissions tests. The key to certification is the engine management system that controls how much fuel is burned and when.

Any modification to the computer system changes the emissions output; hence any changes to the engine require computer modifications. General Motors guards the computer system and its data as though they were atomic secrets. No one is to fool with a GM engine. Period.

Instead of developing the engines in concert with Oldsmobile and then going to an outside source such as TAG (Technique Avant Garde), the French company that does certification and computer work for many high-performance engines, Shelby was stuck with a recalcitrant General Motors.

Whether or not this had any bearing on the horsepower problem was problematic, but it did put Shelby in the hands of and on the timetable of a reluctant partner.

In the search for development partners, Team Shelby approached Alcoa Aluminum. Alcoa had worked with Chrysler Corporation in the development of the Prowler aluminum chassis and expressed interest in the high-profile Shelby project. After meetings with Visconti, Edwards, Harkins, and

Rager, the Alcoa team took the Cad-Key files and went home to figure out how it could participate. The team's response was discouraging.

"We'll be back in 18 months with a prototype and our recommendations," was their offer. On top of that, Alcoa's cost estimate for the development work was way out of line with the Shelby budget. For a car that was originally scheduled to be on the road by the end of 1997, this was impossible, especially since Mark, Mike, and Kirk felt that they were close to having a practical design—one that had been carefully worked out on their computers and with their own practical experience as a guide.

Alcoa could not be a partner. Its corporate culture would not allow it to think like a race car builder. Each year, a racing team fields a car that is almost totally new and improved from the previous year's car. If you fall behind in race car design, you don't win races. Since judicious use of a computer can point out the trouble spots and potential weaknesses, it was apparent that the chassis development partner had to be a company with practical race car experience.

At the suggestion of the Ford Motor Company, Rager turned to Multimatic Corporation in Toronto, Canada. Multimatic had considerable expertise in racing and racing development. The English arm of the company builds shock absorbers for F1 racing teams, and in the United States it sponsored a number of racing cars. Multimatic is acknowledged for its expertise in chassis and suspension design. Since Ford owned the Cobra name and Carroll Shelby was so closely linked with Ford, Ford felt that it was in its best interest to make sure the new Shelby project succeeded. Besides, with the rift between Ford and Shelby being a thing of the past, Ford harbored the thought of possibly sponsoring future projects with Shelby.

Mark met with Hao Wang, Doug Broadhead, and Larry Holt of Multimatic, and solidified a deal in which Multimatic would provide all structural analysis and suspension development. With Multimatic's input, the 18 months that Alcoa needed turned into a few months. Multimatic had turned the solid beginnings of the Shelby engineers into an absolutely first-rate chassis.

The new chassis as created by Shelby and augmented by the finite analysis completed by Multimatic was a world-beater. It weighed just 265 pounds and had a natural frequency of 53 hertz. It also had a torsional rigidity of 12,000 ft-lbs per degree. In layman's terms, this means a chassis that will withstand just about anything before flexing. In practical terms, the chassis was half the weight of the new C5 Corvette that was a new world's high for an open car (23 hertz) and was over twice as rigid as the Corvette.

It also meant that the amount of horsepower that could be utilized in the chassis without further modification was enormous. Carroll felt that the chassis could take an engine of 1,000 horsepower without further stiffening.

The stiff chassis combined with the race car-type pushrod suspension meant that all four wheels would be squarely on the ground more often than those of just about any other car that was designed for the street. The promise of superb cornering ability was going to be achieved. Carroll's race car for the street was off to a great start.

Chapter Six

Assembling a Team of Snake Charmers

O nce Rager moved the Shelby operation to the Valley View site in 1996, work could begin on the new Cobra program. As intriguing as the new Series 1 would be, the backbone of the Shelby car company was the Cobra. It was the car that made Carroll famous and the car he loved.

D'Antonio had just about enough space to set up a production area. To produce a Cobra meant starting from scratch. Jigs had to be made for welding the frames of the 427 Cobra, which was the car selected to continue the marque. There were other Cobras more famous, such as the Daytona Coupe and the 289 FIA cars that swept American and international road racing events. But the 427 was selected because it was generally recognized as the most brutal and hair-raising of all Shelby cars.

The 427 had a monstrously big and powerful engine stuffed into as light a car as possible. It made big noise and was blindingly fast. The 427-ci Ford engine was no longer in production, but a careful search of salvage yards and the inventories of select Ford dealers could still enable a serious Cobra fan to come up with one.

Part of the program of building the new/old Cobra was that the car was to be sold without engine and transmission. The new world of emissions and safety regulations had made the sale of cars like the original Cobra nearly impossible. Adding regulatory necessities like collapsible areas in the front and rear of the car would make the old body obsolete. Steel beams in the doors and crushable areas front and rear would further bastardize the design. The Ford 427 was a gas guzzler and an emissions nightmare.

Virtually every governmental agency involved in environmental and safety issues would climb down the throat of anyone selling a car that had such total disregard for safety and emissions. However, there is a vast kit car industry that offers enthusiasts the opportunity to create or re-create famous cars. (EPA regulations do not apply to kit cars unless someone tries to sell the finished car to the general public.) Usually these are made for show and special racing events. Carroll's continuation model aimed toward this market.

The car was sold as a component package. (Carroll bristled when anyone called his Cobra a kit car.) Shelby dealers around the country located buyers, who then located appropriate engines and transmissions. After the buyer found those, he or she commissioned the dealer to build the car to order. The vehicle was licensed or not, depending on the owner's intentions. If the vehicle was for show or vintage racing only, it would not need a regular license. Unlike all the rest of the Cobra knock-offs that were being built and sold by various kit car companies, Carroll Shelby's cars were the real thing. They were built by Carroll Shelby.

Steve Temple, the recruit from *Kit Car* magazine, took the responsibility of locating dealers and developing a marketing program for the Cobra.

The Shelby car building empire was growing. While the ground had not yet been broken for the new assembly plant at the Las Vegas speedway complex, Cobras were being built, and the basic design for the Series 1 was nearing finalization.

A key component of the Series 1 was the carbon fiber body. Carbon fiber is unusual material. It is extremely lightweight and strong when the components are designed correctly. Suspension parts for Formula One race cars are made of this material. The B-2 bomber utilizes large amounts in its low-profile stealth design. Carbon fiber is also expensive.

There are a couple of key ingredients to making a carbon fiber car body. One is the ability to vacuum-bag the material after it is formed and the bonding resins are applied to the material. By vacuum-bagging the panels, the resin is drawn evenly through the carbon fiber cloth. If it is not vacuum-bagged, the permeation of the cloth by the resin can be uneven, with resulting changes in the strength of the material.

The second item is an autoclave, an oven to cure the finished product. While there were many sources for doing this work on a limited basis, there were few facilities capable of handling large automotive body parts.

Another part of the automobile that had to be created was the interior. Today's automobile interior is a complex affair. There must be seat belts, padding in just the right places, and prescribed distances between head and windshields. Creating an automobile interior is a combination of science, physics, and asthetics. Peter Bryant and Mark Visconti contacted numerous companies about creating the Series 1 interior but got little help. A quantity of 500 units was not much incentive for anyone to invest millions in development, even if the payoff was a high-visibility Shelby product.

The job of Gary Arntson, the retired Oldsmobile engineer, was to help the Shelby engineers through the maze of GM bureaucracy. He also helped locate parts, open the right doors, and guide the engineers through the production process. For his efforts, Gary was to be paid a small retainer and receive a Series 1. It was more than a good deal for Shelby American. Gary's knowledge and patience were worth every cent.

Peter had contacted Magna International about development of the interior and exterior panels. At the same time, Mark was talking to Lear Industries, but that discussion never got past the initial stages.

The next vendor they contacted was Venture Industries, another major Tier I supplier to the auto industry. Mark had been directed to its representative, Bill Young, by Bill Hoffman of Speedline of America, the company chosen to supply the Series 1 wheels.

Venture, a large plastics molding company, not only built prototype automobiles for many clients, but also specialized in interiors. In fact, Venture was one of the giants of the global auto industry. Chances are that if you own a car made just about anywhere in the world, you are surrounded by the products of Venture Industries. Venture's Bill Young came in to assess the Shelby project.

His judgment was that Venture could do the interior and that they might have an interest in producing the entire body. It was potentially an ideal match. Venture was a major auto industry supplier, had plenty of cash to invest, could do the interiors, and wanted to showcase its expanding capabilities by developing carbon fiber technology.

Rager and Visconti toured the impressive Venture facilities in Detroit and determined that the company was more than capable.

The final price of the body and interior components was resolved in a bidding war with Magna. The price started out at $31,000 per car and quickly fell to $19,000, with Venture Industries the low bidder. Venture was now a key member of Team Shelby. Of course, we had no idea of how key it would become.

By the summer of 1997, Vic Olesen and I had just about exhausted any hopes of becoming involved any further with the operation. At one point, we had thought that we could handle promotions, merchandising, and licensing for the new car. We went so far as to develop a complete proposal that would immediately begin to create shirts, caps, watches, and other products in the name of Carroll Shelby and the new car.

In one meeting, Don Rager said that he just didn't want to get into the "rag" business. For many, the rag business means vast sums of money. At every major auto race, there are trailers selling the wares of every major driver and team. Most of them carry sponsor logos. Fans pay millions to wear the insignia and signature of their favorites. A properly executed licensing program could conceivably have paid for the development of the car, or at least underwritten a major portion of the cost.

Should we have gone into rags? Absolutely!

Vic then more or less threw up his hands and decided that any further investment of his time would not be productive, especially since Don was obviously in charge of even the minutest detail. I didn't know what to do. Since I had been the one with the most contact with the dealers, I was the one getting all their phone calls about progress, about prices, about what to do with deposits, and those key matters. Without much of an option other than changing my phone number, I just remained in contact with all parties.

In the meantime, Don had been looking for someone to handle sales of the cars. It was a short-term deal since all the cars were, hopefully, to be assigned to end customers within a year. Don decided to appoint Ray Wilkings to do the job. Ray had been active in the development of the Las Vegas Motor Speedway and his time on that job was coming to an end. Ray's wife, Darlene, was working as a staff assistant at Shelby on a part-time basis. Both the Wilkings were people of consummate ability, and they were about to embark on a new venture, a speedway in Irwindale, California.

However, after looking at their plans, Don realized that they would not be around long enough to complete the job. He had not considered me for the job at this point since I lived in Manhattan Beach, California, and was not about to move to Las Vegas. However, after thinking it over, it made sense for Don to at least talk to me about participation. I flew to Las Vegas, and over lunch in August 1997, I agreed to assume the job of sales director for the Series 1. We made a deal based on a flat amount per car for each deposit. Based on the production schedule as I understood it, the job would take about a year or, at most, 18 months. I could live and work from home and would make a weekly trip to Las Vegas to stay in touch with the project and the people. There was another advantage to my Southern California residence; the Shelby development work was being done at the old facility in Gardena, California, which was about 20 minutes from my home. At last, I was able to lay to rest the issue of my financial compensation for my involvement in the project.

Also, J. D. Power & Associates, located about 30 miles north of Los Angeles, employed me on a part-time basis. While the Shelby project was an active one, it could mostly be done by telephone, and it didn't matter where the phone was located. Besides, I relished the idea of working for two members of the Automotive Hall of Fame (Shelby, of course, and Power, as one of the industry's renowned leaders in quality assessment) at the same time.

I gave Don a recap of all that had been happening on the sales side. He had been up to his neck in negotiations for the new building, in negotiations with suppliers, in securing temporary financing, and in fighting with Peter Bryant. I suggested that Don write a personal report to the dealers, giving them an update on progress. He needed to tell them how their money was to be used and, in general, let them know that he, Don Rager, the president of the company, was active and involved in the sales process.

All the dealers knew me, but few had had much contact with Don, and he would be around long after I had finished my task.

On August 9, Don sent a letter to all the dealers that not only provided an update, but also outlined specifics of the rules. It detailed the deposit process and stated that dealers were to receive a 20 percent sales commission. All checks were to be made payable to Shelby American, and the sales commission would be issued to the selling dealer from Shelby after final payment was received.

He also announced the availability of a show car that had no engine but otherwise appeared to be a genuine Series 1. It was the "pushmobile," and it made its rounds of almost all dealers.

Don further stated that production would begin in the second quarter of 1998 and that full production would be completed by 2000.

The final point in his letter reiterated that the entire project was a team effort. Indeed it was.

The statement about having production competed by 2000 was significant. All cars were to be registered as 1999 models. Environmental Protection Agency (EPA), Department of Transportation (DOT), and National Highway Traffic Safety Administration (NHTSA) requirements dictated that all the cars be built according to the safety and emissions standards of that year. The standards changed for 2000, and the cost of re-certification would be enormous. Certification tests included crash tests and numerous variations of fuel economy tests. These were serious and costly matters, and Shelby could ill afford delays that would cause the cars to miss deadlines. While the car had originally been planned to be equipped with an air bag, the inclusion of the device would have added about $1,000,000 to the development cost. This would have driven the cost of each car up by $2,000. Luckily, the federal government granted us an exemption that lasted until May 2000.

The next step in our plan was an auction. Kruse auctions were the largest auctions of collectible cars in America. Kruse held numerous auction events around the country, but the biggest one was its annual Labor Day weekend event in Auburn, Indiana. It was Don's idea to auction off the rights to buy the first Series 1 at that auction.

It was a substantial risk because if the highest bid price turned out to be less than the anticipated selling price of $99,975, there would be difficulty in attracting retail buyers for more than the auction price. On the other hand, if the car brought a premium—an amount well over the list price—the word would spread rapidly through the collector car world that the Series 1 was a good buy at $99,975.

There was another flaw in the plan. While the Kruse auctions were big, they were not the most prestigious. Most of the cars sold at Kruse auctions were more commonplace than those sold at the major auctions held in Scottsdale, Arizona, by Barrett-Jackson and at the world famous event at Monterey, California. At those events, it was quite usual to see rare and exotic cars sold for millions of dollars. The Shelby was in the wrong venue to bring big money.

However, the fact that the purchase rights to Shelby Series 1, CSX 5002 were to be sold by Kruse generated lots of publicity. CSX5002 was the first production Shelby. CSX5001 was the first car to be built and, as the first, it went to Carroll. Carroll's personal collection included the first of every Shelby car built.

As a highlight car, there was a lot of interest in the Series 1, which was ultimately purchased at the auction for $120,000 by Frank Simoni from Cleveland, Ohio. Part of the auction deal was that any amount in excess of the $99,975 selling price would be donated to the Carroll Shelby Children's Foundation. While Carroll was not generally known for altruism, the Children's Foundation was something of which he was very proud. The money he raised through the sale of personally autographed items and other Shelby memorabilia went to help needy children receive organ transplants.

While there were cars being sold for what was now determined to be a price of $99,975, development work and pricing was still going on. Mark and Kirk submitted a bill of materials and timeline to Don that indicated that the cost of materials for the car would be about $76,000, just about the same amount submitted earlier by Peter Bryant. They also submitted a request for somewhere between 7 to 10 million dollars and 24 months for development.

Don's reaction was immediate. "If that is the final number, let's just shut the doors." In my conversations with Don about the subject, he stated that it was his aim to start the sales rolling with the $99,975 price. Early buyers who were obviously going to have to wait for their cars (longer than we originally anticipated) would be rewarded for their wait by purchasing a car for considerably less than subsequent cars (in effect, an early-buyer discount). He felt that once everyone was comfortable with the final cost of the car, subsequent price increases would enable the project to ultimately come out in the black.

The next event on the schedule was another IRL race at the Las Vegas Motor Speedway, scheduled for October 11. While construction had barely started on the new assembly plant, it seemed a good time to get buyers and dealers together for a groundbreaking ceremony and to enjoy the race.

October 11 turned out to be a bitterly cold day (for Las Vegas) with winds that nearly collapsed the tent erected on the grounds adjacent to the new Shelby building. Steve Temple acted as master of ceremonies and hosted the few press people that attended. There was a brief ceremony in which Don expressed his appreciation for all the support and encouragement.

Carroll's remarks were the ones that had a lasting effect. He announced that a supercharger would be available. While that was ostensibly true, the contract with GM expressly prohibited it. Naturally, his remarks were the only ones that made the press. As expected, Oldsmobile came back to Rager for an explanation.

The supercharger was a touchy subject. (For the layman, a supercharger—sometimes called a "blower"—is a way to force a greater than normal amount of the air-fuel mixture into the engine's combustion chambers to produce more power.) Everyone at Shelby knew that it would be necessary to make the car as fast as Carroll wanted it to be. While the Olds guys gave lip service to the party line that the car would be a "fine performer" without a blower, they knew that Carroll would have a supercharger one way or another. As a matter of fact, when the chassis had been engineered and the necessary new engine mountings had been designed, the engineers had created the mounting space for a supercharger. The mounting was designed into the aluminum casting that held the front of the engine and also provided the locating points for the front suspension.

It was just a matter of time before Carroll got his supercharger and attendant horsepower boost to something in excess of 425 horsepower.

One early buyer, Calvin Folds of Georgia, was totally unprepared for the weather and showed up in a pair of sandals. Bill Fischer, the dealer from Stuart, Florida, appeared with his sales manager, Greg Irmager. The pair used the Shelby festivities as the chance to meet their customer, Calvin, and as an excuse for a Las Vegas outing. Heather McKinnis, who represented the Series 1 project at Findlay Oldsmobile in Las Vegas, was also there.

The other dealer present was Mike Deichmann from New Bern, North Carolina. I had not yet met Mike face to face, but we had begun a telephone relationship many months before.

Locating Oldsmobile dealers who understood the concept of selling an intangible sports car was difficult, and I never expected to find that ability in a small North Carolina town. My knowledge of New Bern existed only as a spot on the weather map in *USA TODAY*. And when Mike called to tell me—in the thickest drawl that I had ever heard—that he was to be my biggest and best salesperson for the Series 1, I had trouble believing it.

However, Mike was not only persistent, but he was also enthusiastic and knowledgeable. He knew about selling to the type of customer that we anticipated would buy our car. While he was a GM dealer, selling Olds, Pontiac, GMC, Buick, and Cadillac, he also dealt in the secondary market for Porsches and Ferraris. On top of that, he was on the board of directors of Fountain Boats, a company that built "sports cars" for the ocean. Mike had come late to the party. There had been no official notification of the opportunity to sell the Shelby car, and Mike had been trying to locate someone who could lead him to us. Fortunately, he finally tracked me down and officially joined Team Shelby in June. By then, we were fast friends. In any event, Mike showed up in a cab for the event wearing a T-shirt. Since there were no cabstands at the racetrack, I drove him back to town so he could buy a jacket and rent a car.

Earlier in the day, Don had arranged to use space in one of the track's garages for a Shelby display, press conference, and dealer presentation. Included in the display were new Cobras, old Cobras, Shelby Mustangs, and the Series 1, which was the subject of photo-ops. The opportunity was also used to make a videotape of the event that included interviews with all the personnel involved. This video was duplicated and sent to all the dealers. Its purpose was to assure dealers and customers alike that there was a real Shelby company and that the company was actually preparing to build cars. Our development partner representatives from Venture Industries were also participants.

Don's remarks were brief but significant in that he publicly announced that the car would be fitted with a six-speed transaxle. We were finally out of the closet with our own transaxle. Oldsmobile be damned.

Wayne Stoker, chief financial officer of Shelby American, spoke his piece about how safe the money would be with him watching over it. Steve Temple gave a little of his background as a journalist, and the newest member of the company, Bob Marsh, the new man in charge of production, explained his anticipated involvement.

I threw in my two-cents worth about sales and turned the mike over to Mark Visconti, who provided the most interesting presentation. He talked about the car and its engineering features. He concluded his remarks by getting into the Series 1, starting it up, and driving out of the building with Bill Young of Venture Industries as his passenger.

The fact that the car was there and drivable was almost a miracle. There had been two cars, but the one that had been in Detroit for the Detroit auto show had been dismantled. The other car, the orange-striped one, had been turned into a rolling lab by the engineers in Gardena, California. This was the car that now had to be put on public display as the real thing. When it came off the truck in Las Vegas, Don took one look and sank into despair. The bodywork in front was damaged, the headlamps were broken, and a hole had been cut in the body to accommodate the gas filler. It was a mess.

In a moment of inspiration, Don and Wayne sent the car to the paint shop where it was touched up as best as possible. The broken headlamps were taped with black, and in a stroke of genius, a sign was added that said, "Do not touch. EPA Test Equipment." All of a sudden, the ugly beast became a true work in progress.

Later that evening, Don Rager drove the car on a lap of the speedway prior to the start of the IRL race. That was the first public outing of the Series 1, and it was reported in a story complete with a color photo in the *AutoWeek* edition of October 27, 1997.

Since Shelby had no facilities of its own at the track, Don arranged for our few guests to be fed at Fred Treadway's hospitality tent. Treadway was an industrialist who had enough of an interest in racing to sponsor an IRL team. At one point, it was decided to link up Treadway Racing with Shelby American for promotional purposes. An alliance with Carroll Shelby would have added luster to Treadway and the IRL, and having a direct racing connection would have added to the rebirth of Shelby as a racing-oriented company. The alliance fell apart in a hurry when A. J. Foyt screamed to Goodyear that Treadway's race cars utilized Firestone tires. It took some fast and careful back peddling on Rager's part to undo the faux pas.

The IRL race was run on Saturday night, and the crowd was sparse. Even though the stands were about 95 percent empty, the track refused to provide tickets to our group, so the Shelby group was forced to watch the race from the infield fence. A Shelby motor home served as a place to keep warm. The crew from Venture Industries brought some promotional jackets. One of those found its way to Mike Edwards, who was also fooled by the Las Vegas chill and had only a T-shirt for warmth.

Steve Temple acted as host for the day. He was nervous by nature, and the frantic arrangements that were made more frantic by Don's constant changes really put him on edge. There were not enough people to handle all the hosting responsibilities, so my wife, Mary, stepped in to help. She had no instructions; she just saw what needed to be done and did it.

Steve Temple didn't know quite what to make of her efforts. He needed more of her help but did not know how to ask for it. Mary and I were sitting together in the motor home, and Steve turned to me and asked, "Would it be all right if I asked your wife to help?"

She turned to him and replied, "Hello, remember me? I'm Mary. I'm right here. If you have a question to ask me, just turn about 6 inches to your left and ask." Poor Steve. I merely said that I had no jurisdiction whatsoever over what my wife chose to do or not to do and that he would be better served by asking her directly since she was merely 3 feet away.

Oh yes, Carroll Shelby was there. Carroll's presence was a big plus for everyone, and as soon as he got anywhere near the motor home, he was besieged by well-wishers and autograph seekers. A new addition to Carroll Shelby's entourage was his new wife, Cleo, and her daughter, Simone.

Carroll's wife of 10 years, Lena, had been tragically killed the past May. While driving on a road near Carroll's Texas ranch, she had been blinded by the sun and veered off the road and into a ditch. She had not been wearing a seatbelt and had been thrown from the vehicle, suffered a broken neck, and died instantly.

Carroll's latest wife, Cleo, was an attractive English woman who had automotive credentials of her own as a racer of Minis, vintage cars, and as a manager of a dealership. Cleo and Carroll had been friends for many years, going back to the days when he was creating Cobras from English AC cars. Cleo was an ideal partner for Carroll, full of enthusiasm, support, and was obviously in love with him and his celebrity lifestyle.

In the collector car business, serial numbers mean a great deal. Having No. 001 adds value to a car. In many instances, the first car off the line is not the best. It carries all the warts, wens, and early mistakes. However, a prototype or an early number has significance to many. To own either the first of a series (or at least a very low number) or the last can add significant value.

Since there were now deposits on nearly 50 of the Series 1 cars, the question was who would get the lower numbers. The first number for sale was CSX5003. (CSX5001 was to be Carroll's, and CSX5002 had gone to Frank Simoni at the Kruse auction in Auburn, Indiana, on Labor Day.) There had to be a fair way to determine who among the early buyers was to have the rights to the first cars.

Don suggested a drawing in which every dealer would participate by the number of cars for which he or she had deposits. If a dealer had deposits on three cars, then he or she would receive three draws in the lottery. The first 10 dealers to have signed up were given the first 10 cars by lottery: the second 10 dealers, the next 10 cars. This process was repeated until the first 50 car numbers were assigned.

A local CPA firm conducted the lottery, and the findings were all recorded. Since it was a sensitive issue with many buyers, Don felt it was necessary to take the precaution of using an independent and unimpeachable third party to handle the drawing.

The first number for a car that was to be in commerce was CSX5003, and it went to Kent Browning, the Oldsmobile dealer from Cerritos, California. Kent had purchased the car for his own collection. CSX5004 was the first of four cars purchased from Findlay Oldsmobile in Henderson, Nevada, by Tom Schrade. Tom purchased four of the cars on speculation that, like all Shelby cars, they would appreciate over time.

As we neared the end of 1997, the design of the car was basically complete, but there was no way that the initial promise of beginning production by the end of the year would be met.

Recognizing it was difficult to sell the Series 1 without so much as a photo, we tried to make do with the best we had. We did not have a car to photograph since the engineers had torn down the blue-striped car, and the orange-striped car had to be used by engineering for development purposes. As an alternative to a real car, Don had a static car built. Using a fiberglass body taken from the original molds of the first two show cars and a wooden platform, an almost perfect replica of the Series 1 became available. Since it had all the cut lines that indicated where the hood and doors would be and a real interior, it could easily pass for the real thing.

The idea was that the car would be available for shows, exhibits, and for dealers to display in their showrooms. We developed a schedule whereby one dealer would pick it up from the previous dealer and so on until it made the rounds of the United States. We were even able to take photos that even the most critical eye could not discern from the real thing. Fulfilling all requests with one pushmobile was difficult at best. Each dealer had an event or a time that was best for his or her particular need. It did not always fit the needs of the other dealers. The car was fragile, had almost no ground clearance, and could not be steered. Logistical problems were exacerbated by the fact that the car was so low to the ground that a jack could not be inserted under it so that it could be towed into position.

Don compounded the scheduling problems. He volunteered use of the vehicle for every exhibition that came along. For example, a dealer in

Florida had booked the car and arranged for transportation and publicity, and Don would announce that he needed it in Las Vegas for a local event. There was nothing to do but call the offended dealer, try to calm him or her down, and reschedule the car at another time. Sometimes Shelby was forced to eat the freight expense that the dealer had incurred.

The worst conflict came in December 1998 when the car had been scheduled for Mt. Vernon, Washington, where the dealer, Greg Hinton, had planned a huge Christmas promotion. The car was to be in the center of his showroom and surrounded by Christmas stuff. The car was sent to him, installed in the middle of the display, and then Don advised me that Oldsmobile insisted on having the car for another event.

It was up to me to call Greg Hinton and tell him he had to rip up his Christmas display. Hinton had a dour personality to begin with and, after begging to become a dealer for the Series 1, had become a skeptic about the entire operation. This was the last straw for him. While I agreed with him that it was a bum deal, Don had promised the car to Oldsmobile, which knew nothing of the Hinton situation. Hinton screamed loud enough to someone at Oldsmobile so that the plans were changed and Greg Hinton's Christmas display was left intact.

The pushmobile almost caused a riot within Shelby. When the car was finished and ready to be delivered to its first destination, Steve Temple made arrangements to fly to California and take some photos. He acted very much the artist and ordered Kirk, Mike, and Mark to push the heavy beast around in the parking lot until he found what appeared to be the best location. He waited until the sun was almost gone—a moment of perfect soft light that photographers call the "magic hour"—then asked the big question: "Is there a store around here where I can get some film?"

The last big piece of Shelby publicity came in the December 1997 issue of *Motor Trend*, in which an interview with Carroll at the Monterey, California, vintage car races was published. In this article, production for the Series 1 was estimated to begin in March 1998, and the price was listed at $100,000.

There we were, raising money without a real car behind us. Were we scared? Not really. We believed so strongly in the project that we knew, some way, somehow, it would succeed. Should we have been scared? We should have been shaking like a badly tuned engine.

Chapter Seven

Parties, More Games, and Big Surprises

In January 1998 Carroll Shelby celebrated his 75th birthday. Better yet, hundreds of fans and well-wishers also celebrated. But it was more than a birthday party; it was an opportunity to spruce up the ugly old Gardena facility. There were many participants in the event, but Carroll's old friends at Goodyear came through and made the old tire warehouse look spectacular (or at least semi-respectable).

They painted the walls and hauled off the junk. Banners from numerous companies that donated time, money, or goods to be auctioned for the cause were everywhere.

The party took place on a Sunday, a day that caused Kirk Harkins considerable anguish. Kirk was a rabid Denver Broncos fan, and his beloved Broncos were playing the Steelers in the AFC playoff game. Kirk was forced to keep track of the action via a small portable TV that he had hidden in a back office.

The guest list was a who's who of the automobile world. Executives, race car drivers, mechanics, journalists, and fans all turned out to help the hero celebrate his first 75 years. Carroll's friend Bob Petersen went so far as to purchase Series 1 CSX5075 in Carroll's honor. The car was destined for the famous Petersen Automotive Museum on Wilshire Boulevard in Los Angeles.

A side benefit of the celebration was that the prototype shop where Mark, Kirk, and Mike worked was cleaned, painted, and polished and finally looked like a real shop. It didn't affect their work, for that was already top-notch, but the shop was prettier.

While the battle of the transaxle was over, there were many more obstacles to overcome in dealing with GM. Horsepower was still a major issue. While the target weight of the car looked like it would be close to its intended number, horsepower was falling behind. The engineers (and Carroll) wanted a car that would accelerate from 0 to 60 miles per hour in about 4 seconds. It needed to be competitive with the Dodge Viper and other performance vehicles.

Beating the Viper was particularly important because Carroll and Kirk had played a role in the development of that car. Chrysler president Bob Lutz, had called on Carroll when the idea of the Viper arose. Carroll and Kirk were directly involved in the creation of the initial prototype. What they submitted to Chrysler and what finally became the Viper were two different cars. Carroll preaches the gospel of light weight and the Viper was a big, heavy car. Carroll's objections to the ultimate Viper vehicle were vehement, and he resented Bob Lutz for making a mess of what he created. Therefore, the Viper would be the target. The Series 1 would be everything that the Viper was not.

In fact, when someone asked Carroll what kind of a car he was building, would it have side curtains like the original Viper, would it look like the Viper, and other related questions, Carroll's only response was, "I ain't building no goddamn Viper!"

Since none of the emissions tests, engine durability tests, or any of the necessary certification procedures could take place until the engine and transmission were finalized, the problem of horsepower was becoming a serious issue.

Carroll knew that the car had to be supercharged. He had earlier leaked his plans for a supercharger to the press probably in hopes of forcing the issue with Oldsmobile. He and the engineers—Shelby's and Oldsmobile's—guessed that by supercharging the Aurora engine, well over 400 horsepower would be available. The 400 horsepower would be enough to let the Series 1 show its tailpipes to just about anything on the road. (Carroll Shelby's gospel is horsepower, and the principal tenet of his faith is that there is *never* enough.)

However, GM Powertrain forbade the use of a supercharger. If Shelby planned to supercharge the engine, the deal was off, and by this time, there was no alternative. Powertrain objected on the grounds of reliability. Supercharging puts a strain on an engine, and Powertrain was not sure that the Aurora V-8 could take the extra strain. Also in the area of reliability was the fact that the engine was vulnerable to detonation. Just a fraction of a second of detonation could mean a hole in a piston. Since Powertrain had never supercharged the engine itself, it was loath to have an outsider do it, especially since it would not release the computer data that would enable a new computer program to be written.

Later, when Cadillac announced the Evoq, a roadster with a super-charged version of the 4.0 liter V-8, the thought came up that perhaps GM wanted to save the supercharging for its own use, and that the Shelby project would have detracted from its potential new model.

With supercharging out of the question, horsepower had to come in a normally aspirated way. Oldsmobile engineers Dennis Weglarz, Vic Ide, Arlen Fadely, and Bill Baker were all involved in creating optional engine programs that might be acceptable. Options included doing special work on the cylinder heads, making new pistons, and grinding special camshafts. All of those options were expensive, and Shelby still did not know exactly how much GM would charge for the engines. However, everyone understood that the engines would be priced at approximately the same cost as a replacement engine sold to a dealer.

The meter was running, and no combination seemed to deliver enough horsepower and reliability and still be certifiable. Don was forced to yell, "Stop! Let's go with what will work and what we can afford."

That turned out to be an engine of approximately 320 horsepower. The horsepower gains came through a simple combination of intake camshafts from the Cadillac STS, a stainless steel exhaust system with special headers, and a revised fuel-mapping program. While 320 horse-power was adequate, it was a long way from the 345 horsepower that the engineers thought would be necessary to propel the car at an acceptable rate. In fact, the Olds engine could achieve 345 horsepower, but in that par-ticular configuration, the torque that it produced would have guaranteed less acceleration.

While Don was struggling on the development and financial fronts, Darwin Clark now had a year on the job as Oldsmobile general manager. During that time, many dealers had begged him to lend major support to the Shelby program. Oldsmobile desperately needed a lift, and the

Oldsmobile dealers involved with the program could see the similarities between Oldsmobile and Dodge.

Both car companies had staid images and had suffered losses in market share. However, with the introduction of the Viper, an exciting car focused attention on a new aspect of Dodge. Olds dealers saw the Series 1 as their Viper, a sign of rejuvenation. It appeared that Darwin got the message. He was a car enthusiast and knew better than anyone of the excitement that was missing from Oldsmobile.

In February 1998, Dennis Weglarz advised Rager that Darwin wanted to meet to review the program. By this time, Don had become a bit feisty after fighting with various General Motors factions over parts, engines, and horsepower. His instincts told him that Darwin wanted to pull the plug on the whole operation. He questioned Weglarz about who would be in attendance and was told that along with Darwin Clark, Dennis Weglarz, and Vic Ide, there would be some merchandising and marketing people and a couple of lawyers.

Don smelled a trap and told Dennis that if there were lawyers present that he would not attend. His assumption was that the lawyers would be there to extricate Oldsmobile from a program that no one wanted and that had become a bastard stepchild when John Rock departed.

Part of the meeting was to be a presentation of a written report on the progress of the program. This report, written by Mark Visconti and Don, covered every aspect of the program with special emphasis on the difficulties in dealing with GM. It was basically an in-your-face document that laid all the problems of the program at GM's feet and defied Oldsmobile to break the contract. Having spent over 20 years working with General Motors, I was leery of Don's position. I asked Don if he wanted me to attend the meeting with him and Mark. I even volunteered Vic Olesen to attend since he had lots of GM experience and a brief acquaintance with Darwin Clark. Rager was adamant that he knew what he was doing and could handle the situation.

The meeting itself was cordial enough, and there were a couple of GM lawyers present. The result was merely an affirmation that, yes indeed, Oldsmobile did intend to honor all the terms of the contract. On the way back to Detroit Metro Airport for the flight back to Las Vegas, Don told Mark, "We've got 'em where we want 'em. They can't back out now!"

It was over a year later when Mark learned from a now-retired

Oldsmobile person who had been in attendance that the purpose of the meeting was to figure out how Oldsmobile could capitalize on the program. Darwin Clark had been prepared to commit millions of dollars to making the Series 1 the "Oldsmobile Viper." The lawyers were there to facilitate the operation.

Darwin had been so offended by the arrogance and general hubris that Don had served up that he never put the Olds marketing support money on the table.

Oldsmobile continued to support the program following the terms of the contract, but a full-scale marketing program was out the window. Such a boost by Oldsmobile would have put the Series 1 off the charts. Instead, the program went on with dealers and customers wondering why Oldsmobile passed up this golden opportunity to reclaim some of its sporty history.

Without the Olds support, the responsibility for merchandising materials fell back to Shelby American, and since I was the one who had the need for selling aids, it was up to me to get something done.

I found a couple of photos taken by Steve Temple. While Steve was a decent press photographer, he was not equipped to do the kind of work that would adequately represent a $100,000 car in a brochure. I took the best that he had and sent them to my friend, Jim Brophy, in Detroit. His family business, Brophy Engraving, was responsible for much of the excellent reproduction work for the Detroit auto industry. In addition to having all the latest computer capability that would turn Temple's photo into a thing of beauty, Jim's daughter, Kay, was an art director at the J. Walter Thompson advertising agency.

With one phone call, we were able to obtain a first-class brochure. Unfortunately, there was little money to pay for it, and it took months of shipping materials to dealers and charging them for it to make Brophy Engraving whole for its efforts.

One of the Oldsmobile promotional programs still available to us was the Chicago Auto Show. While the only vehicle we could send to Chicago was the pushmobile, which was then hidden in a corner of the Olds exhibit, the Series 1 was noted in the Chicago papers as being the hit of the show.

The local Chicago dealer had created a promotional piece that featured the car and distributed them at the show, but selling the car had been difficult for him. Generally, an Oldsmobile dealer was used to selling cars to older people. In most cases, the dealers did not have the customer base or the kind of salespeople who were able to sell a high-performance sports car, especially one that existed only on paper. While the lure of a $20,000 commission per car brought many dealers to the table, the reality of actually making a sale was more difficult than imagined. The chemistry had to be just right. In this case, it was not. Shortly after the show, the dealer and I agreed that his dealership and the Shelby program were not a good match.

In the case of a dealer backing out, he was entitled to have his deposit of $50,000 returned with interest. It took a monumental juggling act by Wayne Stoker to make the full refund, and a few months passed before we could make good on our word.

Over the course of the program only two dealers dropped out. The dealer in Tulsa, like the Chicago dealer, could not develop the necessary sales formula. Again, it took a few months before we could divert enough cash from the program to repay the dealer. We lost a third dealer, in Dallas, when he sold his dealership.

We had been seriously looking for someone on the East Coast who could do justice to the program and had not met with much success. Fortunately, I remembered an Oldsmobile sales department member whom I had met at the SEMA show and gave him a call. He directed me to the Oldsmobile dealer in Milford, Connecticut, who he thought might be interested. The dealership was named Connecticut's Own and held franchises for Volvo and Mazda along with Oldsmobile. The dealer turned out to be a man who was a close friend of many friends of mine.

I didn't grasp the connection at the time, but the dealer, Michael Brockman, had been a darned good professional race car driver. One of his racetrack competitors turned friend and business partner was driver/actor Paul Newman. While Connecticut's Own eventually turned the Oldsmobile franchise back to the factory, Michael Brockman remained a Series 1 dealer. Michael didn't have much time to devote to the Series 1, but having Connecticut's Own on our dealer list gave us some bragging rights.

Sales were going as well as could be expected under the circumstances. One of those circumstances included no delivery date in sight. It was obvious that costs were rising, but exactly what the final bill would be was anyone's guess. Changes in the car, delays, and a multitude of other variables made it impossible for Wayne Stoker and Don to know exactly where they stood.

But a price increase was needed. In early March 1998, another $7,000 bump was instigated, making the retail price $113,975. The sales commission remained at $20,000. In order to stimulate orders, we announced that while the price increase was effective immediately, we would allow dealers until the end of the month to order cars in their own name at the old price by making the deposits themselves. By doing this, we hoped to gain some cash flow. The incentive to the dealers was that they had the potential of picking up an additional $7,000 in commissions since we would guarantee those cars at the old price. "Price protected" was the term we used.

This was an important step for Shelby since the delays had put a serious crimp in the company's cash position. If the original plan had been followed, it would have been dealer money that funded the prototype and customer money that built the cars. Obviously, once the program lagged, all the funds that came in were "catch-up" funds. Once behind, always behind.

Only a few dealers took us up on our proposition. The most prominent participant was Mike Deichmann, our self-proclaimed top dealer. And thank goodness for his enthusiasm, since we repeated the program one more time, and he responded again. Without his participation and support, we might not have met the payroll.

Meanwhile, Mike, Mark, and Kirk were putting the finishing touches on the chassis. The April 13, 1998 issue of *AutoWeek* carried a photo of the bare chassis complete with engine. This photo generated numerous responses from those who knew what a race car chassis should look like. It made the selling job easier when prospective buyers could finally see that the Series 1 was actually in progress and was going to be a race car for the street. One man sent in a check because of that photo. A significant statement in the article came from Don Rager, who was beginning to hedge on the lack of horsepower by talking about the need for a car to be well balanced as well as have a high power-to-weight ratio.

The June 1998 issue of *Motor Trend* carried a nice color spread about the car and made special reference to the Team Shelby concept, in which major suppliers partnered with Shelby to build the car. It also referred to the support of the dealer organization that had been instrumental in the development process.

Ever the promoter, Don Rager secured a deal with *Playboy* magazine to make the Series 1 the car to be given to the Playmate of the Year for 1998, with one of the new-series Shelby Cobras the choice for 1999.

Playboy has a big circulation, and hidden among the teenagers are a few older folks who "buy it for the literature." As part of the package, *Playboy* would provide a free ad in a subsequent issue and editorial coverage in a third month.

At that time, Don was still estimating that the bare cost of the car would be in the area of $75,000, which was about equal to the cost of an ad. By his reckoning, we got three pages of exposure in *Playboy* for the cost of one car. Along with the photo shoot, the photographer would do some studio shots of the car, which was something that we desperately needed. All that was available for the photos was our pushmobile, but it served its purpose admirably. At Don's insistence, the Playmate, Karen McDougal, never posed in the buff with the car. (Family image!)

While none of the *Playboy* activity was ideal for the serious car collector, it did serve to create a buzz and to let people know that the car, while late and getting later, was eventually going to be a reality.

Don seemed to revel in the presence of the Playmates, and he was in his glory when we all attended the Playmate of the Year party at the Playboy Mansion, where he and Cleo Shelby (Carroll couldn't make it) were photographed and interviewed with the Playmate and the car. Carroll's comment was that, in the old days, he would have "had a shot at her."

The pushmobile had been on display at Browning Oldsmobile in Cerritos, California, and Mike Gilligan, manager of the dealership, transported the car to the event. He was treated to a tour of the mansion, including the area in the basement where Hefner's old silk pajamas were stored and cataloged by year and by color.

Response to the *Playboy* coverage was more favorable than I would have guessed. Apparently, people liked the literature. The downside was that the article concluded with "call Eric Davison for more information." My wife, Mary, who had to field most of the calls, did not welcome this.

Ken Gross, a highly respected journalist and curator of the Petersen Automotive Museum in Los Angeles, wrote the follow-up editorial piece. Like every automobile journalist, Ken was a good friend of Carroll. His story was full of enthusiasm, and he wrote very favorably about the potential that was evident from his ride in the first running prototype.

Mark gave Ken a ride in a car that had a fiberglass body pulled from the original mold. It had no doors; the passenger had to climb in. There were black boxes and measuring devices everywhere. But it had the feel of a race car, and Ken Gross reported it that way.

I got my first ride in the Series 1 in that same car. Mike Edwards took me through the parking lot "Grand Prix" at the Shelby Gardena facility, and it was like a kid's first trip to Disneyland. The parking lot was not large, but it was "L" shaped. At one end of the L was the loading dock for the Goodyear tire facility. The outside of the L provided a sweeping left bend with enough space to accelerate to a pace quick enough to demonstrate some serious grip.

I did not think that the parking lot was to be the course when Mark and Kirk strapped me in. The car-building trio—Mark, Kirk, and Mike—had been playing parking-lot grand prix for a week while trying to learn about the car and its capabilities. There was an unofficial competition of lap times, braking points, and so on. I was not aware of this. After a few warm-up laps, Mike cut loose. He approached the first turn with enough speed to generate some serious G-forces. After the turn, he accelerated hard towards the loading dock and what I felt would be sheer disaster.

At the last possible minute, he stabbed the brake, cranked the wheel hard to the left, and jumped back on the gas. Without so much as a mild degree of protest, the car pivoted into a full 180, and we headed back on the outside of the L. It was awesome. It seemed to me that a pretty damned good car was evolving.

Continuing the demonstration, Mike took off down Figueroa Boulevard and down some side streets. We passed a cop on our run, but he appeared to ignore us. I suspect that over the years, Shelby and Shelby people had done enough testing on those streets that the police merely shrugged off the appearance of the latest bit of automotive craziness.

While the car was getting better and better, it was still a long way from production. Dealers and customers were getting restless, and Don was getting nervous about the fact that the new building was not ready for occupancy.

Don could put a positive spin on anything and kept telling suppliers, dealers, and all of the rest of us that the timing was perfect. Once we were in the building in Las Vegas, the parts could all be shipped there and be ready for assembly. All in one fell swoop, the parts would be there, and once there was a roof, we would be off and building our Series 1. Unfortunately, that was little more than wishful thinking, and the completion of the building was way out of our hands.

The industrial park was a great concept. The racetrack would be the core, and the park would be full of the many businesses that go to support the track. Race teams could headquarter there near the track and its testing facilities. Welding shops, machine shops, parts suppliers, anything connected with racing would find a practical home.

Concurrent with the development of the park, Ralph Engelstad became involved in the development of a new casino in Biloxi, Mississippi, which diverted his cash from the industrial park until the Biloxi project was completed. In the meantime, we could not finalize the Series 1 production program, and the Cobra manufacturing program was running out of space fast.

Obviously, casinos generate vast amounts of cash. The story goes that when Richie Clyne coaxed his ex-father-in-law into financing the speedway, they were looking for a second partner. Bruton Smith, one of the best speedway owners and operators, was interested. In addition to owning speedways, Bruton Smith is the owner of Sonic Automotive, one of the most successful automotive retailing chains, and a man of considerable means.

When Bruton and Ralph met to discuss a partnership in the new track, Ralph reportedly said (remember: Las Vegas is the home of rampant speculation and exaggerated rumors), "Sounds like a good idea to me."

He then reached into his desk, pulled out his checkbook, wrote a check for $50 million, turned to Bruton, and said, "Here is my half, where is yours?"

Even pockets as deep as Ralph Engelstad's can have their limits, though, and Shelby didn't get its building until Ralph's new casino was completed. Bruton Smith ultimately purchased the Las Vegas Motor Speedway and added it to his successful string of racetracks.

Chapter Eight

A New Home and a Car that Runs to Perfection (Almost)

By late spring 1998, it appeared that Shelby would soon occupy space at the Las Vegas Motor Speedway industrial park. There was to be an office space, a showroom, an area for Cobra production, and a vast area for Series 1 production. To ease the rent problem, a section of the manufacturing space was leased to Roy Hunt's Finish Line Motorsports. Roy was one of the new Cobra dealers and needed space to do his part in the re-creation of the 427 Cobra.

In all, Don had secured well over 100,000 square feet of space and options on considerably more.

With the new space becoming available and an approaching date when the first pre-production Series 1 would be ready, we decided to have a combination event. We would have an open house and a Series 1 demonstration. All dealers and customers who had made deposits on the car would be invited to have a firsthand look at what their financial support had created.

After conferring with all parties, including the builders and the engineers, we picked July 29, 1998 as the big date.

From the standpoint of the building, we were in the hands of the construction crew. From the standpoint of the car, we were in the hands of Visconti and company and the many suppliers that were involved.

While we had achieved a running chassis in April, turning that into a car that could be demonstrated to the press by the end of July would be a major challenge. We had to build a finalized chassis and complete a respectable prototype body. This meant we needed to form a windshield, install seats, and complete an electrical system along with the wiring harness. In other words, it was a nightmare of pending activity. And the car had to be painted.

All the brackets, hinges, dials, gauges, and linkages had to be in place and working. The gearshift linkage had to be perfectly executed.

One more thing: the car had to be able to withstand the heat of a July day in Las Vegas. It was going to be rough for the next couple of months.

To complicate matters even further, arrangements had been made for *Motor Trend* to do an evaluation of the first pre-production car. On top of having to be complete and look good, the car had to perform. That would require some time to set up the chassis for maximum handling.

From April 1 to the end of July, the crew in Gardena worked almost around the clock to meet the deadline.

The stakes were enormous. Having a major failure in front of the dealers and customers was a potential disaster. Providing a car to *Motor Trend* that was a dud was another form of the same disaster, except in front of a vast readership.

Gary Martiss and Jim Seeling, representatives from Venture Industries, took up semi-permanent residence in Gardena, California, from their homes in Detroit. Hao Wang and his people from Multimatic in Toronto became familiar faces. Dave Lee, an electrical engineer from Vehicle Enhancement Systems, became like another member of the staff.

While Kirk and his crew welded a chassis together, the others were engineering and fabricating the final pieces needed to make the car perform as close as possible to a production car.

Although there were computer measurements for every dimension, the body had never actually come face to face with the chassis. Windshield glass had never been fitted. It was decided not to try to install the side or the top glass, and fitting the stereo and the air conditioning unit was also deemed unnecessary.

As the pieces began to come together in what seemed to be an agonizingly slow process, construction work on the new facility was happening at an equally agonizing pace.

While Don Rager had been involved in construction projects in Las Vegas, the track was in North Las Vegas and different rules applied. There were different people involved. Both Nevada and Las Vegas were behind the Shelby project, but the rules and political pressures did not have the same effect in North Las Vegas. Approvals were slow to happen and grudgingly given.

With two days to go before the big event, the place was beginning to take on a semblance of order. The drop ceiling was in place in the showroom; the floor was painted. Enough furniture was scattered around to give the impression of actual activity.

The shop area that Roy Hunt's Finish Line Motorsports would occupy was where a buffet luncheon was going to be served. Signs and banners from all the development partners were hung on the walls, and tables and chairs were arranged and rearranged to seat the guests.

Invitations had been sent to all dealers and everyone who had purchased a car. By this time, the count of customers was up to 125. Local Las Vegas press was invited, as were the families of the office staff who helped to serve as hosts.

We created special T-shirts with an illustration of Carroll behind the wheel and the words, "Shelby Series 1. First Drive, July 29, 1998."

As the event drew closer, it looked like a horserace between the contractors and the inspectors to see who could become the spoiler. The event was to take place on a Sunday, and on Friday the fire inspector announced that while the sprinkler system had been approved on paper, he had yet to pass judgment on the installation itself.

He was adamant, and no amount of pressure would sway him. By Friday afternoon, all of the tiles from the drop ceiling in the showroom were in piles on the floor. Don Rager was about to go into orbit.

The car was close to being ready. It had been shipped to Las Vegas where there were few tools and shop facilities, but the assembled crew had moved from Gardena to ensure that everything that could be done was done.

Unfortunately, the windshield didn't fit. It was supposed to be a Corvette windshield, but it turned out to be 2 inches too big. Attempts to trim it resulted in cracks. After about four tries and four windshields, one was fitted with only a minor crack showing.

The original schedule called for *Motor Trend* to get some driving impressions before the public event. The *Motor Trend* crew had come to Las Vegas and was standing by waiting to get some track time.

On Friday, when all seemed to be complete, Kirk drove the car over to the racetrack where it was to be tested before handing it over to the writers. As he was about to enter the track, he heard a "crack" and the car sagged. Before anyone could determine that something was wrong, Kirk used his cell phone and asked that a truck be sent out immediately and quietly. If the car had a failure, it was not going to be a public failure.

Back in the shop, someone discovered that the aluminum casting that carried the rear suspension had broken. The part had come from Multimatic in Toronto. Because there had sometimes been delays getting parts through customs, Multimatic's Hao Wang and Doug Broadhead flew back to Toronto to pick up a new piece. Before the crisis was over, Wang and Broadhead would make two round trips to Toronto within less than 30 hours. This time Kirk did not even get out of the shop before the second piece broke. An ominous "crack" as he drove over an air hose indicated that more was wrong.

Bringing in another piece from the same batch of castings would not serve any purpose. It was obviously a faulty casting. Hitting it lightly with a hammer gave off a "thud" rather than the "ping" associated with a solid casting.

The only solution was to disassemble the rear end, remove the casting and try to repair it. With Kirk welding and the others rechecking measurements, a sturdy but hasty repair was made while the gracious crew from *Motor Trend* cooled their heels, unaware of the severity of the problem.

By the big day, the car was drivable but completely untested, and it had to perform test-drives for as many of the dealers, customers, and guests who attended.

About 100 people showed up, and they all received the special "Carroll Shelby Series 1" T-shirts. It was a race to sweep away the thousands of crickets that had hopped in from the desert to view the new building before the guests arrived. The air conditioning had not yet been installed, but big fans kept the desert heat from settling on the party.

After everyone stoked up at the buffet and toured the facility, Don said a few words and Carroll blessed the event. The car was then unveiled, and everyone had a firsthand and up-close look at America's newest supercar. The highlight of the day was a lap of a closed course on the speedway in the car. With the outside temperature about 106 degrees and the track temperature about 130 degrees, it was going to be a difficult day. An air-conditioned motor home was placed trackside for those waiting for a ride, and participants were shuttled back and forth from the Shelby office to the track in air-conditioned cars provided by Findlay Oldsmobile.

To ensure that the car was demonstrated to its maximum potential and to allow Multimatic an opportunity to evaluate the suspension system, Multimatic donated the services of Scott Maxwell. Maxwell, aside from being an accomplished race car driver, was an excellent test driver, and he had the unique ability to translate the car's actions on the track into useful engineering information.

In all, on that incredibly hot day, Maxwell took about 60 eager passengers on one-mile "hot laps" in the Series 1, a car that had never been tested. Not only did Kirk's emergency repair hold up, but the car's engine temperature never exceeded 200 degrees. Both achievements were more than remarkable.

The major complaint of the day was Carroll's, who was besieged for autographs on the special T-shirts. He grouched that they were hard to write on. He was correct, but he was one proud guy when the latest Shelby lived up to its expectations.

A number of dealers attended, including the man who was now the nation's leading seller of Series 1 automobiles, Mike Deichmann. Some of Mike's customers were also on hand to ride in what they had purchased. What started out to be cocktails with his customers turned into a night of Las Vegas revelry. I learned very quickly that a hangover in the Las Vegas heat is even worse than a normal one.

Frank Simoni, who was to be the owner of CSX5002, was on hand as well. Frank was in his mid-70s and had a gruff manner. A collector and hands-on restorer, he had an appreciation of the depth of the project, yet he was skeptical of the company's ability to deliver on its promise: make cars. One fast loop of the test track with Scott Maxwell at the wheel, and Frank was calmed down. Temporarily.

Business Week sent an editor who was doing a story on exotic cars as executive toys. He was impressed with the Series 1.

The dust had hardly settled from the "first drive" affair when the car had to be turned over to *Motor Trend*. Fortunately C. Van Tune, the editor in chief, and Matt Stone, feature editor, knew enough to appreciate that they were getting their hands on a work in progress. And they were well aware of the beating that the car took over the weekend.

SNAKE BIT

Carroll Shelby's abilities with the press came in handy as *Motor Trend*, while acknowledging all of the obvious faults with the prototype, wrote of the car in the most glowing terms.

The story, which appeared in the November 1998 issue, featured a photo of Carroll in the car and a cover blurb: "Exclusive First Test: Shelby Series 1. As great as promised?" The eight-page feature led off with the statement that the Shelby Series 1 was "the most significant car Carroll has ever produced."

It covered all aspects of the development of the car down to the last detail. It was a wonderful revelation of the product. As usual, Carroll provided a salty quote or two, especially when he sent the editors off to drive the new creation.

"'Break the shit out of it,' Carroll growls. 'This is the first car,' he reminds everyone in the room. 'You're going to break every damned thing in the car in testing. You have to in order to know if it's any damned good.'"

Motor Trend did find fault with the brakes. Eventually this was traced back to an engineering selection of an inappropriate master cylinder that didn't put enough pressure on the rear brakes. Once this was corrected, the braking power became almost legendary.

Motor Trend ran some acceleration trials, and was concerned that the car did not perform to expectation. While the times were good—0 to 60 in about 5 seconds—they were not what the Olds engineers, the Shelby engineers, or the public would expect from this car. Since the car now weighed 2,650 pounds and the horsepower was 320, there was no way in which the car would perform as anticipated earlier when the weight was planned to be 2,400 pounds and the horsepower 345.

However, after discussion, *Motor Trend* agreed that the expectations of the car were better than the figures that it obtained and some negotiated numbers were determined. *Motor Trend* ascertained that a feasible 0 to 60 acceleration time was 4.4 seconds. The reasoning was that the car had not been properly set up and had come to them completely unprepared for maximum horsepower and for maximum road holding. In addition, Las Vegas is 1,700 feet above sea level, and better times would have been achieved at sea level. The final variable considered was the track temperature of well over 100 degrees (more likely 120 degrees), and heat is another big enemy of horsepower.

All in all, *Motor Trend* was generous. Let's face it: no one wanted to put a bad hit on Carroll's new car.

As part of the *Motor Trend* show, Don had arranged to have the engineering and development cars on hand. These were fiberglass-bodied cars that had been involved in development. They had been used at the GM proving grounds for a variety of purposes, but they made an impressive showing since they were full of instruments and measuring devices. They also ran well, and Don took the opportunity to run laps on the high-banked Las Vegas Motor Speedway's 1.5-mile oval track.

His propensity for exaggeration was evident when he reported that he had lapped the track at 160 miles per hour. Kirk, Mark, and Mike could hardly contain themselves. Mike estimated that if Don had even tried to run speeds in excess of 130 miles per hour, he would have been dead. As Don repeated the story for other audiences, the speed crept up to "over 165 miles per hour."

Following the *Motor Trend* program, the car (dubbed "PP1" for Pre-Production No. 1) was sent to the Venture Industries facility in Troy, Michigan. The objective was to take all the critical measurements required to make the final body molds. This assumed that the chassis was perfectly straight and that all the dimensions were exact, right to left, top to bottom, and front to back.

While hopes were high that the Series 1 was now ready for production, those hopes were quickly dashed. Using its sophisticated jigs, Venture found that the Series 1 chassis did not match front to back, side to side, or any other dimension. While the jigs that were made to hold the aluminum tubing were accurate, the heat of the welding process put incredible forces on the jigs, and the chassis were distorting.

The process for making the chassis was relatively straightforward. Pre-bent square aluminum tubing was clamped into a jig where the welders performed their task. After welding, the skeleton was sent for heat-treating. Heat-treating was necessary to equalize the temperature variances and to remove the internal stresses that had resulted from the welding. Once the chassis was heat treated, it was put back into the jig and aluminum honeycomb panels were glued into position. The honeycomb panels were, in fact, the same kind of panels that are used in commercial airliners. They are lightweight and provide incredible rigidity.

The problem turned out to be that the force of the metal as it was heated in the welding process was greater than the strength of the jig that held it. The result was a very small amount of distortion, enough to make measuring the chassis for final body molds impossible.

It was a contentious issue about who was to blame. A number of months passed before the cause was determined, a few more before a solution was agreed upon, and even more months before an absolutely true chassis could be sent back to Venture for final measurements.

While in Detroit, the car was to take part in the Woodward Avenue Dream Cruise, a spectacular street event that occurs each August in the Detroit area. The Woodward Cruise is unique. Woodward Avenue—from Ferndale to Pontiac—was the scene of street cruising, where kids in cars followed girls to drive-in restaurants and where kids with hopped-up cars would meet to arrange drag races at red lights. "Cruising Woodward" was something that just about every suburban Detroit teenager did from the 1950s to the 1970s.

Nostalgia-minded promoters turned a revival of cruising Woodward into a major event, with participation by over a million people who either cruised or watched the cruising. It is the biggest event of its kind in the world and rates high on the scale of enjoyable automotive events.

The Olds dealer in the area was Suburban Olds in Troy, and the general manager, Dave Butler, arranged for a tent to cover the Series 1 placed at a high-traffic location on Woodward near 14 Mile Road. His publicist arranged for photos in the papers and for TV and radio coverage.

Jim Seeling of Venture was like a father to the car (he had sweat through the worst of times along with the Shelby engineers) and volunteered to get the car from Venture to Woodward.

Late Friday night, just prior to the big day, the only spot on the rear suspension carrier that had not been welded and reinforced by Kirk Harkins gave way. At that hour of the night, there was no one at Venture who could re-weld the casting, so Jim, with the help of someone who happened to be at hand, saved the day with a giant C-clamp.

The Series 1 drew a big crowd at its static display. Whenever the crowd began to thin out, Jim Seeling would start the engine, and the delightful roar of the tuned exhaust would bring a new crowd.

Following the Woodward event, PP1 was shipped to Multimatic, which used a local test track and Scott Maxwell's expertise and input to establish the optimum settings for the suspension. Tuning the suspension was critical for obtaining maximum handling characteristics. The shock absorbers were adjustable so the ride could be firm or soft. The springs were adjustable so the height at which the car rode was adjustable. All the hot laps that Scott Maxwell had run at the speedway during the first-drive program came in handy, and the experts at Multimatic finished their assignment by giving Shelby an absolutely first-rate car in terms of ride, handling, and cornering capability.

The next stop, while in the eastern half of the continent, was a day at the Waterford Hills racetrack. Waterford Hills is a delightful 1.5-mile road racing facility about 40 miles from downtown Detroit.

It is a favorite place for journalists to test cars as well as the home of a road-racing club. The course is tight and twisty, and an ill-handling car's faults will be exposed quickly. The Oldsmobile engineers, knowing that the car would be in Detroit, felt that it would be a good opportunity for Oldsmobile executives to test the car. They particularly wanted Corvette engineers to attend.

The Corvette group had been especially opposed to the Shelby project. They felt that the Series 1 might take some luster from their new C5 Corvette. This had been a bone of contention when Shelby was looking for a transaxle and suspension components and the use of Corvette parts was denied.

Naturally, it was the Corvette engineers who had the most fun. They had the most insight into the nature of the project, and when they drove the car, most came away with a grin. The Corvette group provided some excellent advice and recognized immediately that the Series 1 was a race car in street clothing and the Corvette was an elegant sports car. They appealed to different kinds of buyers. Besides, with a production run of 500 units and a price tage of $100,000, the Shelby was not a competitor of any sort for the Corvette at 35,000 units and $40,000. Olds chief Darwin Clark was there and drove around at a very sedate pace considering that he was the car enthusiast. Tom Binasio of Delphi went too fast too soon and spun at the tricky Waterford Turn One.

Of all the events that took place in the Detroit area, none was more important than a dinner that took place with Bill Walker, the Venture auto enthusiast who had lobbied for the Shelby project; Chuck Hunter, president of Venture; Don Rager; and Mark Visconti. This dinner took place following the day at Waterford Hills where all involved Venture parties went to watch the proceedings. Venture's role in the program was significant, as the body and interior program was the largest single expense. The total cost per car for what Venture provided was $19,000, and by this time, Shelby was well behind the schedule that called for periodic payments.

Mark and Don knew that the dinner could not be a purely social and relaxing recap of the apparent success of the track day. Right they were, for the concept Venture wanted to put on the table was that Venture Industries was interested in buying Shelby American.

It came as a surprise to Don. He had considered selling the company but only down the road. He wanted to finish the Series 1 and then, when the car was a success, see if other projects could be sold. Selling the company might take Shelby American out of its financial bind, but it would certainly change the nature of the beast. Don's report to me about the meeting and about the prospect of working with Venture was one of great enthusiasm. Don was especially elated by the fact that Venture knew that the program could not be profitable and that the Series 1 would be finished as planned so that future projects could be developed.

The team of Mark, Mike, and Kirk was a good one. Ford had begun to make noises about building a new Shelby Cobra. Shelby's own Cobra business had potential, and there seemed to be an abundance of strategic partnerships with other auto companies or engineering projects that might carry Shelby American into the future without financial help.

On the other hand, the Series 1 was late, the costs overran expectations, paying bills was a juggling act, and there seemed to be no end in sight. Additionally, Venture knew exactly what the financial condition was. As the largest vendor, it was the most behind in receiving progress payments. Its finance guys were obviously very familiar with the Shelby situation.

The concept was intriguing. Don reported that Venture stated it wanted to become more entrepreneurial, and the example of hustle and free spirit displayed by the Shelby organization might serve as inspiration for Venture.

It was a surprising turn of events and a concept that was especially interesting to Carroll, since he owned 100 percent of the stock in Shelby American and somewhere along the line he had to be able to cash out. After turning 75, his need for a thriving business was not as great as his need for a big estate.

While that concept was left to simmer, the next event on the calendar was the 1998 SEMA exposition. Rager had reserved space to display the car and to give key suppliers the opportunity to show what part each of them had played in the development of the car.

The display itself was a patched-together conglomeration of carpets, lights, signs, and racks collected from a variety of donors. As makeshift as it was, the display drew large crowds. On display was the Series 1 from the summer's activities (PP1) along with a bare chassis that showed the wares of the key vendors from Multimatic, M.C. Gill, Goodyear, and Speedline. Multimatic was chassis refinement and suspension; M.C. Gill was the aluminum honeycomb sub-structures supplier; Goodyear supplied the tires; and Speedline provided the wheels.

The body was shown on the complete car, PP1. One of the problems with PP1 was that the body didn't fit worth a damn. It was the first prototype body, and had been a force fit in many instances. The interior was also a bastard; the instrument panel was a jury-rigged substitute for what was to come.

Fortunately, Jim Seeling and Gary Martiss were there from Venture to explain away the problems. The two did more than that; they dug in as though they were already owners, and hands-on owners at that.

During the show, I spent a lot of time with them. They were personally aware of the shortcomings of Shelby American when it came to finances and to the ability to manufacture. My question to them was, "Why in hell would Venture want to buy Shelby American? Is it going to be a tax write-off? Is it to protect its investment to date in body and interior tooling? What was it that would drive this interest in a company whose biggest asset was a 75-year-old man with transplanted body parts?"

The reply was: "I guess Larry just wants to own a car company."

"Larry" was Larry Winget, sole owner of Venture Industries, a Detroit company that he had created and grown from a small plastics molding manufacturer in Ohio to a Detroit company with a billion-plus dollars in sales to the global auto industry. It was quite an achievement—Winget was a self-made man, with one of the great private fortunes in America, and it had been reported that he had billions stashed away somewhere.

Apparently Winget had not even heard of Carroll Shelby until the Series 1 project was in the house, but Bill Walker, one of the Venture executives responsible for overseeing the program, was a Shelby fan. Along the way, Walker introduced Winget to the legend of Carroll Shelby. Walker was, himself, a car enthusiast and amateur race car driver and could see the potential of a Venture and Shelby collaboration, one that built specialty cars and utilized the global facilities of Venture Industries. Walker's tales of Carroll Shelby's exploits struck a chord with Winget. He responded to accomplishment.

While Winget did not know much about Shelby American or Carroll's exploits, he was a fanatical golfer. So much so that he purchased a large tract of land in the Detroit suburb of Rochester, where he built his own country club. The story told to me was that he took a two-year sabbatical while he designed the course itself and worked with the architect to create the clubhouse. Along the way, he decided that he wanted the golf cart paths, the driveway, and the parking lot paved with bricks. When he received the estimate for the work, he decided that the bill was too high so he purchased the company that did the work. The estimate dropped considerably after that. The only people who were allowed to become members were his friends and close personal business associates. The country club is named Wyndgate, and it is spectacular.

Wheel of Fortune had planned a week in Las Vegas, and the show's producer contacted Don Rager to see if a Series 1 could be purchased as a prize. Don agreed that he would sell them a car for $50,000, which was considerably more than the show had ever paid for a prize. While *Wheel of Fortune* has a large and devoted following, it was not necessarily the place to attract Series 1 buyers. However, featuring the car appear on the show would add credence to the fact that it really did exist and was not just another bag of smoke.

PP1 was wheeled out of the SEMA show after it closed on Thursday night and driven to Las Vegas Boulevard on the western end of town, where the famous "Welcome to Las Vegas" sign is located, and Vanna White was taped for the show's promo.

The only risk involved was the day when the car was won. If the car stayed around all week waiting to be won, there would be lots of television exposure. As luck would have it, the car went on the very first night.

After the successful presentation of the car at the first-drive program and after the highly favorable report in *Motor Trend*, expectations were high that production would soon begin.

Bob Marsh had hired some key people to train in the assembly of the car, and Brent Fenimore had come on board as the man in charge of Series 1 production. While Brent was an extremely capable young man, he exhibited some alarming characteristics. Nothing was his fault, and he was the one to remedy everyone else's faults. This manifested itself in unfortunate ways, causing conflicts within the office and with other members of the production staff.

Brent was skillful, but he was terribly young. It was too easy for him to use his authority to belittle and to browbeat his subordinates. He was also too quick to run to Bob Marsh or Don Rager with a complaint about another worker. Don referred to this as his ability to "throw people under the bus."

A particular target of his was Gary Patterson. Gary was a Shelby aficionado and high-speed fanatic. Gary owned an older Corvette and a hopped-up Mustang, both of which he drove in the same manner: foot to the floor. Gary had joined the Shelby organization as the man in charge of purchasing for the Cobra program.

Gary was personable, knowledgeable about cars and the history of Shelby, got along well with customers, and was a damned good driver. When the purchasing assignment grew and required more experience, Don moved Gary over to a merchandising assignment. Officially he was in charge of public relations, marketing, and all sales-support activities. It was a full plate, and with Don as changeable as he was, it was damned near an impossible task.

A typical situation: Gary would be given an assignment that required the help of production. Halfway into it, Don would call and tell him to drop everything and do something else. This would, of course, leave Brent holding the bag to finish the first assignment. The net result was that Brent would spend a half-day "throwing Gary under the bus" for leaving him alone to finish the original task. After a few episodes like this, Gary, with the help of Brent, gained the reputation of being the company "fuckup." Gary was sanguine about it all. "I can only do what I can do, so let 'em complain."

Another newcomer to the program was Tom Conley, who joined in November as the man in charge of Cobra sales. Steve Temple, who had spent about two years on the job, realized that he was more of a journalist than a salesperson, and a particularly tempting opportunity arose with a local magazine. That left the door open for Tom.

Tom had retired after a successful career in automobile sales. He had worked for General Motors, Toyota, and Isuzu in senior sales positions. He also had import and sports car sales experience that dated back to the infancy of the import business. Most important of all, Tom Conley was a Cobra fanatic and avid Shelby enthusiast. We had known each other for about 20 years, and the opportunity to get Tom's enthusiasm and abilities at a cut-rate price was almost too good to be true. For Tom, the chance to be involved with the resurrection of the Cobra was a once-in-a-lifetime opportunity.

At one point in his life, Tom had been the owner of a 427 Cobra. While visiting a friend in San Francisco in 1967, the car disappeared from his friend's garage. After giving up hope of ever getting the car back, Tom accepted a settlement from the insurance company. Even after the settlement, he never quit looking for CSX3113, the serial number of his car.

It was an odyssey that lasted for 30 years and almost came to a successful end when in 1989, through the help of the Shelby American Automobile Club, the FBI, and some clever sleuthing, a chassis that, in all probability, had been the underpinnings of his car was located. Using FBI techniques for exposing the original numbers that had been stamped into the chassis, all that could be verified were the letters CSX3—with the remaining digits too blurred to verify. While the history of the chassis indicated conclusively that the car had been Tom's, he didn't feel that he could ever prove the point beyond all doubt and gave up his quest.

For me, having Tom aboard was the chance to work with an old friend and to bring some serious automobile sales professionalism to the party.

I introduced him to Don Rager, and Tom was instantly part of the group. Our birthdays are a day apart. By chance, we were in Las Vegas for both of our birthdays when he officially became a member of Team Shelby.

Chapter Nine

Hidden Snake Pits

B y December 1998, we were no closer to building the Series 1 than we had been in August. Although an assembly program was in place, tooling for the chassis was not complete, and many parts were still not engineered, priced out, or produced.

Pat McClure was the new purchasing agent, the man in the middle. Production was screaming at him for parts, and he was screaming at engineering for specifications. Of course, I was screaming at everyone because customers were screaming at me.

Gary Patterson would greet me every time I came to Las Vegas by imitating one of the more rancorous customers by snarling, "Where's my car?"

Dealers were calling me at all hours of the day and night. Since most of the dealers were not involved on a daily basis, they gave their customers my name and number. This was fair and it was part of the job, but when delivery dates for the car kept falling by the wayside, some of the phone calls were rough. Since we used customer money to buy parts, make payroll, and finance other things, it was a delicate tightrope to walk when some customers asked for their money back and we had no reserves from which to give them a refund. Refunds had to come from the proceeds from new sales, and these funds had already been committed to parts, payroll, and so on.

The answer was always, "Of course you can have a refund, but this is going to be one helluva car." There were few instances in which customers actually did want their money back. Their complaint was almost always that they were not kept informed.

We had originally announced that it would be about 18 months from design to production with a build rate of about 50 per month. Normally it takes at least four years to accomplish the chore of getting to production. If someone spoke out too loudly about how long it was taking to get his or her car, I sometimes had to say, "If you are that unhappy, why don't I send your deposit back?" No matter how hard the bitching was, the offer of getting out was always met with a statement to the effect that, "Shelby needs to get off its ass and get the cars out, and I want mine soon."

Most of our buyers were very knowledgeable about the auto business and knew that it would be a miracle if the car would make it to them on the original schedule. They understood the delays and were expecting them despite our optimistic forecasts. The most critical dates were those surrounding certification. The end of 1999 had been drummed into everyone as *the* date. If all cars were not completed then, at least enough needed to have been completed to assure that the vehicles met the 1999 standards for emissions certification.

One early purchaser backed out—twice. The purchase agreement spelled out very specifically that $10,000 of the initial deposit was non-refundable. We did this for a number of reasons. First, it kept the dilettantes away, those who would make a deposit just to see what would happen down the line. We needed serious and committed buyers. Second, it was a major pain in the rear to do all the paperwork. During the early part of the program, we had few defectors and each one got their money back—somehow. It was hard work for Wayne Stoker, who had to juggle funds in the most creative ways, but we never wanted anyone to feel that Shelby American ever took advantage of anyone.

However, in one instance, we almost slammed the door. The buyer, a rabid enthusiast, heard about the car and made a deposit. Then he told his wife, and she put up a fierce line of resistance and he folded. He called and begged for the money. The heat at home was more than he could handle.

At that point in time, we had to stall him because we had no cash to return. We did assure him that he would get his money, despite the "no refund of the initial $10,000 clause." Before we could start the refund process, he called and asked if he could change his mind and could he bring his wife to the Gardena facility to see what she was depriving him of.

I arranged to meet the man and his wife. They took pictures of the prototype, he had her sit in it, the engineers walked her through all its marvels, and they left arm in arm. He called me the next day and said that the deal was on again. "Fine with me," I said.

This time the deal lasted for about two weeks. Then it was, "Please, oh, please, I have decided against the car, and I have to have the money back." This time we decided that while he would get his money back, he was going to have to sweat. Wayne dribbled the payments out to him over six months. Every month, we would get a call from him about how much he really wanted the car, but "you'll never know how much heat I am getting." Poor guy—if he had actually gotten the car he probably would have suffered even more.

By now it was evident that the most prolific salesperson for the Series 1 was Mike Deichmann. Others did well, too. Greg Ryan, a boyish dealer and entrepreneur from Billings, Montana, had gotten off to a good and enthusiastic start. He was the owner and general manager of his dealership. Mike Juneau from Milwaukee was in the same position, as was Tom Emich from Tucson. If the dealership was too big or one of a number of dealerships that was owned by the Shelby dealer/agent, then the process was either turned over to someone, such as a salesperson who was an enthusiast, or became a general assignment. In either case, the process lacked the personal touch of the dealer who had contacts in local industry and local society.

If the dealership was too small, or the dealer had too many other things to do, the Shelby project stayed on the back burner until someone walked in the door with a check in hand.

Mike Deichmann, though, stood head and shoulders above all the others. Literally. At 6 foot 4 inches, he was hard to miss. He was a former amateur boxer and had a booming, infectious laugh. He had been married twice, divorced once and separated once. That he was still married but separated gave him far more freedom than most adult males ought to have. While he was 55, he was a young 55, fit and athletic. What he liked most was "havin' fun." He also figured that real fun would be selling 100 cars, which at $20,000 commission per pop would net him a cool $2,000,000 that would enable him to retire all the debt from his dealership and go about the rest of his life with ease.

To Mike, everything could be turned into fun. "Sellin' these cars is fun." "Ah know a great bar that is really fun." Or, "Let's go have some fun," which could be anything. Hard work, if approached properly, was "fun" for Mike. For example, "I got up at five this morning to get a hold of all those folks back east, and I think I sold another car. That sure was fun!"

Being a great salesperson takes more than the ability to present the product. In the case of serious "adult toys" such as expensive sports cars, it takes the ability to respond properly and to close the deal. While the dealer group ran collective ads in the *duPont Registry* and the *Robb Report*, Mike took out full-page ads in those same publications that proclaimed, "Mike Deichmann at Trent Oldsmobile is the Number 1 Shelby Series 1 dealer in the country."

When he received a call, his staff was trained to contact him immediately, no matter what time of day or night. Mike immediately followed up with a phone call and had an information package overnighted to the prospect. He followed up the package with another phone call. With his engaging personality, he usually made a friend of the prospect. He worked hard at the program and developed a list of hundreds of prospects.

As it became apparent that Mike was just about the only dealer who could afford to make the Series 1 a full-time gig, he decided that it would be best if he set up his headquarters in Las Vegas. The best way to sell the car and to get a check was to get someone either behind the wheel or in the passenger's seat.

In February 1999, Mike took up temporary headquarters in Las Vegas. His girlfriend, Paige Livengood, came along as companion and helper. They rented an apartment and furniture, and both became fixtures at the Shelby factory at the speedway.

While we had become solid friends over the phone and in our few personal dealings, our friendship grew when he moved to Las Vegas. My schedule called for me to go to Las Vegas on Monday morning and return to California on Tuesday evening. Monday night was always dinner and "fun" with Mike and Paige that usually consisted of dinner and looking for some good jazz.

In January 1999, the big promotional effort was the Barrett-Jackson auction in Scottsdale, Arizona. The people who attend these auctions go to see and purchase exotic automobiles. They were a natural collection of Shelby prospects for both Cobras and the Series 1. Our involvement came through an association with the Titan Motorcycle Company.

Through the Titan publicist, Stefani Paulus, a meeting was set up with Don Rager to explore the possibilities of a Shelby/Titan joint promotion. What came out of that meeting was the idea for a Titan Series 1 motorcycle painted and marked the same as the Series 1. In addition, the Series 1 bike would have a serial number to match the Series 1 car. What a concept—a matched pair of automotive icons!

The Titan Motorcycle Company was the property of Frank Keery, who had never sat astride a motorcycle until a few years ago. He had spent most of his life telling his son Patrick not to ride the damned things. Both the Keerys were successful people. Frank had been an investment banker who had engineered some major resurrections of dying companies. Patrick had also been in finance and had done well as a consultant.

However, Patrick was more inclined to ride motorcycles than anything else, and the pair teamed up to create the Titan Motorcycle Company. Titan was, like many other such companies, created to ride the boom that Harley-Davidson had created for big American bikes. The Titans were special. The engines were balanced, the chassis were beautifully finished, and there were abundant amounts of billet aluminum work with surfaces polished to mirror-like perfection.

Titans were expensive, individualistic, and high quality. Don Rager thought that doing a Shelby/Titan bike would be good for the Series 1. It would also bring a nice royalty to Carroll, especially with a retail price in the neighborhood of $50,000.

Stefani Paulus had arranged a cocktail reception at Scottsdale's Montera Restaurant overlooking the vast grounds that housed the auction area and the hundreds of cars that were waiting to change hands.

The Series 1 was on display along with a Cobra and some Titan bikes. Since there was no display facility for the car on the grounds, we had assumed that the cocktail party was our exposure. However, the Series 1 caused a real stir, and Shelby was offered the chance to place the car in the midway area where parts, accessories, and other paraphernalia were displayed.

The decision to display the Series 1 within the grounds was made late at night, while Mike and I were exploring Scottsdale. I slept in (until 9:00 a.m.) and ambled over to see the cars and to watch the auction. When I arrived, I found the Series 1 on display and Gary Patterson all alone with a big crowd around the car. While I could help by getting names and providing information, it was the perfect opportunity for Deichmann.

I called and roused him from a very dismal hangover with news of the opportunity. He was there within the hour. He may have been the sickliest looking car salesperson that I had ever seen, but he was also the most hyperactive and must have passed out over 100 business cards. After two hours of torture in the boiling Arizona sun, he headed back to his hotel for a nap and some Pepto-Bismol. After that, it was back to normal—promoting like crazy for the rest of the weekend.

There were complications about that as well. Because the grounds were leased to Barrett-Jackson, any automobile sold within its territory was subject to a 10 percent commission to be paid to them. No one had bothered to explain that to any of us, including Mike. As it turned out, he had only been able to gather names for future contact. Visitors to Barrett-Jackson were far more interested in classic cars than new sports cars. The audience was right, but the timing was wrong, although Mike did gain a few prospects.

At the auction grounds the Shelby Series 1 was adjacent to an exhibit by Bruce Canepa, a well-known designer. His products were displayed under the canopy and inside his semi with an 85-foot trailer. The rig was beautiful. While there was room for only three cars, it had an area for storage of tools and equipment, a kitchen with refrigerator, microwave oven, sink, and cabinets. There was also a luxurious lounge complete with leather sofa, desk, TV, stereo, and a toilet. The way the trailer was laid out had room for one car on the level with the kitchen and two cars on the second deck. The rear tailgate turned into an elevator for raising and lowering the cars. There was even a stairway to the roof, on which there was a viewing platform. In all, it was a dazzling set up.

When Don learned that Canepa wanted to sell the rig, he grabbed Carroll and they went into a huddle to figure out how to obtain it. Shelby American needed a rig. Auctions, vintage races, and similar events were the places that potential customers for the new Cobras and the Series 1 were found. We needed a way to transport the vehicles and to display them properly. In addition, Don needed a place to do business, and Carroll needed a place to both rest and to entertain his friends and followers. Another potential use was that of delivering Series 1 cars to customers. Series 1s were sold for pickup in Las Vegas, but Shelby would arrange to deliver the car to the customer's home for a fee if he wished. While the purchase of an elaborate and expensive rig seemed questionable for a cash-poor company, we struck a deal. The "show rig," as it came to be called, became a part of the company along with the driver, Rick Johnson, and his wife, who often accompanied him to events.

While Deichmann was selling cars at an enthusiastic pace, other dealers were not, and everyone at Shelby genuinely appreciated Mike's efforts. He claimed to be an introvert and to not like being around people, yet he was one of those who ate up a room. He was like a staff member of Shelby American and demonstrated cars and conducted plant tours for customers of other dealers as well as his own customers. If this was the definition of an introvert, the world would be a jollier place with more of them.

When his customers came to see the plant, he took them on a guided tour and all those in the shop greeted him by name and helped him convince his prospect of the superiority of the vehicle. In return for all their help, Mike was likely to buy a pizza lunch or a case of beer. He believed in returning favors. He was also generous to a fault and, on many occasions, loaned money to those who couldn't make it to the next payday. If he was not going to be in town, he would hand the keys to his new Corvette to someone and ask that person to drop him off at the airport and to pick him up when he returned, which may have been a week later.

The rest of the time, when he was not selling cars, he was busy exploring Las Vegas. He was not a gambler, but he enjoyed the Las Vegas scene.

He quickly discovered Piero's Restaurant, the favorite haunt for Las Vegas' most prominent citizens. Show business people of all kinds dined there, as did politicians, sports figures, gamblers, and those on the edges of respectability.

Presiding over Piero's was the owner, Freddie Glusman. Freddie had once been married to Diahann Carroll, so he was accustomed to being around celebrities. Freddie's raspy voice and gruff demeanor belied his masterful management of the complicated restaurant. The menu was superb, but the choice of seating was a matter of incredible politics. The front room, where the bar was located, was the place to be seen. Who sat there was decided by Freddie, and there was little argument about who got the "A" room. Freddie decided. On more than one occasion, noted guests who complained about not getting preferential seating were told to sit where they were placed, shut up, or leave. Freddie was king.

Mike was an enigma. He would go into Piero's with Paige and sit at the bar and mind his own business. Usually he was dressed in Levis. He always tipped well, he took all his out-of-town guests there, and never asked for any favors. This must have been a shock to Freddie, because in Las Vegas, everyone has an angle. Mike did not, and I think that his friendly manner and lack of pretense made him, at first, a curiosity and then, once it was clear that Mike was not on the make like the rest of the town, friends with Freddie and with the rest of the Piero's regulars.

Mike was full of good old boy homilies. My favorite was "never write a check with your mouth that your ass can't cash." In all his dealings with his customers, the Shelby people, or the citizens of Las Vegas, I never heard him promise something that he did not do. On the other hand, he was particularly critical of anyone who wrote a bad "verbal" check.

In his exuberance, Don Rager promised damned near anything without thinking of the consequences. Since Mike was the man bringing in the customer deposits, he always had Don's ear. Mike explained to Don that he would be flying people to Las Vegas to drive the car and so, once he promised a ride in a car, a car always had to be available. He made it very clear that if he had a few days' notice, he would reschedule the visit.

Don would say, "Mike. You've got it. There will always be a car there for you. We have PP1 available and X1." (There were a few more pre-production cars that were built.) "Say the word and a car will be at your disposal." Naturally, the customer arrived by plane from somewhere distant, and Don had sent the cars elsewhere. Mike never went as crazy as he might have under the circumstances, but he lost faith in Don's word.

Don made certain that Mike's position as the number-one salesperson of the Series 1 was recognized. One of Mike's ads showed Mike and Rager shaking hands in the Las Vegas showroom with the Series 1 and about 50 employees in the background. Don was quoted as recognizing the leading Series 1 salesperson.

The deal with Venture Industries was still pending, but it appeared that it would actually happen. The lawyers were still chewing over the details and would continue to do so for months, but all parties were trying to learn about each other. One evening, Don asked me to have dinner with him and Gary Millard. Millard Design was an Australian company that Venture had recently purchased. Its business was automotive design, and while Gary Millard had been bought out by Venture, he was still directly involved in the company. How Millard and Shelby might work together in the future was important to Gary.

continued on page 129

The history of the Shelby Series 1 is contained in the following four magazine covers.

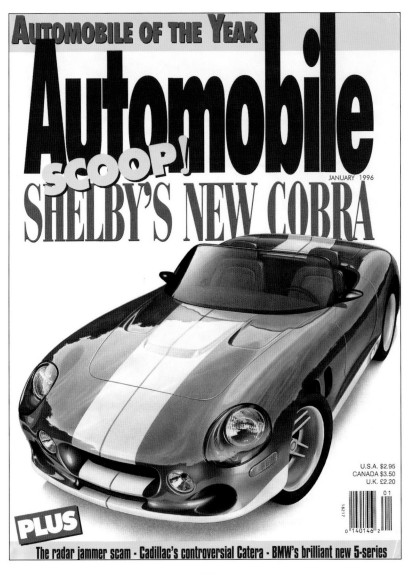

Automobile *Magazine, January 1996, announced the possible arrival of an important new Shelby sports car.*

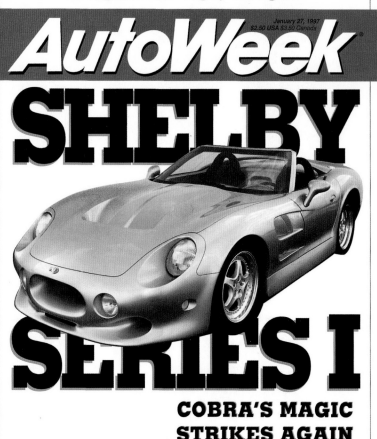

AutoWeek, *January 27, 1997 showed the first prototype and expressed hope that the car would be great.*

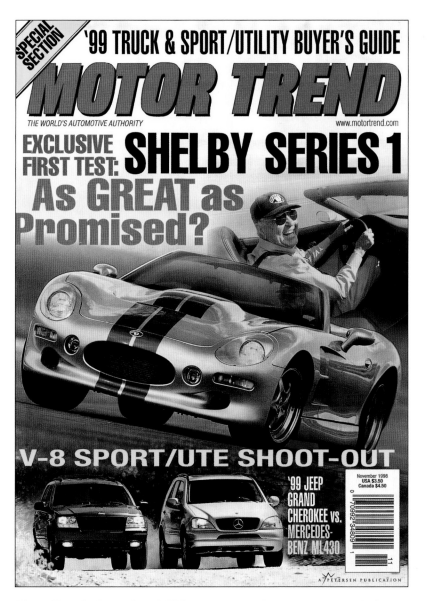

'99 TRUCK & SPORT/UTILITY BUYER'S GUIDE

MOTOR TREND

THE WORLD'S AUTOMOTIVE AUTHORITY

www.motortrend.com

EXCLUSIVE FIRST TEST: **SHELBY SERIES 1**

As GREAT as Promised?

V-8 SPORT/UTE SHOOT-OUT

'99 JEEP GRAND CHEROKEE vs. MERCEDES-BENZ ML430

November 1998
USA $3.50
Canada $4.50

0 70992 34809 1

A PETERSEN PUBLICATION

Motor Trend, *November 1998, gave an exclusive report on their first impressions of the new car. The summation: it will be great once it is developed.*

AutoWeek *in May 1999 announced that the car had potential once it was developed, and every magazine story that followed repeated that theme until production ended over two years later.*
David Newhardt

The first mockup of the Series 1 was created at the men's correctional facility at Willow Springs, Nevada. This photo was taken in November 1995 when, during the SEMA convention, the Shelby team took Oldsmobile project engineers to the prison for a preview of what was to come. From left: Neil Cummings, Tom D'Antonio, Don Rager, Carroll Shelby, Dennis Weglarz, Vic Ide, Arlen Fadely, Vic Olesen, Peter Bryant, Bob Marsh. Shelby Automobiles, Inc.

John Rock standing between Peter Bryant (left) and Don Rager (right) on the occasion of the first presentation of the prototype to the Olds dealers in Las Vegas in April 1997. Rock and Shelby drove the car into the meeting. Neither man could fit into the car. Peter Bryant

Prototype mockups were being prepared for the Detroit and Los Angeles auto shows. At this time it had not been determined whether the car would be a roadster or a coupe. This is a rare photo of the potential coupe that was looked at and discarded in favor of the roadster. Peter Bryant

The lack of sophisticated labs did not impede progress. Here is a make-do test lab on the apron to the entrance of the Shelby operation in Gardena, California, with an engine and transmission undergoing durability testing. Mike Edwards

All official testing for the various certifications was completed at the General Motors proving ground in Arizona. But the parking lot of the Shelby Goodyear Tire distributorship and the freeways of Los Angeles had enabled the engineering team to gather some instant feedback. Mike Edwards

The first public appearance of the Series 1 was at the Los Angeles Auto Show, January 1997. Carroll Shelby is shown talking to Dennis Weglarz of Oldsmobile and the author. Shelby Automobiles, Inc.

The final aluminum Series 1 chassis. The bare chassis weighed 255 pounds.

A drawing for the first and lowest serial numbers was held in late 1997. Since collectors feel that serial numbers have significance, the drawing was held under the supervision of an accounting firm and the results published. Shown here are Wayne Stoker and Eric Davison of Shelby with Gary Lein, a Las Vegas CPA enlisted to certify the proceedings. Shelby Automobiles, Inc.

The first-drive day was a big success. The car, patched up rear suspension and all, ran faultlessly. Mike Deichmann, the number one sales agent, is shown here dressed for the weather. The track temperature at the Las Vegas Motor Speedway was close to 130 degrees, and the fear was that the car would overheat. It did not. Shelby Automobiles, Inc.

The members of the staff are shown here on the big first-drive day.
From left Dave Lee, Gary Patterson, Mike Edwards, Scott Maxwell
(Multimatic), Mark Visconti, and the author.

Carroll Shelby learned long ago that his fans were what made his fame lasting. Here he is shown autographing the instrument panel of a customer's car. Carroll's signature on a car adds materially to its value. Gary Patterson

Don Rager was a tireless promoter. He is shown here addressing the press and a few owners on the occasion of the first delivery of a Series 1 to a customer. It was nearly a year later before the next cars were delivered. Shelby Automobiles, Inc.

From humble beginnings in Gardena, California, the Shelby facility became a bona fide car assembly operation in Las Vegas. Gary Patterson

SHELBY SERIES 2 COUPE
THE MILLENNIUM

One of the good projects that never came to fruition was the Millennium Cobra, a project that would have reunited Carroll Shelby and Ford. This rendering by Lavin Cuddihee was one of the contenders under consideration. The project was originally designated Shelby Series 2. Lavin Cuddihee

Frank Simoni purchased the right to own the first Shelby available at a Kruse auction in 1997. Nearly two years later he took delivery. Gary Patterson

1/4 Mile - 11.35 Seconds @ 124 Mph

Shelby Series 1

Carroll Shelby's cars are supposed to be fast, and after many frustrating setbacks Carroll was finally able to get his supercharged Series 1 completed. With Gary Patterson at the wheel, the car achieved an officially timed acceleration for a standing 1/4 mile of 11.35 seconds with a 0 to 60 time of 3.2 seconds. Shelby Automobiles, Inc.

Details of the Shelby Series 1. David Newhardt

Details of the Shelby Series 1. David Newhardt

We had dinner at the MGM Grand. The conversation took an interesting twist, and neither Don nor I understood its full implications until many months later. Millard said that one of the worst things that had happened to him was that he had sold to Venture. He said that Venture bought his company because it felt that Millard Design could add a dimension to Venture and that Millard Design could teach it some new ways of doing business. What happened, he said, was Venture took over and enforced its own culture on Millard Design. The net effect was that Millard Design was just another part of a politically driven Venture. Rather than imparting methods and knowledge to Venture, Venture smothered Millard. In effect, Venture bought a company when it could have started a company of its own for considerably less money. "Watch out" was his admonition.

A lot was happening by early 1999. Mark Visconti moved from Los Angeles to take up residence in Las Vegas, where he could be involved in engineering the details for production. Gary Martiss from Venture also set up a semi-residence in Las Vegas as its representative on the spot.

Don Rager was an indefatigable promoter. The opportunity arose to participate in a CBS ice-skating special. Entitled "Battle of the Sexes," it would feature male and female teams of Olympic skaters competing against each other. It was a hokey concept at best and was made even hokier by the fact that the honorary judges were going to be Frank Keery of Titan Motorcycles, Don Rager, and a couple of Playboy Bunnies. Not what you could call skating authorities. The big event would take place at the MGM Grand Hotel.

I shuddered when Don waxed rhapsodic about this big deal and the resulting network exposure. My experience told me that this was network "filler" and that the ratings would be extremely low. I could not see how that kind of exposure would benefit the Series 1. A quick check with one of my media-industry friends confirmed my position, and I called Don to warn him. His feeling was that it was a cheap deal and that the price justified participation. The price was the use of a car for a year by each of the winning skaters, of which there were to be three (one for each team member), and two other vehicles for show personnel. This meant that five cars (and the capital) would be tied up for over a year.

By my reckoning, the use of a $100,000 car for a year was worth about $1,500 per month, or $90,000 for the package. We could have bought commercials on the show for considerably less. Anyway, it was too late. The show went on and received horrible reviews in the Las Vegas newspaper. Within a few weeks, I began receiving calls from skaters and their managers about when they could pick up their cars which, of course, were nowhere near entering production.

Shelby also began the "delivery program," the program that was part of the purchase process. When buyers bought a car, we offered them the opportunity to fly to Las Vegas to take delivery. We put them through an "indoctrination" program and presented them with a beautiful leather jacket designed by Jeff Hamilton, the maker of jackets for celebrities. The jackets were an exclusive design of silver and black with the Series 1 emblem on the front and an image of the car embossed on the back. The jacket was numbered to match the car's serial number and autographed by Jeff Hamilton and Carroll Shelby. The jacket alone had a retail value of $1,500.

However, the pièce de résistance was a driving lesson from Davey Hamilton. Hamilton was a superb race car driver and had done well driving for A. J. Foyt in the CART series and later in the Indy Racing League. He was a Las Vegas resident and, when not in the race season, had spare time during the week. In addition to his driving skills, Davey was an outgoing man who had plenty of great racing stories to tell.

His role was to take the new owner on a road course at the speedway and demonstrate the incredible capabilities of the Series 1. After a few laps with Davey behind the wheel, they changed places and Davey acted as coach and guided the new owner for a number of laps. While, in the end, the car was overweight and underpowered, it had superb handling, and any shortcomings of sheer acceleration that the car may have had disappeared immediately when Davey Hamilton put his talents to work on a tight road course.

Everyone who rode with Davey raved about the car. Of course, that was our plan.

We offered the delivery program to buyers as a way of proving that the car was actually being built. A ride in the car was an ideal way to forestall complaints about the fact that the car was late. After the Davey Hamilton test drive, enthusiasm was rekindled, and the buyer was safe from defection for at least a few more months. Two early buyers who came out on the same day for their predelivery demonstration programs stepped out from behind the wheel and wrote checks on the spot for second cars: one to drive and one to put away for an investment.

It was a strange phenomenon. Many of our buyers were men who were too young and poor to afford Shelby Cobras in the 1960s. Now that they were older and successful, they weren't about to pass up the opportunity to own the newest Shelby. The temptation was to park it and wait for the appreciation, just like the old days. However, once behind the wheel, the temptation to drive the car was too much and the checkbooks came out.

While we had promised Davey Hamilton, he was not always available. At those times, Gary Patterson was pressed into duty. He was not a professional driver, but he was an experienced one and had accumulated enough track time to be the equal of Davey on that particular road course. This did not sit well with Brent Fenimore. "That goddamn Patterson is just running around out there fucking up the car. Every time he goes out there, I have to drop everything and fix something." Although Gary did sometimes forget to check out all systems before he did his driving duty, he was always available when Mike had a prospect that needed a convincing demonstration.

Then came a big event for Shelby, an auction and *concours d'elegance* on Amelia Island in Florida. Carroll Shelby and his Cobras were the honored marque for the event, and Carroll was the grand marshal, a significant honor in car collector circles. The new transporter was used to haul a Series 1 and a couple of Cobras to the event. The Cobra dealer from South Carolina was there with a couple of cars. Shelby American was assigned to a tent at the entrance to the golf course where the *concours* entrants were displayed. The Shelby hauler sat in a field adjacent to the lot where people parked to be shuttled to the event. In all, the Shelby presence was dominating.

Mike Deichmann and Paige were there, and this time we were joined by Greg Ryan from Billings, Montana, and Bill Walker from Venture Industries was present to learn what one of our premiere events was all about.

The Amelia Island event was a big success for Shelby and a lot of fun for those of us who attended, yet it was almost a financial disaster. Don promised the last five Series 1s to Dean Kruse of Kruse auctions. While the sale of five cars could be considered a success, Don promised them to Kruse for $100,000 each. This was downright scary since the last of a series of anything collectible usually brings a premium. The last five Series 1s would certainly bring a premium, but the premium would go to

SNAKE BIT

Dean Kruse and not the cash-poor Shelby American. Luckily, Don never started any paperwork and never asked me to send contracts to Kruse, so I just let it pass. I had already turned down premiums for the last car and saw no justification for giving the money to someone else.

Chapter Ten

Dollars, Cents, and Finger Pointing

Building a car from the ground up is a far more complicated task than most people can imagine. It takes an army of engineers to create the next Chevrolet, and the crew members that are employed to develop a new race car are usually numerous. Shelby American was creating a unique sports car with a mere skeleton of a crew.

Since production was screaming that not all parts were engineered, and purchasing was screaming that they couldn't get prices and delivery dates until the parts were designed and spec'd out, there were a lot of fingers pointing at the few engineers. They desperately needed help.

While the deal with Venture was still pending and small amounts of cash were coming in from customer deposits, the program could not begin to right itself until cars were delivered and the final 50-percent payments came in. Wayne and Don were doing their damnedest to keep afloat and to keep the credit line active, but the fact of the matter was that engineering help was needed.

Mark wanted five more engineers and additional computers. Is there anyone who does not appreciate the value of computers, especially in this highly technical field? A smart engineer with computer skills is the equivalent of a couple of engineers and an army of draftsmen. A computer is cheaper than a good drafting table, and a drafting table requires more hours of labor from the engineers.

Unfortunately, Don was one of those rare individuals who did not appreciate the value of computers. Mark presented his needs at a regular Monday morning staff meeting. Usually the meetings started at 10 a.m. so Tom Conley and I could catch an early flight from Los Angeles and attend. While the concept of a staff meeting was good in that everyone had a chance to find out what was going on, what was needed, and to agree on critical dates, they quickly deteriorated into monologues by Don.

On this particular Monday morning, Don took off on computers. "Computers are both running and ruining our lives. We are dependent on the damned things. They are expensive," and on and on for at least 20 minutes. Mark, who was taking heat from everyone about missing details from engineering, could not get a word in edgewise.

The upshot was that Mark got a tentative OK to hire a couple of apprentices and buy one more computer. Rather than scream to the heavens and cover his ass by documenting his obvious inability to get the job done without the tools in hand, Mark simply dug in and worked as many hours as he could. In the end it really didn't matter, because body parts and tops were delayed far more than his engineering drawings and specs were.

The reality of all the delays was that the engineering crew was short-handed, and the development timetable was condensed. The request for five or more full-time engineers turned into an intern program with Loyola University, and the 24-month schedule became 12 months. That anything was ever built and ever actually ran was a miracle.

While Don got high marks for his aggressive development of the program, he was an incessant meddler when it came to engineering the car. Like many people who get involved in projects of this nature, they do it for the love of the car, for the thrill of creation. It is sometimes difficult for them to realize that their expertise is not in the physical creation, but in the vision to move ahead in the first place.

One particular problem was the transmission. Converting the five-speed to a six-speed was one difficulty; creating the linkage was another. And there were even more problems because 500 transmissions were more than had been created for anyone before. Usually purchases of ZF transmissions were in amounts of 10 or 20 units. Five hundred was considered mass production.

The first units were prototypes, and they had been installed in the first prototype cars. From these first applications, it would be possible to see what changes and revisions were necessary for the production run. As it turned out, none of the first units were the same. Shifting was different for each, and there were problems in selecting reverse gear and in locating the next gear in the shift sequence.

Don panicked. For him it was a catastrophe. The engineers merely shrugged, noted the problem, and moved on. This infuriated Don. Each night he took a car home, and each morning he stormed into Mark's office with the latest shortcoming of the Series 1. Mark had to drop everything and try to respond. Don sent people to Roy Butfoy's factory in Texas to try to sort things out. He had Davey Hamilton drive the car and give his impressions, and then determined that Davey's race engineer could help. All the while, Kirk Harkins just smirked. He knew that all they needed was time; the gearbox was sound and the adjustments that he and the engineers had planned would take care of the problems. While the transmission problem was vexing, it was more a matter of becoming accustomed to the shift pattern than anything else.

Another important subject was that of crash testing the car. Originally the engineers determined that it was not necessary and, indeed, the concept of crashing two hand-built sports cars was a little unnerving. Crash testing is not required if enough supportive data that simulates what would happen in a crash can be shown. The downside to this is, if something happens that was not indicated in the engineering data, then there can be big trouble—as in major liability and insurance woes.

Therefore, it seemed prudent, though expensive, to crash two cars, one car for front and rear impact and the other for side impact. Our Oldsmobile friends were skeptical about how many cars it would take to get through the tests. We were told that GM could crash up to 25 cars in order to get satisfactory results.

The cars to be crashed had to be exactly as they were to be delivered to the public. This meant a full-court press by the engineers who had to hand-build some parts to ensure that all the components were exact since many of them were not yet in production. We were nervous. All the engineering data indicated that the car was solid and crashworthy, but a 30-mile-per-hour front impact can upset a lot of data.

In May 1999, we delivered the two cars to the government-approved facility near Riverside, California, and the smashing took place. The results were heartening. Mark reported, "The cars did great but the passenger died." The only failure was in the seatbelt recoil system, which was easily replaced with by a less-complicated and more reliable system. After a 30-mile-per-hour frontal impact, the front wheels would still roll, which is extremely rare.

After the rear impact, the car is put on a rotisserie and turned upside down. If more than a minimal amount of fuel leaks out, the critical fuel system fails the test. Almost no fuel escaped from the inverted Series 1. The side impact tests are equally severe, but the strength of the chassis was evident when it was determined that the driver and passengers would have suffered only bruises when being T-boned. Fortunately, all the time devoted to designing and engineering the safety systems in the car was well spent.

The seatbelt system was another example of our government at work. Race cars use a five-point system: five anchor points are used to attach the belts that keep the driver in place. There are two lap belt anchors, two for the shoulder harness, and one for a belt that goes over the crotch to the floor in front of the driver. That belt keeps the driver from sliding forward and down (submerging). It is about as good a personal safety system as you can get. The intention was to offer a four or five point system on the Series 1.

The Department of Transportation and the National Highway Traffic Safety Administration rejected our application to install these systems because the four- and five-point systems had not been government tested. (They had only been tested by *thousands* of race car drivers and fighter pilots.) So much for common sense.

Shelby American was a lean operation. Just about everyone did double and triple duty. Don was a whirling dervish, a man who seemed to enjoy punishing himself. He claimed that he flew red-eye flights to save money, but it seemed more like his hair shirt; it gave him bragging rights for being the most penurious when it came to creature comforts. On the other hand, he was always careful to show at least a veneer of opulence under the right circumstances. His office and the accouterment of position were first-rate. His office was filled with mementos and photos of himself and Carroll and with various other celebrities of politics, racing, and show business.

With Don's health being what it was, it seemed foolish that he would punish himself with late-night flights, missed meals, and limited sleep. Typically Don's lunch was a cookie from the vending machine and a Diet

Pepsi. For a diabetic with a transplanted liver—with skin cancer to boot—it seemed like a one-way ticket to a hospital. Or worse.

But that was Don's style and he was not about to change. He claimed that he would die happy if he died in his office doing what he liked best. With his life a dither, there had to be someone who could keep track of things such as meetings, deadlines, and schedules.

At first, when the operation was starting out, Don's wife-to-be, Nancy Ekezian, came in to the office half-days to cover the phones, type, and help out as needed. For the second half of the day, it was Darlene Wilkings. As needs expanded, it would have been ideal to have more of Darlene's time. She was an accomplished businesswoman and knew her way around the performance and racing industries. Unfortunately, she and her husband departed to Irwindale, California, to create the new speedway there.

To replace her but on a full-time basis, Don hired Carlotta. Carlotta was a New York-raised woman who had no trouble taking charge. She had a great sense of humor and seemed willing to step in and make things happen. However, as is the case with many take-charge people, only one person can be in charge. After a few months and many skirmishes with Don, she was history.

Next into the seat was Jane. Jane was an attractive blonde who had once been a model, was married to a retired air force colonel, and had been a practicing psychologist. (I often thought that she came to Shelby to gather a case-study portfolio.) She was bright and cheerful and seemed to jump at the opportunity to take responsibility.

Ask her for something, and the reply was always, "You've got it!" At Carroll's insistence (he liked blondes), Jane was named managing director of operations. In effect, she was a secretary, but Carroll felt that she was smarter than everyone and, therefore, should take charge. At one point, he wanted to make her general manager but sanity prevailed.

As it was, people who were merely directors had their noses a bit out of joint. It didn't take long for problems to arise. The phrase "You've got it!" really didn't mean much more than, "I have taken note of your request and if I remember it tomorrow, something may happen."

She would send out memos saying, "Don wants you to give him a report on [whatever]." Then, one of the memo's recipients would go to Don and say something like, "Don, we already talked about [subject].

Why do you need a written report?" He would shake his head and say, "I don't know a thing about it." He would then ask Jane, who would say something to the effect that that was what she thought he wanted. It was perplexing, especially to Wayne and Mark who felt that she was isolating Don from the realities and creating chaos.

Jane sometimes started a project, and when the day ended, the project was over, never to be looked at again whether it was completed or not. "Oh, that, I took care of it." This problem became more curious than anything else. Meetings that weren't scheduled, memos that weren't written, and a variety of apparently mixed signals were Jane's way of doing things.

Sarah Moore had been hired by Wayne Stoker to work in the accounting department. She was bright, capable, and discreet. Jane often gave her Don's letters to type. Although Sarah had no particular reason to do so, she usually accommodated her, but Jane never acknowledged her assistance. One day Don Rager stopped to chat with Sarah just to pass the time.

Jane discovered them in conversation and later admonished Sarah to "never again talk to Don, it is not your position to do so."

God bless Don. His sense of humor overcame his anger and frustration. He started keeping track of the mix-ups and labeled them "Janeisms." At one point, he called Jane in and asked if she had set up the meeting with Mr. Jones. "Of course I did" was her reply. "He is coming in this morning at 10:00 a.m. and I have arranged to have coffee and donuts."

"But Jane, there is no Mr. Jones and there is no meeting scheduled. Why did you give me that answer?" There was a muddled response from her. Fortunately, she left shortly thereafter, and it was a number of months before all her hidden land mines were located and cleaned up.

Sarah Moore took over as soon as Jane departed. She was a miracle worker. Wayne and Sarah had worked together at Deloitte & Touche and later in the auditing department of Hilton. Sarah was slightly overweight and wore round glasses that made her look prim. Since she had been recommended by Wayne, who was a very strait-laced Mormon, we thought we were in for solemnity.

When she was first hired, Sarah was part of the accounting department and stuck in a back room with no chance to let her personality come through. Her sense of humor remained suspect, as a friend of the usually ultraconservative Wayne.

However, once she broke clear of accounting and took on the responsibility of keeping everyone straight, she became a different person. I had jokingly taken to calling her "Lady Sarah" in deference to what I thought would be her dignified demeanor. Was I ever wrong. A lady she was, in every respect, but she showed us a delightful sense of humor, patience with everyone, and incredible organizational skills.

With Lady Sarah installed as Don's caretaker and with the responsibility of keeping us all pointed in the right direction, life became easier for everyone. We didn't mind that she terrorized the highways with her Firebird Trans Am. Sarah was like a sponge that could absorb every task and make it look easy. She took on the job of scheduling buyers for their delivery program, which meant making sure there was track time, that someone could meet their airplane, that their hotel room was booked, a lunch ready, a driver on hand, and that their Jeff Hamilton jacket was ordered. That, plus being mother confessor to the troops, was enough to keep anyone occupied full-time. She managed it all with no complaints. What a refreshing change!

Tom Conley's job as the man in charge of Cobra sales was not an easy one. While the Cobra was a famous car and there had been a solid cadre of dealers formed out of the original recruits, delivery was a terrible problem. With money short, the purchasing guy, Pat McClure, could not order anything in quantity. Therefore, he had to wait until there was a backlog of orders for some of the specialty parts to be manufactured. If cars had been ordered and the missing part was not available, the components were shipped to the dealer for assembly. But dealer assembly could not be completed until the missing part was available. Naturally, the missing part made the car undeliverable and that held up the cash flow. It was a vicious circle.

Carroll, in his usual flamboyant manner, made an announcement: "Now that we have the 427 program up and running, we will soon offer the 289, the 289 FIA version, and the Daytona Coupe." While those cars were in future plans, they were not yet even on the drawing board, and the announcement that the most famous Cobras of all were going to be available nearly shut off the tap for orders on the 427.

The Daytona Coupe was the most famous Shelby car of all. Only six had been built, and the last Daytona Coupe sold brought $4,000,000 at auction. A genuine Carroll Shelby continuation of that line would be a winner.

The 427 orders slowed but did not stop, and a decision had to be made about how to transition from the 427 to the 289. D'Antonio was put to work creating the 289. He was virtually alone on the project. While he had original cars to copy, each part had to be drawn, fabricated, and its specifications recorded and submitted to purchasing for bid and manufacture. While Tom D'Antonio was a fabricator of incredible skill, what he was doing was time consuming in the extreme.

Meanwhile, Tom Conley felt that it was time to have a dealer meeting so that the Cobra dealers could see the new facility, review the progress on their back orders, set sales objectives for the future, and see and drive the 289. Don vehemently opposed any dealer meeting. He felt once all the dealers were together in a room, there would be chaos and the meeting would get ugly.

Neither Tom nor I agreed with Don. Both of us had spent our working lives in dealer meetings of one sort or another, and the idea of 12 Cobra dealers getting together sounded like a very productive process. Don finally gave in to our dogged pursuit with the caveat that, "Carroll hates the idea." I seriously doubted this since Carroll knew better than anyone how important it was to have dealers who were confident and informed.

After discussions with Bob Marsh and Tom D'Antonio, we set a date for early June. The availability of the 289 was key, because after the premature announcement from Carroll, dealers had begun taking orders.

The June date would give D'Antonio almost three months to get the 289 on the ground and running. Bob Marsh promised that he would get all the help he needed since the 289 was a priority for the company. As the meeting date grew closer and closer, there seemed to be little evidence that the 289 would be done in time. It became a joke and the subject of an office pool. Tom D'Antonio kept saying that if he got help he would make it. Bob kept saying that he would get him some help. Help never arrived, the 289 sat unfinished in the shop, and everyone, Bob included, screamed at Tom. He merely shrugged his shoulders and said, "With the help I was promised I would have made it."

Despite the lack of a finished 289 Cobra, the meeting was a success. The unfinished car did provide an example of what was to come. We shared ideas and agreed to a general direction for the future. We established future goals, most of which would never be met.

The fact that Roy Hunt's Finish Line Motorsports operation was under the same roof as Shelby American was cause for concern. The other dealers feared that any prospects that walked into Shelby American looking for Cobras would automatically be referred to Roy and that he would have an unfair sales advantage. Shelby American and Roy agreed that he should find his own home.

Money was always a problem, so when a bill arrived from GM for 530 Aurora engines, there was widespread panic. Engines would not be delivered until the bill was paid. At approximately $4,000 per engine, it was a sizeable bill. Wayne could do nothing more than shrug his shoulders, and Don could only try to scheme up some way around the bill, especially since it represented little or no savings. That was the price that any dealer would pay for a replacement engine. On top of the $4,000, Shelby American had to add the cost of doing the modifications to reach 320 horsepower. Partial payment would have seemed to be a logical response, but for some reason, GM wanted it all. We thought GM had taken advantage of us; $4,000 per engine hardly seemed like the "grandfather" deal that Rock had envisioned!

Deichmann was an unofficial member of the staff by now and was party to all news, good and bad. Upon hearing that GM wanted to deliver all engines at once and wanted payment in one lump sum, he offered an alternative. A quick call to his parts manager at Trent Oldsmobile, his dealership in North Carolina, revealed that he could supply the engines for just slightly more than the price from GM, and he could order them in any quantity and pay for them as ordered. It seemed a good way to circumvent the GM system and to ease the cash burden on Shelby American.

After reviewing all the clauses in the contract and after pleading with GM, they delivered the engines with no up-front payment.

Cash was a never-ending problem, and the Venture deal was still iffy. At one point, Carroll's dear friend, Robert Petersen, the magazine publishing giant, was about to step in and make an up-front purchase of 50 cars. This would have provided Shelby American with just about enough operating capital to make the program a success. The down side was that the cars were to be sold to him for a price considerably lower than the retail price at the time. It would have resulted in a nice profit for Petersen and kept the company afloat, but the Venture deal was too close to being consummated to allow it to happen.

Despite the fact that the Venture deal was not completed, it was close enough to a done deal to feel the company's influence. In May, Venture began to funnel cash into the operation. Obviously Shelby needed it. However, there were strings attached. According to the terms of the purchase, Venture had agreed to fund the company. That is, it had agreed to put in enough operating capital so bills could be paid and Shelby American would be current with all its legitimate supplier bills and payroll.

What happened instead was that Venture decided what bills were to be paid and only put in enough money to cover the most pressing accounts. Wayne Stoker, rather than making the decision about what bills had to be paid, had to justify each invoice to Venture and let it decide who was to be paid. It left Wayne no room to adjust to keep the promises that had been made. The Venture decisions had nothing to do with individual cases. Its decisions were based to some extent on how fair it thought the price was.

Multimatic, for one, incurred Venture's wrath. Venture looked at the price that Shelby was paying for shock absorbers and suspension components and went nuts. Its purchasing department determined prices which were fair and that became the measure of worth. However, the concept from the outset was that suppliers paid development costs and recovered those costs in the unit price. Multimatic had been one of the key development partners. It had provided hours and hours of time on its computers to do the finite analysis on the chassis. It had done the final development on the suspension system. It was Multimatic's work with Mark, Kirk, and Mike that made the Series 1 chassis a superior element of the car.

Negotiations with Multimatic went on for months, with Multimatic refusing to ship components until some sort of agreement was reached. While a settlement and resumption of shipments resumed, the relationship was acrimonious.

We sensed a major indication of the future when the manufacture of the chassis became a critical subject. According to the NHTSA, DOT, and the EPA, the cars were supposed to be completed by the end of 1999. A liberal interpretation of the rules gave Shelby the leeway to have the chassis completed and the engines all converted to comply with the 1999 safety and emissions regulations. Going at maximum pace, it would be fortunate if 200 chassis were completed in the Gardena facility.

As it was, the Gardena facility was a nightmare. If any safety inspector or OSHA representative ever appeared on the scene, the operation would have been shut down without hesitation. It was that bad.

To resolve this problem, Don instructed Mark, Bob, and Wayne to locate an alternate source. Since welding the chassis was a precision job, they did not expect to find anyone outside of the Southern California area, where the aircraft industry had created the need for aluminum workers. However, they discovered a remarkably efficient and professional company, Metalcraft Technologies in Cedar City, Utah, that had the exact capabilities that we required. After reviewing all the specifications and the timetable, Metalcraft submitted a bid that appeared to all Shelby parties to be acceptable in every dimension: quality, price, and delivery schedule. In addition, the Metalcraft operation was geographically much closer to the assembly operation in Las Vegas. By turning the chassis work over to them, the inefficient operation in Gardena could be closed down. If the work were to continue to be done in California, a new and larger facility would have to be located, leased, equipped, and staffed. All of those steps would take time and money, and there was assurance that Metalcraft would meet the standards. A handshake agreement was reached and a written contract was in development.

In May 1999, the contract was all set with a schedule that would deliver the last chassis to Las Vegas before the end of the year. While the contract with Venture to acquire a controlling interest in Shelby was not officially in place, Venture was beginning to assert its influence in decisions affecting the bottom line. So Don called Venture to report his next step (the Metalcraft contract) towards completing the project.

Within an hour Don received a phone call from Larry Winget who stated that he wanted Venture to make the chassis, that they had the capability and available personnel. His idea was that the more vertical the process, the more control that Venture would have over the project. Don had no choice but to agree. This was just the first of many Venture overrides of Shelby decisions, and it left Wayne with the unenviable task of backing out of the contract (and his personal handshake) with Metalcraft.

As it turned out, Venture had no capability to weld the chassis.

Venture's first attempts were a disaster even though it had created the accurate and excellent tooling that enabled Kirk and his crew to finally build chassis. In the meantime, while Venture learned how to fabricate the chassis, time—too much time—passed. The curious thing was that

Venture had the capability to produce almost anything and to do it extremely well. It seemed to take Venture so long to do things because it always learned the hard way. Once Venture learned that everything was not as simple as it initially appeared, the chassis that it built were excellent.

Don and the California crew had to find a facility that had the capabilities of handling the work and would be suitable to Venture. Each time they found one, something was wrong. The lease terms were not appropriate, the electrical system was inadequate, the location was wrong. And each time Venture found something wrong meant another delay.

Finally, we found a new location in Cerritos, California, in December 1999, and by January 2000, Kirk and the welders could begin to work. However, Venture already had found a new source in Michigan that could handle the job, and Kirk shut down the chassis assembly program in March 2000 with only 235 chassis produced (somewhat beyond the December 31, 1999 deadline).

While all of the chassis components were represented by Venture to be fabricated and stored by the critical date, the first Venture-built chassis did not appear on the scene in Las Vegas until well into 2001, when the supply of 235 Shelby-built chassis was finally exhausted.

While all of this time and money was being wasted, Venture was poring over the books to find out why car production was encountering so many cost overruns. Once again, it was "those idiots at Shelby."

We had been warned that Venture was a very political company with most executives vying to be closest to Larry Winget. The first casualty of the new alliance was Gary Martiss. Gary had been assigned to be the liaison with Shelby, which meant that he divided his time between Las Vegas and the Venture offices in Detroit.

While Gary was a competent man, he could not refrain from involving himself in the inner workings of Shelby. He maintained a desk in the production area and spent all his time with Brent Fenimore, who had already proven himself to be a political animal. It appeared that Brent would feed all the dirt on what and who he felt were problems to Gary. Gary would carry the dirt back to Detroit and use it to ingratiate himself with his superiors who, in turn, passed it along to Winget. There was constant carping and backbiting. Shelby personnel appeared to be portrayed in Detroit as hopeless boobs, incapable of doing anything right.

It didn't take too long for Don to figure out what was causing the disruptions. Gary was reassigned to Detroit, and Brent was temporarily set aside as head of Series 1 production.

While Venture Industries was the supplier of the carbon fiber body components, it had little or no experience in working with the material. Instead of learning the process, it purchased a factory in Mexico that claimed to have the necessary capabilities.

When the first body panels arrived, they were awful. They were uneven, poorly finished, warped, mis-sized, and on and on. Since lightweight body panels were part of the Series 1 package, the Shelby engineers threw up their hands, screamed, yelled; they tried anything to get the travesty corrected. It was obvious to anyone who saw the body panels that those making them did not have a clue.

Rather than acknowledge the problem, Venture accused the engineers, Mark Visconti in particular, of being stubborn and unyielding. At one point, one of the visiting Venture "firemen" lectured Mike Edwards and Mark Visconti on the properties of carbon fiber and how to properly lay it up.

Edwards, who had worked on the B-2 bomber that utilized high levels of carbon fiber, was not amused to be lectured by people who were trying to pass off substandard work as first-rate.

One of the young Shelby engineers, J. T. Lyons, a top-notch composite specialist with impeccable credentials, was even more upset about the quality of the body panels, especially when he learned that they were set out in the hot sun of Mexico to cure rather than in an oven. The Venture heavy hand silenced—quickly and rudely—his sincere attempts at trying to explain what should have been done.

The parade of visiting experts from Venture in Detroit was incessant. They came in like a conquering army, found faults in the program, promised to fix everything, and then disappeared, never to be heard from again. This made life difficult for everyone. Even worse was what seemed to be an ongoing game by the Venture troops. They came to Las Vegas, found fault, promised to help, and then returned to Detroit to take part in the bashing of the entire operation and contributed nothing to the solution.

At one point, Bill Walker called me to ask who in Las Vegas was complaining about the body panels. My response was "everyone," since everyone from Don Rager to the floor sweeper could see the incredibly bad mess that was being passed off as quality body panels.

Walker was insistent, "Who is it? Mr. Winget wants to know." "Why?" I asked. "Well," he told me. "Mr. Winget wants him fired."

I repeated, "*Everyone* is complaining."

The only continuing positive link between Venture and Shelby American was Joe Tignanelli. Joe was Larry Winget's son-in-law, and all of his experience was in the backrooms at Venture, the manufacturing side. Like everyone else at Venture, he had no experience in sales or marketing. Joe and Mike Deichmann became instant friends, and Mike occasionally treated Joe to one of the genuine Cuban cigars that found their way to Las Vegas.

One of the most curious aspects of the Shelby arrangement with Venture was that Venture did not seem to have a clue about what it had purchased. To many auto enthusiasts, Carroll Shelby is the supreme being of American racers and car builders. Larry Winget did not seem to have any idea about the significance of Shelby's accomplishments. He did know that Carroll had, on his own, achieved greatness. Winget seemed to respect and admire that, whatever it was that Carroll had accomplished.

In the main, Venture was a manufacturing company. It made "stuff" for the cars of the world and did it well. It grew by acquisition. It dealt with purchasing agents and engineers. If a specification changed, it negotiated a new contract. Life for Venture was simple, a black-and-white affair. In taking charge of Shelby, it faced a brand new set of rules and issues: consumer contracts, consumer protection laws, and responsibilities for warranties. Servicing all these seemed to baffle Venture. Not one of the Venture people could understand that things could not be done with consumers the way they were with purchasing agents.

Many of the Venture folks would listen to the rules of consumerism, but even when the facts were overwhelming and the consequences apparent, they would always come back to something like, "I know, but that is not the way Larry wants to do it."

It was like Dorothy, Toto, and friends dealing with the Mighty Oz.

This turn of events with Venture was very surprising. Everyone at Shelby had high hopes about the Venture takeover. Larry Winget had a reputation for doing things right and for not being afraid to spend to make things happen. Engineers anticipated help, the production people hoped for some serious expertise, the finance and purchasing guys looked forward to going ahead with real support. Don and Carroll anticipated that the Series 1 would finally get all the kinks ironed out and become what it was intended to be.

On top of that, Winget's reputation with his staff was that of a guy who backed his people to the hilt. Therefore, there was nothing but blue sky ahead for Shelby American.

Don Rager was expert at promising everything to everyone, and there were times when the pigeons came home to roost. Every automotive enthusiast magazine wanted to do a story on the Series 1. When *Motor Trend* received an exclusive on the first prototype, *AutoWeek* was miffed, and rightly so. Since it had been the most frequent reporter of Series 1 news, it had, as a result, been promised the chance to report on the first car. *AutoWeek* was a weekly that had considerably less circulation than the monthly *Motor Trend,* so a story in *AutoWeek* would not have devastated *Motor Trend.*

By April 1999, five months after the appearance of the *Motor Trend* article, there was still not a car for *AutoWeek* to test, and its West Coast editor, Mark Vaughn, was champing at the bit. To try to compensate for the fact that he did not give Vaughn the lead story, Don promised him the chance to drive the first production vehicle. The *Motor Trend* article had been written about the first running prototype (PP1).

However, by April, a production car was still months away (nearly a year!) and Don wanted publicity. Rather than give Mark Vaughn a car to test, he offered to let him come to Las Vegas and take part in the delivery program, a program geared more to the starry-eyed buyer than the savvy professional.

This was a terrible idea. Mark Vaughn was a shrewd editor, and he wanted a Series 1 to evaluate. Hiding the lack of a finished car behind the glitzy delivery program seemed to me to be an invitation to disaster. Don was adamant that he could pull it off, directing Mark to a story about the delivery program rather than the car itself.

The Series 1 appeared prominently on the cover of the May 24, 1999 edition of *AutoWeek* with the headline, "Are We There Yet? The Shelby Series 1 will be super, when it's finally ready for production." Recognizing that the car was a long way off, Vaughn did his best to compliment the progress, but he also stuck a needle into Don's proclivity for deflecting every question about apparent faults.

His last paragraph was a zinger:

"After a while, you get the sense Rager can deflect any question.

'Hey Don, the car is fully engulfed in flames!'

'That's just our heater. It works good, don't it?'

Okay, so we made the last one up."

Don had also promised a car to *Road & Track* for a road test. *Road & Track* positions itself as a sophisticated publication with more engineering orientation than its competitors. Giving an unfinished car to the magazine was another invitation to disaster. But charge ahead we did.

One of the big concerns of everyone at Shelby was the fact that the initial prototypes were heavy. Venture did not have a handle on body panel production. The *Road & Track* road test would surely yield something considerably slower than the announced expectation that the car would accelerate to 60 miles per hour in just over 4 seconds. With lots of cars yet to sell, a bad report in *Road & Track*—the purist's bible—would be a serious problem.

The only way to overcome high weight is to increase horsepower. Therefore, we decided to modify the standard Series 1 engine to compensate for the weight gain. Obviously this had to be kept a secret because it was cheating. Cheating on road test cars is fairly commonplace. Any car that is given to any magazine by a manufacturer is gone over from bumper to bumper, and if anything can be done to enhance performance, it is done. Usually these things are either cosmetic or superficial, so the case of a souped-up engine was certainly more egregious.

The car that was to be turned over to *Road & Track* was the same one that Mark Vaughn had driven, with all the faults he had uncovered. The car was delivered to the *R&T* offices in Costa Mesa where it was to be looked over, passed around among the staff, and then taken to Pomona, where the magazine would utilize the drag strip for its performance testing.

Fortunately for everyone involved, *Road & Track* called Rager to say that it did not feel that the car was sufficiently completed and that an analysis in the magazine would not be fair to the car, which was, as Mark Vaughn reported in *AutoWeek*, a work in progress. This was fortunate in another way, as the so-called special engine eventually swallowed a valve about a week later.

The relatively kind treatment by the magazines was curious. While Don had done his best to make certain that Carroll was far removed from as much of the project as he could, Carroll's influence was pervasive. Don wanted to be the spokesperson, to be the man to give the details of the Series 1 to the press, yet the press regarded him lightly. Carroll Shelby's aura protected us. But how long could we count on that?

The fact that *Road & Track* and *AutoWeek* didn't lambaste the car and Shelby American for presenting it to them in such an incomplete and desultory fashion was a tribute to Carroll's relationships with the editors. Even though all of the press knew that Carroll fed them a lot of nonsense most of the time, they loved the fact that he was up front and spoke his mind. There was also a great respect for his accomplishments, and no one wanted to rain on his parade. Courtesy to Carroll dictated that they refrain from a test that would harm his cause.

Following the latest foul-up with the press, I wrote Don a private memo. I suggested to him that things were getting out of hand. He was forcing promises from his staff that they could not meet, he was stretched too thin, and he needed someone to back him up. I also told him that I felt that Mike Deichmann, as great a guy as he was and as important to the company as he was, had assumed too great a role in the inner workings of the company. Mike, as the most productive dealer, was in a position where he could see all the warts and wens of the company. He knew too much for *our* own good.

Mike's influence was everywhere, and both Don and Carroll treated him like royalty. Carroll vowed to help Mike get a Jaguar dealership. Mike was told to move to Las Vegas, that there would be big rewards for him on future projects.

While Mike could not help but be flattered, his head was on pretty straight. He was enjoying all the excitement of Las Vegas and the attentions of Carroll, but he also knew he had a very comfortable business in North Carolina. The Shelby program was a one-time thing as far as Mike was concerned. He also figured that once all the cars were sold, and by the time his involvement was over (he had sold over 70), there would be a continuing business of service and reselling. He had advertised extensively, and within the small community of dealers and public that knew of the Series 1, Trent Oldsmobile, Mike's dealership, was well known.

Don never commented on my letter except to say that he agreed with the fact that Mike was an incredible salesperson.

Rager's health continued to vex him. In the spring, he went back into the hospital for skin grafts on his head. The cancerous condition was worsening. Naturally, he came back to the office too soon, and the combination of medicines that he was taking seemed to cause unpredictable behavior.

In one staff meeting, he began to discuss all that was wrong: the delays, the press problems, the engineering lags, everything. As he did so, he became more and more impassioned, his timbre rising and his face becoming flushed. The staff could only sit there. It was a most uncomfortable and embarrassing scene to watch, as he became more and more enraged. As he reached what we thought was the fever pitch, his cell phone rang.

"What was that!" He leapt up and thrashed papers around on his desk until he could locate it. When he found it he threw it to the floor to silence it.

He looked at the wreck of his phone and tried to compose himself. He made an attempt to conciliate the group and sat down. Within three minutes, he was sound asleep in his chair.

Later, he approached Mark Visconti, who had been the object of most of his diatribe, and said, "I hope we woke some of those others up!" Mark was stunned and offended by the entire outburst and was even more stunned by Don's attempted rapprochement. Wayne Stoker later asked Don if his medications were affecting him. Don's reply was "Oh, no, everything is under control."

Even when Don was not exhibiting difficult behavior resulting from his medical condition, he did things that caused serious problems with credibility and morale. At one vintage race, Don spotted a Whizzer motorbike. Whizzer was a company that took ordinary bicycles and converted them to motorbikes. Whizzer bikes were a big rage during the period right after World War II, and a company was now capitalizing on the retro craze of the 1990s by recreating the Whizzer motorbike. Don saw one and had to have it. He rationalized that it was "hip," and people would know that Shelby was up on the latest fad. He also rationalized that it would stop the company from having to rent golf carts to get around the grounds of the events we attended. The price of a Whizzer was about $2,400. While this was not a lot of money, it was an enormous amount for a company that had no cash and whose engineers were in need of computers that it couldn't afford.

Therefore, when Don denied Visconti's request for a desperately needed computer and then instructed Wayne Stoker to cut a $2,400 check for a Whizzer, there was considerable resentment. It's a wonder there wasn't a mutiny.

Chapter Eleven

Getting Frayed around the Edges

After the Ford Motor Company and Carroll had kissed and made up, there were conversations about what they might do together and how. The most natural thing was a new Shelby Cobra.

Shelby, Cobra, and Ford were three words that just seemed to belong together.

The Ford link with Shelby was so strong that I received a number of calls about the Series 1 in which the caller did not want to do anything more than berate me because the Series 1 utilized an Oldsmobile engine. "It can't be a Shelby if it doesn't have a Ford engine" was the typical comment.

Mark Visconti and Mike Edwards worked on plans for a new coupe that would utilize the Series 1 chassis but would change all the other components from GM to Ford. Millard Design and others drew up some sketches of what the car might look like, and there were several meetings (in secret, of course) to discuss the issue.

These meetings began in late 1998 and involved Don, Carroll, and John Colletti, Ford's manager of performance operations. Later, as the Venture deal began to solidify, Venture people participated. The talks and discussions dragged on for months until they ended with "no deal" in early 2000.

Apparently, Ford wanted the Shelby name, something that it should have secured many years ago. Ford wanted to purchase the name and arrange with someone to build new Cobras. It had no interest in the Las Vegas facility and wanted the Series 1 program to be finished. The new Ford Shelby Cobra would be built somewhere, by Venture or someone else, but Carroll would have been out of the car-building business and Venture would no longer own "Shelby." It appeared to be the ideal proposal for Carroll: cash out and watch his famous Cobra come back to life with Ford. In the end, it appeared that the price that Venture put on the name was too much, and Ford backed away.

While the Ford deal never came to pass, the discussions were an undercurrent that directed attention away from the Series 1 project.

Don's helter-skelter management style caused mass confusion. No one was in charge, yet everyone was in charge. With production partially underway, the phone was ringing off the hook with customers calling about their cars. I had no answer to give them. The only person I could go to was Bob Marsh, and he usually provided a meaningless date.

On a couple of occasions, I went to Bob to see if a second or third prototype would be completed by a certain date. A dealer would want it for an auto show or an exhibition. I always posed the question as, "Bob, dealer X wants a car for a show on [date]. I can tell him no, and he won't be angry. If I tell him yes and we can't make the date, then he will be angry. It will be better for us if we have a car there, but it will be worse if we say we can and then fail. What should I tell him?"

Bob would look at his production chart and say, "We've got to start producing these cars. Tell him, yes, we'll have one." Without fail, the deadline would approach, and there would be no car. "What happened, Bob?" I would ask. He would then tell me that such and such part didn't arrive or come up with some other lame excuse. It was my personal nightmare.

The best example of corporate miscommunication came in May 1999. There was the usual serious staff meeting in Don's office about the start of production. Don exhorted everyone to meet the challenge, and a date was set for June 15. Everyone agreed that June 15 would be *the* date. I walked away feeling great. At least there was a real date, and I could begin to tell customers and dealers to be ready.

I walked past the office of Pat McClure, the purchasing guy. He saw me smiling for a change. "What's up?" he asked.

"Well, I just got a commitment that everyone signed off on that cars will be rolling in June," I replied.

"I don't know how that can be, we won't have side glass for the doors for another couple of months," said Pat.

Another shattered dream and more of those personal nightmares.

In an effort to clear up my own confusion, I asked Gary Martiss for his opinion on when cars would be complete and ready for shipment. "I guarantee that Venture will have body panels by July," he said with the proviso that, "if the details are engineered, then we can have cars by the end of July."

I next had dinner with Gary Arntson, the ex-Oldsmobile engineer who was close to the details. His response: "By July you should have a good car ready to go."

To add further to the confusion, I went to Don and said that I had learned that side glass was still not available and would not be for some time. He acted like this was fresh bad news, went into another one of his "stop everything" programs, and directed everyone to work on the problem of side glass.

The side glass problem was a strange one. The original plan called for the car to use the side windows from the Corvette.

Obviously, utilizing something that was expensive to recreate but was already available made good sense. Therefore, when the original design was created, the car doors were engineered (by Venture) so that the curvature of the Corvette windows would be correct.

But early on, a committee decision mandated a more dramatic curvature on the sides of the car. The doors were re-sculpted with no one bothering to recheck the dimensions. Of course, when the finalized doors were being produced and the Corvette side glass was installed, it wouldn't fit.

Eventually the problem of the side glass was resolved but not until much later than July 1999. Naturally, the cost for creating the molds and for casting new side glass added considerably to the bill. The curious thing about the glass problem was that the doors were supposed to have been engineered by Venture. Naturally, Venture shifted the blame to Visconti.

The contract with Venture was clear about who was to engineer what, such as hinges, door handles, and body mounts. Once Venture became the boss, anything that was undone seemed to be the fault of Shelby American, and the engineering buck stopped with Visconti. To me it seemed terribly unfair. Mark, Mike, and Kirk had created a fantastic car. The faults that were arising were the result of a lack of development and testing time. Venture was supposed to be supplying expertise. Instead, it was supplying criticism and applying blame. The crew who created the car that made Venture want to become involved was now the object of scorn and derision. The Team Shelby concept that had kept the whole mess together was now on the trash heap of corporate cover-your-ass.

At one point, shortly after Don's tirade and phone toss episode and another blame-assigning episode with Venture, Mark was ready to throw in the towel. It was a totally normal reaction to a terrible situation. We went to lunch one day, and he vented his frustrations. While I could not help but agree with him, I urged him not to quit. To leave before the project was over would mean that any and all of the problems would be blamed on him. The chassis and the work that he, Mike, and Kirk had done was significant and important.

If Mark left in the middle, Venture could say that it had to step in and clean up his mess. If he stayed to the end, the project would always carry his name. He deserved plenty more than blame, and he agreed to stay until production started.

The convertible tops were another problem. The top had been an exclusive design executed by Dura, a company that makes convertible tops for some of the world's best cars. The Series 1 top had to be special. First of all, it had to be light in weight, and secondly, it had to fit into a shallow space behind the cockpit. The bows were made of aluminum and were designed to fold inwards rather than scissor in the normal fashion. The result was to be a top that, when collapsed, would only take up about 5 to 6 inches in depth. The weight was to be about 26 pounds, about 20 pounds less than a Corvette top.

Since there was no consistency in the body panels, the top, which was built without an adjusting device, would not fit each car. There was always a gap on one side or another. While most convertible tops on sports cars do leak some, this one in particular was a major problem. Dura kept claiming that it couldn't deliver tops until the cars were consistent, and Shelby kept insisting that the cars were consistent but the tops were not. It was not until June 2000 that tops with built-in adjusting arrangements were delivered in quantity to Shelby. In the meantime, the few cars that were completed either sat waiting for tops or were delivered without tops that would be fitted later.

The supercharger issue kept rearing its head. Everyone involved knew that a supercharger was necessary. After Carroll had publicly announced that there would be one, a vast majority of the buyers wanted assurances that a supercharger would eventually be available. Deichmann had personally guaranteed to some of his customers that it was coming, and naturally, my phone was constantly ringing with supercharger questions.

Carroll Shelby wanted it, therefore it was bound to happen. Don Rager turned a deaf ear to the subject. There were obvious questions about certification and the ability of a manufacturer to offer one when the car was certified without one. There was also the issue with GM Powertrain about offering a blower. The whole subject made Don nervous.

The answer was to offer it as an aftermarket option. Properly done, it would meet the necessary emissions tests and be certifiable as an accessory. Visconti, who had done a lot of feasibility work on the subject and intended to set up his own engineering company at the conclusion of the Series 1 program, saw this as an opportunity.

Visconti, along with Mike and Kirk, began by setting up an engineering company, Red Shark Engineering, and they set out to spec out a supercharger program. Obviously this was of great interest to Mike Deichmann, and he expressed not only his support but also his willingness to invest in the company and to take part in the marketing of the package.

It all made sense. The operators of Red Shark knew the car and the engine as well as anyone on earth. Mike wanted to have continuing involvement with the car after the program was over, and he had generously included me in the ongoing activities. Also, the supercharger plan kept Shelby American out of the loop of commerce and away from liability and government regulation.

Mark showed his presentation to Mike and me. We thought it made great sense and that the development could begin right away. We told Mark to submit it simultaneously to both Don and Carroll. Don had a way of turning aside that which didn't fit his agenda, and because of his apparent lack of enthusiasm, we felt that this too would find its way to a pile on his credenza. But we also knew that Carroll would have immediate interest.

Unfortunately the "nice" streak in Mark took over, and he presented the proposal to Don alone. His personal ethic dictated that it would be disloyal of him to involve Carroll when Don was clearly trying to keep Carroll out of the loop. Both Deichmann and I told him to kiss the supercharger goodbye when the proposal went into the "ignored" pile on Don's desk.

To keep the pot boiling, Deichmann would bait Don about the supercharger. Don would tell him such things as, "Oh, I've talked to Carroll about it, and we have a plan." Or, "I have talked to three companies about it, and we can do it for $5,000." All of which was nonsense since he hadn't talked to anyone and the bare bones cost was about $10,000.

Don Rager had obviously been working beyond his capacity. While he was extremely bright, energetic, and dedicated to his cause, the problems that faced him were taking an obvious toll. His health was a disaster. He was medicated all the time for his transplanted liver. As a diabetic, he should have been eating better. His skin problems continued. The promises he had been making to customers and vendors were due, and he was furiously trying to put together the Ford program while managing the Shelby business.

If all that wasn't enough, *Playboy* Playmates were calling about when they could collect their cars, ice skaters were calling about when they could collect their cars, and the *Wheel of Fortune* winner wanted his car. Their respective agents were calling regularly.

Things were crumbling beneath Don's feet, and I told him to get help. He said he could manage. The man who was most upset by Don's troublesome ways was Mike Deichmann. By this time, he had sold over 70 cars and his customers were getting antsy. Facts were needed, and Don was equivocating. Mike used every sort of cross-examination to try to get the truth out of Don, but no story ever matched the previous one. Since Mike had the run of the place, he knew from the guys on the floor what parts were missing, what part worked, and what the exact problems were.

Out of frustration, Mike began to express his displeasure to Joe Tignanelli. Joe kept reassuring him that Venture was aware of the problem and was preparing to act. The actions it took were about six months away, and in the meantime, all hell was breaking loose.

As difficult as things might have been for Mike Deichmann, he continued to be the best salesperson the Series 1 had going for it. One story is legendary. It is the story of how one Series 1 got "unsold."

Part of the selling process was getting the buyer to make a deposit. The logic was that once a deposit was made and a serial number assigned, the buyer was hooked. The best way to keep him hooked was to get him behind the wheel. The Series 1 represented serious automotive fun and even the most jaded found it a real joy— unless, of course, the car was a mismatch for the driver.

In this instance, Mike extracted a deposit from a buyer, assuring him that it was required to secure a place in line. The buyer agreed, sent his deposit, and made arrangements to fly to Las Vegas to test the car with the proviso that his money would be returned if he did not like the car.

When the customer arrived at the factory, it was apparent that the car and the driver were not a good match. The buyer spent a great deal of time making critical comments about things he would have done had he designed the car.

When he got behind the wheel, the mismatch was even more apparent. He tentatively took hold of the gear lever, holding it gingerly from the top by his fingers. He seemed intimidated by the performance and the quickness of the steering.

It was fun to watch because I knew that Mike was going to have to return the man's deposit, and being the competitive animal that he was, this would make Mike very unhappy.

Finally Mike came to me and said, "Damn, I know I'm going to have to return his money and the thought of it pains me." My suggestion was for Mike to take a positive stance and force the customer's money back on him. Tell him he can't have the car.

Mike thought about it overnight and then called the reluctant buyer. "George," he said, "I watched you with that car yesterday. I saw the way you looked at it and the way you drove it. I've decided that I'm sending you your money back. That car ain't for you. The Series 1 is a man's car."

That was late in the week. On Monday I called the man's office to ask where to send the check. His secretary answered the call and asked, "Oh, how did you know?"

I was perplexed and asked, "How did I know what?"

"That he had a heart attack and died over the weekend" was her response.

From then on I accused Mike of using too much pressure and that his tactics were killing the customers.

The most upsetting event happened in August 1999, when Don announced that Larry Winget had come to the conclusion that the cars had been priced too low and that he intended to retroactively increase the price. Even though we had not delivered cars and purchasers had signed contracts and paid deposits, Winget felt that it was "the thing to do."

Deichmann and I were dumbfounded. As far as I knew, a contract was a contract. Don went ballistic, and Carroll took pains to reassure Mike and me that this would not happen. He recounted again the fact that Winget knew full well that the car was a money loser when he purchased Shelby. "Over my dead body," was the phrase he used to state his antipathy for Winget's concept. That anyone would even think of taking such an action threw a pail of cold water on everyone.

While there was a loophole in the purchase agreement that would allow a nominal price hike, raising the price on those who had purchased cars almost three years ago seemed like bad business. If Venture bought into Shelby, it could not have been because it saw a big profit opportunity in the manufacture of 500 sports cars.

The negative publicity that would arise would be considerable. Mike, while agreeing that it was a really bad idea, was immediately drawn into what he felt would happen to his reputation as a dealer if he had to go back to his customers with that kind of bad news.

Besides, Carroll had stated emphatically that it wouldn't happen.

It was an interesting concept to consider. Most of the buyers of Shelbys could certainly afford to pay more. However, most of them were very successful businessmen who would take a very dim view of being duped by a bait-and-switch scheme.

With all the apparent negatives, I didn't give the idea much more thought. It was too preposterous to consider. A retroactive price increase just could not happen.

One of the many Venture troops who visited Shelby American was Nelson Gonzalez. Nelson was a Brazilian who had spent many years with General Motors. His forte was manufacturing, and because serious manufacturing expertise was sorely lacking at Shelby American, I guessed his visit was a prelude to further involvement and more help in getting cars out the door.

Nelson spent an August day at the plant quietly observing. One of the eye openers for him was a demonstration by Don Rager. As he usually did, Don drove his Series 1 home each night and would report the faults to engineering and manufacturing each morning. On this particular day, it had rained in Las Vegas and the streets carried a nice slick of surface water.

Driving hard as he always did, Don found the Series 1 a handful on wet pavement. As is always the case with a light car with a lot of horsepower and wide tires, traction in the wet is a problem, and power has to be applied carefully.

Don came dashing in to the office screaming for Visconti. "Get out here right now," he demanded. "We have a real crisis."

"Watch this." He shouted as he jumped back in the car and began to accelerate wildly, making the car spin in almost uncontrollable loops in the parking area.

He parked the car and ordered a meeting to take place "Right now!"

"Call Goodyear, Mark, we have to do something, *now*! This car is unsafe, people will be killed." And on and on like a man possessed.

This was Nelson's first exposure to Don and his modus operandi. He looked at Mark and commented that the only thing wrong with the "wet test" seemed to be the driver. After quietly interviewing most of the staff and watching Don in operation, Nelson passed his judgement on what had to be done to get production underway.

While it had not been officially announced, Nelson was to be chief of production and preside over the Las Vegas operation. As his first official act, he gathered the staff in Don's office and announced that Don's new assignment was to sell future projects for Shelby American and that production was to be undertaken by Bob Marsh and Mark Visconti without further assistance from Don.

This was a crushing blow to Don. But he was not a manufacturing man; he was an accountant with a marketing flair. He was not involved full-time. He was into a multitude of other projects, including organ transplant, and his management style almost prevented production from moving ahead. However, the effect of the demotion by Nelson seemed to galvanize his feelings about Mark. He appeared to feel that Mark was to blame for his situation, and from that day on, he took every opportunity to push blame for everything to Mark.

Production still languished. The Las Vegas crew claimed that the parts weren't designed right, and the engineers from Gardena claimed that the Las Vegas crew was inept.

In a move to resolve the issue, Kirk and Mike took up headquarters during mid-summer in Las Vegas under a special but temporary arrangement to get production rolling. The three (Mike, Kirk, and Mark) teamed up and, in Kirk's words, "Kicked some butt." After a few weeks of extreme pushing, it appeared that cars were ready to roll.

Obviously all the delays generated great frustration. I was caught in the position of having to explain each delay to dealers and customers. We had tried to use a newsletter to keep people informed, but all it seemed to be was written evidence of our ineptitude. The same was true for our website. We would post a production schedule and then, three weeks later, it would only show how little progress had actually been made. The only thing I should have done was change my phone number.

One customer would call me every week to see if his car was any closer to completion. While I would do my best to tell him the truth, he never believed me. He said he was a businessman, understood manufacturing, and could not believe that any company could be so inept. Therefore, I was lying to him. He just could not believe that I wasn't lying, and that, yes, we were that inept.

Deichmann kept asking about the supercharger, and Don kept telling him conflicting stories. The stories varied from "We can't talk about it," to "I've got it all handled." He told Mike that he had many conversations with John Middlebrook from Vortech, the supercharger manufacturer, and that the "deal was done." Mike knew better because he had been discussing the supercharger on a regular basis with Visconti, who was the only Shelby person in direct contact with Vortech.

Eventually, Mike took Carroll aside to ask what in hell was going on, since Don had also told him that he and Carroll had it all worked out and that (depending on the day) Mark was going to do it or Mark was not going to do it. All of this came as a surprise to Carroll. Don had told him "it was all handled." He knew nothing of Mark's Red Shark proposal or about any negotiations or discussions with Vortech. He promised to get in the middle of it, which he did.

To assuage Mike and to get a better picture, Carroll invited Mike to accompany him to Oxnard, California, to visit Vortech and to move ahead on the supercharger. By now, Carroll was totally vexed by Don's behavior. He came to the conclusion that Don wouldn't know the truth if it "bit him in the ass."

By early August there were a couple of cars that Don decided could be delivered and that, by delivering cars, we would take some heat off. The four cars that were to be delivered were Carroll's CSX5001, Frank Simoni's CSX5002, Kent Browning's CSX5003, and Tom Schrade's CSX5004.

While Frank Simoni was a delightful man, he had been waiting for two years for his car and never hesitated to call and scream about where in the hell it was. It was important to get a car to Kent Browning because his dealership, Browning Oldsmobile in Cerritos, California, was located in the biggest sports car market in the world. With a car on display in his showroom, the number-one market would have a chance to see an actual car.

Don planned a big affair for the official delivery of the cars. All participants were invited to attend as the first cars rolled off the line and into the semis for delivery.

To say that this was a sham would be an understatement. The cars barely made it to the factory door. Since Carroll's car was part of the family, its state of completion could be faked until all was right. Kent Browning was on vacation, so his car could wait until he returned to his dealership. For purposes of the show, Schrade's car was pronounced ready. Tom Schrade was a Las Vegas resident, and his car could stay in the factory for completion. It was only Simoni's car that had to be ready to go.

With the local press on hand, Don, Carroll and I expressed thanks to all for their patience and wished our new buyers a bon voyage and happy motoring. Photos were taken of the activities and of the lines of cars in the background. Carroll autographed each man's car and it was a happy occasion. At least we wanted everyone to see it that way.

Brent Fenimore and I stood together as the happy owners (Frank and Tom) bathed in the glow of new ownership. The thought hit us both simultaneously: what in hell do we do next? We had just announced to the world that cars were now on the way, yet we knew it would be months before the next car would be ready to go and *some of the parts had yet to be engineered.*

A little knowledge is not just a dangerous thing. It can be downright terrifying.

Chapter Twelve

Deliverance...
into More Trouble

T he first cars that we delivered were more trouble than the ridiculous exercise that got them out the door in the first place. Two days after his vacation, Kent Browning called me and asked that I come to take a look at his car. Since it was only a 40-minute drive to his dealership in Cerritos, I was there within the hour. I was apprehensive about what his complaints might be and feared the worst. While everyone at Shelby had signed off on the car, including the Venture advisors, I had an uneasy feeling that there were a few things that we had overlooked.

Gary Patterson had the assignment of final sign-off, and he was a stickler for perfection. He believed that anyone paying $100,000 should get a car as close to perfection as possible. He had even withheld his sign-off until a number of quality issues could be resolved.

Gary had substantial misgivings about the car that we eventually delivered to Browning. Don expressed the view that early cars are expected to have flaws. The Venture position was that too much money was being spent on cars that would never achieve perfection under any circumstances, and the only remedy was to scrap the car and build another one for Browning. This was, of course, correct but not a financially sound option.

Browning's car was particularly important since it would be the only Series 1 on display in the entire Los Angeles metropolitan area for some time. The good news was that there was a car on display. The bad news was that this was the car on display.

Kent Browning is an avid car collector and restorer who does much of his own restoration work. Therefore, he was more knowledgeable about body fitment and paint quality than most people. He walked me around the car and pointed out the unacceptable flaws. He was not upset, but his point was that this was to be the vehicle that would demonstrate to the Los Angeles market that the Series 1 was a quality car.

"Would you be happy with this as a representative automobile?" was how he put it to me. I could not help but agree that this was not our best shot and made arrangements to ship the car back to Las Vegas where I knew that someone would point a handful of critical fingers at me for incurring further expense.

While there were a few "fish eyes" in the paint, the biggest complaint was that pinholes in the flared areas around the wheel openings appeared. These pinholes were not apparent when the car was painted. I had examined the car carefully myself and had not noticed them. Nor had anyone else.

The car went back to the paint shop where the faulty areas were sanded, filled, and repainted. Before reshipping the car, the pinholes reappeared. We eventually traced the problem back to a flaw in the preparation process that allowed paint to be sucked into certain areas. The experience with Browning's car saved a lot of future headaches, but for some time, Gary Patterson and I were accused of being too cautious and nitpicky about quality.

It took another couple of months to finally finish Tom Schrade's first car. Schrade had purchased four cars from Findlay Oldsmobile in Las Vegas. In fact, the car that was posed in line and photographed as his was not the car that he ultimately got. The car used for the event eventually wound up being used for engineering and test purposes.

Carroll's car also became an engineering "mule." It had its body panels replaced and was used as a prototype for the supercharged car.

The one car that actually made it to an owner was CSX5002, sent to Frank Simoni, our first buyer from the Kruse auction almost two years earlier. I thought to myself, "Wow, now maybe I won't get so many angry phone calls from Frank."

I was half-right. Frank called almost immediately to apologize for being such a "pain in the ass" and asked me to tell everyone that he loved his car. It was perfect except for a number of flaws he listed. He was so happy to have his car that the flaws were of minor importance to him. He had raced up and down his street, and he appeared in a couple of Cleveland auto shows where his car was the center of attention.

About three weeks after Frank received his car, Don Rager called me in a panic. "Larry Winget needs to have a Series 1 in Detroit in two days." Apparently he wanted to show it to a prospective customer for his molded plastic products.

The plea to me was, "Can we borrow Frank's car since Cleveland is only a few hours from Detroit?" They told me that the car would be in Detroit for only two days and that they would truck it back to Frank for the weekend. I called Frank, and he reluctantly agreed to loan us his new toy for three days.

When the car arrived at Venture in Detroit, Larry Winget hit the ceiling. In his eyes, the car was a piece of junk. The paint was bad, the body panels didn't line up, and many of the basic functions, such as wipers, didn't work.

He interrogated his staff about the body panels: "Why would we ship panels as bad as these to a company we own? We sure as hell wouldn't ship them to Ford or Chrysler or anyone else?" He then ordered that the car be made as perfect as possible before returning it to Simoni.

As far as I was concerned, Winget's sentiments about the car were on the money, and if he would personally step in, we finally had a chance of achieving quality cars. The Venture staff went to work to right Simoni's car. It was almost totally disassembled, the body panels realigned, and it was repainted. This was all great except that no one told me or Frank that this was happening.

The first I knew of the situation was when I received a call from Frank. He started off with, "You sonsabitches, you stole my car. You told me it was only going to be two or three days and now those bastards can't even tell me when I'll get it back. I'm gonna call the sheriff and report that you and that goddamn Rager stole my car. I want it back now!"

All I could do was try to find out what had happened. The answer was that Larry Winget didn't want the car on the street because it was so bad. Frank Simoni didn't see it that way. It was his car, and he loved it.

Fortunately, Frank and I were good friends by now, and he realized that there was nothing I could do. The car was in Detroit and would stay there until it was as good as Venture could make it. It took about 10 days.

After returning the car, Nelson Gonzalez volunteered to call Frank and explain Venture's good intentions. Nelson was more than welcome to call Frank because Frank would be delighted to hear from someone other than me—especially someone from Venture.

Nelson got an earful and told me that he never wanted to talk to Frank again. He reported that Frank used the term "stupid sonsabitches" 11 times in the first three minutes and that Nelson really didn't feel like taking any more of that kind of abuse (Welcome to the club, Nelson!).

Frank called to tell me that some stupid son of a bitch from Venture tried to bullshit him about his car. He told him that they completely repainted it and refitted the body, but he "didn't see nothin' different."

Eventually, Frank called me back to tell me that, yes, the car did look a lot better and to apologize for directing his volatile Italian temper at me.

After spending countless hours trying to make the first cars look like real, production-line automobiles, Venture stopped everything. It was a wise move, since Venture spent a lot of hours producing cars that were simply God-awful. There was no way all the body panels could be made to align properly.

The alignment problem was mostly chassis related. There were a couple of critical dimensions where the windshield and front door posts were mounted, and where the rear door posts were attached. A fraction of a difference in key measurements from chassis to chassis would mean serious gaps in body panel alignment. With a chassis that underwent so many steps in its assembly process, it was impossible to control all dimensions within a couple of thousands of an inch. A thousandth of an inch off on the right door could turn into a quarter inch on the left side. It was a nightmare, and something had to be done before any more attempts were made to mount bodies to chassis.

In essence, these cars were retro-straightened. The main fix was to develop a tool that assured that all chassis parts were in the same place, front to rear, right to left, and top to bottom before any body parts were fitted. The jig that was created allowed for shims to be used to adjust for any differences. The first 50 cars that were in the system were either hand-fitted or had been retrofitted for panel alignment. From 50 on, everything was properly aligned from the get-go.

Some of the first cars were awfully rough. Bill Ockerlund was a Cobra dealer as well as a Series 1 buyer. In fact, Bill had purchased two Series 1s. His first car was CSX5011, and he desperately wanted it. While his car was complete, it lacked a top, and it appeared that it would be months before tops were available. Because he had experience as a Cobra dealer and knew that sometimes paying for things didn't always mean that the goods were delivered, Bill declined to pay for his car until the top was available. In the end, this was a good thing. On my next trip to Las Vegas, Gary Patterson drew me aside and suggested I have a look at Ockerlund's car. Gary told me Don and Venture had passed it, and that it was ready to ship except for the top.

In a word, the car was horrible. There was a gap of at least 1/2 inch all the way around the hood. It was like a rain trough between the hood and the fenders. It would have been an embarrassment to have that car on the street. To compound the embarrassment, Bill Ockerlund was a Cobra dealer, one of the family, and had purchased two cars.

Everyone insisted that the car was ready to go. My job was to get Ockerlund to pay for it and then to agree to wait and have his top retrofitted when it became available. This was a tough assignment, not one I was sure I could accomplish because Bill had become a friend.

Those ill-fitting tops were a source of difficulty and argument. The plan was to build the cars anyway and then send someone around the country with new tops and install each one on a customized basis. Venture changed its mind because of the expense and then went back to the original plan.

The arguments about the car's suitability bordered on the absurd. Rager claimed that since the car cost only $100,000 versus the current price of $135,000, Ockerlund shouldn't expect to have a car of the same quality as a car at the higher price. He also opined that early cars always had flaws and that those flaws made the car more valuable. Venture just wanted the car out of the plant. It was taking up space. In addition, since Venture had really been pressing the assembly teams to complete cars, having a car sit around for weeks after completion sent the wrong message to the workers. Ockerlund's car was so bad that we eventually decided to not ship it at all and to substitute a different car instead.

Lou Adimare's car, CSX5009, was another car that I hated to see shipped. Lou was a purist and expected a perfect car. He had owned many high-performance cars, loved to drive fast, and had the speeding tickets to go along with his persistent love of speed. While Adimare had been an early buyer, he also had a relatively high degree of skepticism about the ability of the company to deliver a car. More than once during the program, the dealer had to use his or her best and highest powers of persuasion to keep him involved. I believe that he finally decided that, if the car was any good but he did not like it, he would be able to sell it. I don't know how many times his salesperson, George Nelson from Coulter Oldsmobile and Cadillac in Phoenix, called me to get updates on the status of Lou's car. If he called when I was in Las Vegas, I went out to the shop and reported on exactly what was going on at that moment.

Things like the chassis alignment jigs and the realignment of cars made explanations pretty difficult. "Oh, yes, Mr. Adimare, your car was having its body panels mounted, but we discovered that nothing fit so we are remaking the tooling. Your car should be along in another three or four months." That kind of stuff didn't go on too long before even the best of customers became skeptics.

The stability of the company was always an issue, especially when car production fell further behind schedule. In truth, the company was always hanging by a thread, but there was comfort in the fact that Carroll always had someone in the wings to bail it out. When Venture came along, it seemed like a godsend because, to be blunt, Venture had money. However, the Shelby/Venture agreement stipulated that there would be no mention of the change of ownership for two years. I have no idea why this was part of the deal, but Venture was very sensitive on the subject.

To comfort the skeptics, I explained that Shelby had taken on a development partner whose primary goal was to ensure that the cars were built. While I never named Venture, I did say that the company involved had deep pockets and was a prominent supplier to the global auto industry.

Among the Venture army that descended on Las Vegas was Gary Pniewski, a Venture engineer who had spent the past few years in Australia. Pniewski, like many of the Venture staff, had been lured away from Ford. Winget seemed to reward those with whom Venture had worked at client companies with high-paying jobs when their usefulness ran out with the mother company. Pniewski's initial job on the Shelby project was manager of production. While he was an engineer, he knew nothing of production management. Learning on the job on the Series 1 project was no easy task.

All of the Venture people were accustomed to big-time manufacturing and assembly. They had all of those skills and background. But the Series 1 was a car of a different genre. The Series 1 was essentially a race car, designed to be hand built. The man eventually entrusted to the task of assembling the cars, Nelson Gonzalez, had earned his stripes managing production for General Motors X-cars: Chevy Citations, Olds Omegas, and the like. There was a difference in the two classifications of automobiles. However, Nelson eventually made sense of the production mess and departed with a respectable-looking assembly program.

The Venture guys seemed to want to line up everything, press a button, and have the parts fall neatly into place and the car to proceed out the door as a perfect automobile.

Bob Zientek was a Venture man but a genuinely helpful one. Like many of the Venture people, Bob was a retired General Motors production executive. While he was another part-timer as far as the Shelby project was concerned, he was like a Dutch uncle to the production staff. He had been around enough to know that not everything could be measured in terms of black and white, and he had a good sense of humor. His knowledge enabled him to look at a problem and to find logical and practical solutions. His sense of humor enabled him to look at each crisis with the degree of panic that it deserved. Most thought that he was the most constant source of reason and common sense to come from Venture.

The answer to the issue of the woefully sad body panels was to try to salvage them by using body filler to make them smoother and more even. A primary feature of the Series 1 was that it was light, in part because of its carbon fiber body panels. Initial calculations estimated that the car to weighed 2,400 pounds. Final calculations indicated that the cars would go out the door at 2,650 pounds. With the body panels now a mixture of carbon fiber and fiberglass, and with the heavy body filler added in liberal amounts, the first cars weighed over 2,900 pounds. An early buyer, David Hill, eventually sent me an e-mail saying that his car weighed 2,982 pounds with a full load of fuel. With the top added, the weight rose to over 3,000 pounds. The extra 300 pounds was a terrible performance burden for a 4.0-liter motor.

Venture never appreciated the significance of weight for the Series 1. Detroit auto industry types never worried about extra weight unless it upset fuel economy or certification. As far as Venture was concerned, if the Series 1 cars looked good, they were all right to deliver, which missed the point. The Series 1 was a race-bred car and weight is always a critical issue for any such car.

Since manufacturing was now in control, the engineers could only speculate on what was happening. It wasn't until Carroll's car was in the hands of Mike Edwards and Kirk Harkins that Carroll learned how fat and overweight his Series 1 had become.

All of those issues had become battlegrounds for Mark Visconti. He stayed until after the late summer push to get production started. With that behind him, he figured his job was done. Unfortunately, we witnessed an uncharacteristic abandonment of his generally pleasant demeanor. He yelled at the Venture folks, saying that they were "just too fucking stupid to build this car." That was the end of it for him; he just couldn't stand the backbiting and arbitrary decisions.

As I suspected, all the blame for the program's shortcomings fell on Mark as soon as he left. Don went out of his way to blame Mark for all the screwups. Mark and his small crew had achieved incredible results with the design of the chassis and drivetrain. Many of the serious ills were in body manufacture, and that ball fell squarely in Venture's court. However, Mark became a convenient scapegoat, and the word passed back to me through Don was that Larry Winget didn't want Mark Visconti to have any further involvement with the Series 1 or with Shelby American. All the supercharger development work that he had done would have to be redone simply because Mark had done it, and now he was gone.

While the design of the Series 1 was not perfect, Kirk, Mike, and Mark had created a basic vehicle platform that was the equal of any sports car in the world. The problem was that they received little help with the details and the final execution.

Mark immediately took an assignment with Multimatic where his talents as an engineer and race car designer were put to good use as program manager for the Ford "Petunia" project. Petunia was the code name for the project that became the Ford GT40 show car, which was the hit of the auto shows in 2002.

When it became apparent that Venture was selectively paying bills, I went to Don Rager to make sure that my own payments would be safe from its accounting procedures. My involvement in the project was longer than anyone else's since I had been active before there was a project. Yet, my pay had been minimal. Vic Olesen and I had been paid for setting up the dealer organization and all my out-of-pocket expenses were paid in a timely fashion, but I had received little in the way of compensation for what had turned out to be one very difficult job.

While we had first agreed that I would be paid for each deposit on every car that was received, the money was so tight that I deferred income until we could actually deliver cars. I had received a few token payments along the way, but in the main, they were way behind.

With Venture now in control and my agreement having been made with Don Rager, I felt that I would be even more stupid than I had been if I didn't get my financial oar in the water and darn soon.

Don agreed and suggested that I give him an up-to-date invoice for everything the project owed me. Don passed my invoice to Wayne for payment.

Wayne issued me a few checks as his financial plan would allow. Then came the brick wall: no more checks.

The issue of repricing cars came up and drove a wedge between Winget and me. Winget was adamant that the clause in the Series 1 purchase agreement would allow a significant price increase. His attorneys had reviewed the agreement and concluded that the price was not fixed until Venture and Shelby American could determine the final costs of certification and other unknowns. Don Rager, who had assured me from day one that there could be no retroactive price increase, was now saying things like (as he had said about Ockerlund's car), "I know I can sell a price increase; collectors will be willing."

I was incensed. For the past two-and-a-half years, we had been stalling buyers who made deposits in good faith. We had reassured them that their cars were on the way and that the price would hold. When all that was going on, we had no money to make refunds. Finally, the first cars were done, and they were bad cars to boot.

Winget's idea was that the price of all cars to the dealers would be $110,000, beginning with the first cars. The dealer could make whatever he or she wanted on top of the $110,000. All customers would be advised of this policy, and any customer who did not want to pay the extra amount would get his money back.

I wrote a lengthy memo to Don and wrote that the concept of raising the price retroactively was not only unethical but probably illegal in most states. I suggested that dealers would probably sue, as would customers. I believed that states' attorneys general would get involved, dragging the reputation of Carroll Shelby through the mud. I concluded by saying that not only would I not take part in this activity, but that I would also repudiate it. Don passed the memo along to Carroll and the Shelby attorney, Neil Cummings. Carroll had previously said "over my dead body" when discussing the retroactive increase with Mike Deichmann and me.

The memo went back to Venture in Detroit and my checks stopped. Wayne's last request for my funds was greeted by an e-mail from Jim Butler, a Venture accountant. In it he said, "You have no authorization to pay Eric. It appears that he will not present our price position as we want." Never mind that I had a signed and approved invoice from Don who was still the president of Shelby American. Never mind that the company owed me money for work that I had already done.

In the meantime, just about everyone was trying to find ways to get Larry to change his position. I submitted numerous alternate proposals to Joe Tignanelli, who presented them to Larry. Included were proposals to increase the price of the cars not yet sold in an amount that would allow the required net income to be reached. I discussed these proposals with Mike Deichmann because he was the one who would most likely take the biggest sales load. I tried to keep the other dealers out of the loop since I was certain that a revolt would happen if they were aware of the battles within Shelby.

I could not continue to sell cars without knowing the real price. With no price and no pricing policy, I had nothing to say to dealers and potential customers. For every car that was sold, there would be another potentially angry customer.

Another ramification of the proposed policy was that if a customer backed out, the dealer would lose a sale that he had already made and for which he was expecting to earn a $20,000 sales commission.

Having sold the most cars, Mike Deichmann had the most to lose. Mike had become so well known for his Series 1 efforts that *Millionaire* magazine had done a feature story on his Shelby sales efforts. Mike also had an overdeveloped sense of fair play. His position was simple: he had promised cars to his customers at an agreed-upon price and was obligated to deliver at that price.

Mike and Joe Tignanelli discussed this many times. Mike made a proposition to Joe, "You hold the price on the cars, and I will sell the remainder of the cars for you with no commission. I will cut my commissions and do anything necessary to help you make money on the program. But I can't raise the price to my customers."

Don's reassignment didn't keep him from being front and center at the January 2000 events, the Kruse and Barrett-Jackson auctions. Before he was reassigned and while he was working hard to solidify his position as president, Don turned to Stefani Paulus to arrange a press tour for himself in Phoenix where two auctions were to take place on successive weekends. He wanted to be on TV and in the press with the message that Shelby American was on the move. He had Stefani prepare a color picture of Carroll and himself in front of a Series 1. The photo, to be used as a press handout, identified Don as president and CEO and listed Carroll as chairman.

Don went so far as to keep the press tour plan to himself. At least he tried to keep Carroll in the dark. Carroll found out about it when he asked Stefani to do something for him during the same time. Stefani innocently asked, "Are you and Don doing this together?" One question led to another, and the cat was out of the bag. Carroll was livid, and he instructed Stefani that anytime Don was to have a press interview, that he, Carroll, was to be there as well.

Carroll also ordered that the pictures of him and Don posing together be destroyed.

Chapter Thirteen

We'll Fix this Thing with a Sledgehammer

By now I was so deep into the program and was owed enough money that I had to hang in to protect my interests. I also believed there was a chance Larry Winget would come to his senses and realize that retroactively raising the price would have dire consequences. Everyone seemed to be against it. Even Venture staff members appeared to understand the negative ramifications.

My questions were simple. How could such a successful businessman as Larry Winget have purchased Shelby American without knowing that the Series 1 program was a money loser? Venture lawyers, accountants, and other advisors had been on the premises and in the books for months. Venture personnel had said as much before the company and Shelby American became officially joined. Both Carroll and Don had said many times that Larry Winget knows this car will be a money loser and the profit will come on the *next* car.

Having made the purchase and the decision that it was a fiscal loser, why was it not smarter to smile and make the best of it rather than risk destroying the entire operation over what appeared to be about a $10 million swing? Using the numbers Joe Tignanelli provided, the total revenue returned to Venture by the program was $55 million. This meant that the wholesale price of each car should be $110,000. Since about half the cars were now sold with wholesale prices that ranged from $80,000 to

$115,000, it didn't take a genius to figure out how much had to be charged for the remaining cars.

If the dealer commission remained at $20,000, the new retail price should be $165,000. While that number seemed too high, there was plenty of confidence among the dealers that the car could carry that price. There was also talk of adding value and making the price even higher.

Larry didn't want to take the chance the cars could be sold for $165,000; retroactively raising the price made him more comfortable. In addition, Don Rager had assured Larry that he could sell a retroactive price increase to the dealers and customers.

With all that staring us in the face, Shelby American moved into the new millennium without having delivered more than a handful of cars and with an uncertainty about the price.

Larry Winget started the New Year 2000 with a bang by finally visiting the operation that he now owned. I found the fact that he had never visited the operation astounding. While he was reputed to be a billionaire many times over, the investment in a car company, no matter how small, was not something to be undertaken without at least a cursory inspection. Of course, Don Rager was nervous about the visit. The gossip was that major personnel decisions were to be made, and the most rampant rumor was that Larry would replace Don as president of the company.

The staff prepared for the "big visit" by upgrading all that they could. Because Tom Conley and I never had any kind of office accommodations, some kind soul went out and bought two small desks, which were shoved to the back wall of the showroom. It was certainly a cozy place for an office, right in the line of tourists who were given a Shelby plant tour each day at 10:00 a.m. ("Just look to the rear folks, over there behind that white Mustang and you will see two old geezers posing as sales executives.")

On the appointed day, Larry arrived by car from his winter house in Phoenix. He rarely flew and used his V-12 Jaguar for the haul from Detroit to Phoenix and, from there, around the West.

No one bothered to officially introduce Larry Winget to me or to Conley. Both of us did, however, intrude on conversations to at least shake the hand of the man who was now in charge of the Shelby legend. Those in power, including Carroll, disappeared into Don's office for a meeting that lasted a few hours.

Both Tom and I had to return to Los Angeles that night, so we had to wait until Don could give us his version of the future.

According to Don, he had gotten just the job he wanted. He was to be head of worldwide sales and marketing for a new Venture company, Venture Design International, and responsible for all sales worldwide for Series 1 and Cobra. In addition, he was to "open doors" and sell Venture's capabilities around the world. He parroted what seemed to be the party line, that Venture was the manufacturing company, that the groundwork had been nicely laid for it to finish the Series 1, and that he could move on to bigger and better things. He promised that both Tom and I would continue to work for him and that this would mean good things for all of us. No one else said anything, so all we had was Don's word, which, by this time, was highly suspect.

In fairness to Don, he was never a production man. His strengths had been in pulling the act together and getting the car into production. It was time for production professionals to take over. If the new assignment ever materialized, Don would be good at it. He was, after all, a terrific salesperson.

Gary Pniewski's deficiencies as a production man had become apparent almost immediately. He wasn't inept; he just had no experience. Right man, wrong job. So, Nelson Gonzalez took over as president of Shelby American (actually Venture, Nevada LLP, the entity that held Venture's ownership shares). Gary Pniewski was appointed business unit manager for Series 1, and Bob Marsh carried the same title for the Cobra program. Brent Fenimore resumed his position as the guy in charge of Series 1 production. With these changes, the entire emphasis at Shelby American in Las Vegas shifted from the promotional atmosphere of Don to a strictly production atmosphere.

While I knew little of Gonzalez, I was delighted to see him in his new post. He was a professional automobile production man, seemed to be a straight shooter, and apparently was able to speak his mind to Winget. Perhaps someone could finally convince Winget that the bodies were overweight and of poor quality. Although my opinion of Gonzalez being a straight shooter later changed, he remained the consummate automobile production professional.

The subject of the poor quality of the bodies attracted lots of attention, yet nothing seemed to be working in the direction of improvement.

Fenimore made numerous trips to the body plant in Mexico City. There were improvements but not the sort needed to cut a couple of hundred pounds from the vehicle weight. Nor were there improvements that would make the irregular panels that were coming through smooth and even.

The Barrett-Jackson auction was held in Scottsdale, Arizona, the week following the Kruse auction. Since the Barrett-Jackson auction was the big auction of the year, Shelby forces were out in force. The show rig was well placed, and the display area was full of cars. Carroll was there part of the time, and when he was not there, Cleo was. She made sure that any time Don was near the press or a microphone, she was by his side.

Cobra dealers came from all over. Jim Harrell came from South Carolina, Karmen Cusak was there from Colorado, and Roy Hunt brought cars from his place in Las Vegas. Don Rager was there acting as though he was in charge of everything (which was not the case), and Venture was represented by many people, including Larry Winget, who drove from his winter place in Phoenix to see what the program was all about.

Carroll had to leave to attend a dinner where he was to receive yet another honorarium, and he left Cleo to represent his interests, which meant shadowing Don Rager to ensure that he made no further claims to the presidency of Shelby American. It wasn't that Carroll couldn't trust him. Well, maybe it was.

In February 2000, Don called a meeting of all those who had been involved with the Oldsmobile negotiations. The purpose of the meeting was to give depositions to a Venture attorney who was collecting all information to determine whether there were grounds for a lawsuit against GM/Oldsmobile for breach of contract. Don had convinced Winget that the reason the car was late and over budget was because of all the promises made by GM that were not fulfilled.

This was difficult to fathom. The person closest to the contract other than Don was Mark Visconti. While Mark had expressed many frustrations with GM over execution of the contract, he never believed that it failed to fulfill any part of the agreement. The only area of which I had any knowledge was the cost of the engines. At one point, John Rock had said that he would try to have them grandfathered to Shelby. This might be interpreted to mean that he would see that they came to us for the lowest possible price or even given to us. This was nebulous at best and certainly no grounds for legal action (in my opinion) since all the details of the agreement were in the contract that all the parties had signed.

Olds had promised to sell GM parts to us at dealer net prices, and had done that. Olds had promised a certain number of man-hours for help throughout the GM system, and had delivered on that promise, too. The only legitimate question involved the interpretation of "a certifiable engine." Interpreted one way, the agreement might have meant that the engines were to be sent to Shelby certified and ready to be installed. The other interpretation was that the engines, as supplied by Oldsmobile and with the modifications recommended by Oldsmobile and executed by Shelby, *could be* certified.

It was an unfortunate splitting of hairs. As it happened, Shelby had to spend extra money to revise the engines and have them certified. GM appeared to be wrong, and the resulting cost to Shelby was considerable. In the total scheme of things, it was probably no more than pocket change for Oldsmobile, but it meant a lot for Shelby. The delays certainly cost time in finishing the car, and the lost time meant lost money. However, it was extremely difficult to speculate on what actually transpired. The most frustrating part was the ever-changing personnel roster at GM, which meant it was hard to find anyone there who really knew what GM intended.

The one area in which Oldsmobile really dropped the ball was that of participation beyond the contractual agreement. Had John Rock remained involved or had the GM system been more welcoming to a project such as the Series 1, the Series 1 would have been a success for Shelby as well as for Oldsmobile.

As it was, when John Rock left, the Series 1 program became a hot potato. No one wanted to touch it. GM lived up to the contract in the narrowest sense, but the program remained a bastard. It is possible that had Don Rager's fateful meeting with Darwin Clark turned out more positively, coopération and enthusiasm would have spread throughout Oldsmobile and GM. Since Darwin Clark was soon reassigned to another job and the Oldsmobile assignment fell to yet another new face with another new agenda, it is futile to speculate on the fate of the Series 1 within General Motors if things had been different.

In the meantime, Mike Deichmann continued to ask for an audience with Larry Winget. He wanted to tell him to his face that retroactively raising the price was a bad idea. He wanted to tell him that he, Deichmann, would take less than his promised commission and would help sell the balance of the cars for nothing if the price to his customers was not raised.

Knowing that I was adamantly opposed to the price increase, Nelson Gonzalez pressed me about whether or not I would continue to participate in the program. He suggested it would be good if I would go to Detroit to meet with Larry and express my feelings. Of course, in another breath, he told me Larry wouldn't listen to me, anyway. To address my point that the proposed increase was immoral, he said it was immoral to have priced the car so low, at a level that would guarantee a loss. He told me that Larry Winget felt that both the dealers and the customers had taken advantage of him because they knew they were paying far too little for a Shelby automobile.

He also said that all car dealers were dishonest and that they became rich by not being totally honest. If the Series 1 program became too much of a bother, he related that Larry would just shut the doors and everyone would be out in the cold.

"Larry Winget didn't get to be a billionaire by being totally honest, and Mike Deichmann didn't become wealthy by being totally honest either," was how he put it.

How could I possibly respond to that? A sweeping generalization about car dealers was irresponsible, and as far as I was concerned, Mike, like every other car dealer who had become a friend, was totally honest. The saying that Mike lives by, "Never write a check with your mouth that your ass can't cash," is important to him. The proposed Shelby American policy was going to make him look like a fool with those customers to whom he had promised to deliver cars at an agreed-upon price.

Gonzalez told me there was not a judge in America that would make you sell a product for a loss. I guess he never ascribed to the philosophy that a deal is a deal. All Larry had to do, said Gonzalez, was tell dealers, in his down-home Ohio farm boy manner, everything he had done to save the program and the dealers would accept his position without question. "Customers will pay any price for one of these cars because it has Carroll Shelby's name on it."

Even the name "Carroll Shelby" has its limits.

As a final point, Gonzalez accused Carroll Shelby and Don Rager of conspiring to bankrupt the company so they could buy it back from Venture at a bargain price. I had no idea whether Nelson was setting me up for something or if he was serious. I could not help but wonder if these opinions were being delivered to Larry Winget as good advice. I sure hoped not, because everything that Nelson was stating was not going to lead to good future relations with customers, dealers, or with Carroll and Don. In the end, I put it down to arrogance.

I said I would think about it. It was now totally apparent there would be an attempt to raise the price retroactively. There was going to be a mess. Angry customers, bad press, and of course, lawsuits.

Sales slowed to a crawl because no one knew the real price. While the price of a new car jumped to $134,975, there was gossip that more was yet to come and that there was trouble at Shelby.

In order to prevent a total disaster, Carroll enlisted the services of Joe Molina and his JMPR public relations firm. It would be JMPR's responsibility to save the program with some kind of positive spin.

In a meeting in the offices of JMPR, I outlined my fears for the reputation of Carroll and for the future of the Series 1 program. Using what information I had to offer and what JMPR had gleaned from others, a plan was formulated—one that resulted in a couple of favorable articles in trade publications.

It had come to this—desperately trying to save the whole program by the sleight of hand known as public relations.

I then met with Joe Tignanelli and some of the other Venture people. They wanted me to help convince the dealers to accept the new price. No one seemed to understand there were moral issues at stake. The Venture people wanted to make the Series 1 program a financial success, no matter what the cost in terms of fairness or the reputation of its inspiration, Carroll Shelby. Venture had apparently bought a pig in a poke and when its analysis showed that the program was a financial disaster, it wanted to have the customers pay for its mistake.

I thought a trip to Venture would give me the chance to speak directly to Winget. I had no illusions about changing his mind, but I wanted to express my feelings directly to him. It was not to be, and my meeting was with Joe, Jim Butler, the finance guy, and Scott Pickelhaupt, the marketing director. During the meeting I got the feeling that they all knew the road ahead was full of bumps, but since Winget had made the decision, it was up to them to make it work. To put it more bluntly, it was up to them to please Larry Winget.

They assured me that the company's lawyers were certain the price increase was within the scope of the purchase agreement. However, Jim Butler expressed some skepticism about the viability of the anticipated 37 percent increase. It came as no surprise to me that the attorneys had checked into the possibility of raising the price in North Carolina, Mike Deichmann's state. Deichmann was the top volume seller and had the most potential liability with his customers. The lawyers thought Venture could get away with raising the price retroactively in North Carolina.

I still had a host of personal issues to resolve. I wanted assurances I would be paid what was owed me. I also wanted indemnification. I knew that if Venture went forward with its program, there would be lawsuits, and I wanted protection. The meeting concluded without a satisfactory resolution. I never presented my case to Winget, and I received nothing in writing to ease my financial difficulties and potential legal woes.

On the way back to California, I stopped in Las Vegas. Two dealers, Cliff Findlay from Las Vegas and Tom Emich from Tucson, were there to meet with Nelson Gonzalez and Wayne Stoker to discuss the price increase. While Mike Deichmann was in Las Vegas and was invited to attend, he declined. He knew he was too emotional and far too involved in the program. I was scheduled to attend, but said that I would not unless I had a letter of indemnification. After all, I had been the guy who had been telling the dealers and customers for the past three years that everything was going to be all right. Even though there was little chance anyone would hold me responsible, I had little desire to stick my neck out for a cause in which I didn't believe.

Lawsuits were a way of life for Venture and Winget. Joe Tignanelli had told Deichmann one evening that whenever someone sues Venture, Larry "sues 'em right back."

Since I didn't receive a letter of indemnification, I didn't attend the meeting with Findlay and Emich. Wayne and Nelson reported to me that the meeting was amicable with no raised voices. However, the two dealers later met with Deichmann in the parking lot, and that discussion took on another dimension.

Cliff Findlay's view was simple. "No sense arguing. The minute they put their program in writing, I turn it over to my state attorney general." Tom Emich volunteered basically the same approach and Mike told them that he had already reviewed his options with his attorney general, who had assured him there were many breaches of North Carolina law.

Nelson and Wayne were both aware they were walking on eggshells, but neither felt they had a choice if they wanted to keep working for Larry Winget.

The following week I met with Joe Tignanelli, Wayne, and Nelson. The agenda was simple: Will you stay and help us work this thing through?

I was firm. I would not consider anything until I had an agreement about what was owed me, a schedule of payments, and a letter of indemnification. When pressed for an answer on the spot, I said I wanted to discuss the matter with Carroll. After all, he was the reason I was involved, and I wouldn't do anything until after I had reviewed my decision with him. We shook hands, and I returned to Manhattan Beach. I had no desire to continue working with them, and I used their need as a lever to try to get paid for my past services. Under the circumstances, I thought that was fair.

The next morning, Wayne faxed me the letter of agreement, but the matter of past pay and future services were tied together. This was not acceptable, and I called Wayne, who immediately rewrote the letter to my satisfaction. While I had not consulted a lawyer officially, I had asked my brother-in-law, Charlie Clippert, a prominent Detroit attorney, for advice. I read him the letter over the phone and showed it to Vic Olesen over our morning coffee. At least I wasn't totally reliant on my own naiveté for the contents.

After reassurances that the letter contained all I wanted, I called Carroll and told him what was going on. Bless his heart. He told me, "I sure would like you to stay, but you gotta do what you think is right. No matter what you do, you'll always be my friend."

I thanked him and told him I was probably inclined to leave; it ran too much against my grain. I then called Wayne, told him that I just could not go on, and sent him a letter to that effect. Naturally, the first of my scheduled payments for past services never arrived. So much for contracts and handshakes.

I was now out of it, or so I thought. I was genuinely concerned about ever being able to collect on my years of work. I called Charlie for more advice. He suggested I cool my heels for a short time to see if any money came from them. In my original contract and the letter of agreement, Venture had clearly acknowledged I was owed money and I could take them to court for payment. Charlie reminded me that going to court was an expensive procedure, and even if I won (which was likely), there was no assurance Venture would ever pay without repeated and costly court action. His was good advice; within a few weeks Wayne called me to say that even though I had disappointed a few people, he would pay me on a different schedule.

While I was officially gone, in actuality I was not. I still fielded calls from dealers and customers. Since I had not been replaced, there was no one else at Shelby American who could give them answers.

Then came the meeting that seemed to set the tone for the future of the Series 1. It was April 13, 2000, and Larry Winget had finally agreed to address the dealers. He never agreed to *listen* to the dealers, but that's another matter. It was Larry's opportunity to explain why he had to raise the price.

Had Venture held this meeting six months previously, the dealers might not have been so agitated and been more willing to have a more amicable discussion. The length of time between the initial feelers about raising the price and the meeting had been extremely costly. Dealers lost faith and customers became worried. Sales stopped.

All dealers were invited. Seventeen attended. The session started with a tour of the plant with an emphasis on all that Venture had done to bring the project along. After the tour, the meeting commenced in an area of the plant normally used for display. All employees had been sent home so there was no possibility of the proceedings being overheard.

The general agenda for the meeting had been set by a story that had appeared in *Automotive News* on April 3. The story was about the lengths that Venture Industries was going to in order to save the Shelby Series 1 program, and that part of recouping all the excess expenditures was a retroactive price increase to $129,975 ($109,975 plus commission of $20,000). Because just about every car dealer reads *Automotive News*, the dealers were prepped for the confrontation.

Scott Pickelhaupt started the meeting with a fairly simple presentation of the facts according to Venture. The dealers, who were primed for a more straightforward, get-to-the-point meeting, did not sit still for long, and the focus of attention turned quickly to Larry Winget and his intentions about the price. While no one doubted the program was losing money at the initial prices, there was almost universal questioning of the efficacy of raising prices on cars that were already sold and under contract.

California dealer Avery Greene stepped forward with some overhead slides of his own and showed how the desired net revenue could be obtained by Venture without raising prices retroactively and entering into serious controversy. It didn't take a brain surgeon to figure out that this is what should have been done, and it was yet another restatement of the formula that had been worked out earlier with Joe Tignanelli and Mike Deichmann.

While Nelson Gonzalez had previously stated that "car dealers are dishonest," it was the car dealers who were justifiably concerned about their reputations should they have to go back to their customers and tell them if they wanted their Series 1, they would have to pay considerably more than the contracted price.

George Berejik, in particular, was crestfallen. While he had not sold many cars, he had put the offer of the Series 1 in front of his special customers and friends. While others were engaged in a verbal battle with Winget, Berejik was calculating how much of the increase he could eat because he would not go back on his word to his customers. Mike Juneau was also going through the same arithmetic, and in his case it was worse since he had sold more cars. I don't know how many others in the room were going through the same mental process. From the comments I heard later, this was a universal concern.

At one point, Winget stated in a truculent manner, "We don't need you to sell the cars, I have an offer to put them all through an auction and have been guaranteed $125,000 each for them."

By this time, the dealers were on their feet and accusations were flying every which way. At one point Larry seemed ready to walk out. In the end, logic prevailed. Had Larry walked out, lawsuits would have followed and the result would have been the untimely demise of the Series 1 and the end of Carroll Shelby's legendary run as a car builder.

When the shouting finally died down, they came to an agreement: the price of the car for new purchases would be $165,000 and the dealer commission would remain at $20,000. There were other contentious issues. Prior to each price increase, dealers had been offered the opportunity to purchase cars at the previous lower price if they would make deposits on those cars. Shelby American did this to raise cash. In turn, the dealers were to have the opportunity to make the additional profit based on the spread between the new price and the old.

Mike Deichmann had brought extra cash to the table on a couple of occasions. He believed in the car and wanted to help Carroll. His dealership was not a large one, but he managed to put out about $200,000 along the way with the promise he would be rewarded with the difference in the point spread between the current price and the newly increased price.

With Venture having established the cost at around $110,000, and with over 100 cars sold at a retail price of $99,975, Venture was looking at a direct loss of $30,000 on each of the first cars. The price to the dealer was $79,975. Winget looked at all the money the dealer was making and all he was losing, and it didn't go down well. He took an even harder look now since the retail price of the car was (before the bump to $164,975) $134,975, and the spread for dealers on early cars could be as much as $54,975 per car for those dealers who had made deposits on cars that had dealer costs of $79,975.

With a retail price of $164,975, a dealer who had ordered an early car and made the deposit to hold it could conceivably earn nearly $85,000, which was now the spread between retail and wholesale. This concept was too much for a man who was looking at a major loss, and the meeting ended with this issue unresolved. There were only a few cars that fell under this umbrella but enough to make Larry Winget feel that he had been had.

There were other issues. When the program began, Rager had announced that cars would be delivered to customers' homes as part of the deal. While the contract clearly stated that the cars were to be picked up by buyers in Las Vegas, there was a little confusion, and a few customers were left with the impression that freight was included.

The cost of paint stripes was yet another bone of contention. Originally the plan was not to offer any paint stripes. However, the cars displayed at the Detroit and Los Angeles auto shows had stripes, blue in Detroit and orange in Los Angles. Also, the car *Motor Trend* featured in November 1998 had a burgundy stripe. It was only natural that customers would demand the paint stripe that sold them in the first place. This may seem trivial to those outside the business, but a stripe on a race car means a lot.

After checking with Bob Marsh, Shelby American determined that it could do the paint stripe profitably for a $1,200 retail price. In some cases, such as the burgundy-striped car for *Motor Trend*, the stripe ran over the nose. For the blue and orange striped cars at the auto shows, the stripe ran from a power bulge in the hood, back to the windshield, and then on from the cockpit back to the rear of the car. In either event, over the nose or from the power bulge back, Marsh was confident that the $1,200 fee would cover it.

However, the demand for the stripe became greater than anticipated, and Shelby American really didn't want to go through the bother of striping the cars. So the price jumped to $2,500, an amount so high we figured it would discourage orders. Unilaterally, Venture decided all paint stripes were $2,500, even those that were promised at $1,200. To me it seemed silly to alienate customers when there was profit to be made at $1,200, but I was out of it and all I could do was commiserate when dealers called to ask me to intercede.

Since the official Series 1 color was Oldsmobile Centennial Silver, someone determined there would be no variations from this. However, a few customers had made a special color part of their condition of purchase. With the need for sales desperate, there were a few situations in which Rager bent and allowed the application of another color.

One of these cases was a customer of Deichmann's. The buyer, a dignified and wealthy car enthusiast, specified a certain red. His order was accepted, and he was notified there would be an additional charge of $7,500 to have the color of his choice applied. That price had been established by Shelby production people and the painter and was given to the customer in writing.

Venture made a decision that the price was to be $30,000 because of the difficulty in obtaining a good paint job with the specified color. Gonzalez had told me that the silver was very forgiving and that the red requested by the customer would show every flaw in the body. The additional $23,000 was to cover the extra labor required. It didn't take any genius to figure out that it would allow a $50 per hour painter 600 hours to accomplish this task. This was outrageous. The customer stood his ground, and there was yet another threat of a lawsuit before Venture backed down and honored the original contract. I had to wonder: could Venture have tried any harder to alienate customers and invite needless litigation?

The "big meeting" ended with only the resolution that there would be no retroactive price hike, but the new prevailing price would be $165,000. Venture promised to send the dealers a written recap—minutes, if you will—of the meeting.

Mike Deichmann was not at the meeting. He had initiated a complaint through the state attorney general's office in North Carolina. The attorney general's office submitted an inquiry as to the practices of Venture Nevada, LLP, the company owned by Winget, that were affecting the business of North Carolina resident and businessman, Mike Deichmann.

Attached to the complaint were many documents, including letters from Don Rager and myself to dealers that stated that there was to be price protection for those who stepped forward with deposits on cars.

For some reason—and to this day I don't know what it was—Venture did not want the dealers to know about Venture's ownership interest in the project. One of the documents that went with the complaint was a memo to Wayne, apparently from one of Venture's lawyers, instructing Wayne to refrain from being truthful (that is as delicate as I can be on the subject) about Venture's connection to Shelby. Wayne had drafted a letter to be sent to all dealers stating that Venture had purchased a majority interest in Shelby, which they had clearly done, but the higher-ups would not let the letter go out.

Perhaps because there were major issues of liability, Venture did not want it known they had purchased the company. At the time of purchase, there was to have been a two-year period in which Venture was to have been a silent partner. Still, instructing Wayne to withhold the truth is another matter.

The crux of the memo was that Wayne had to redraft his memo and deny Venture's ownership of Shelby. Someone (not me) who remains anonymous to this day (the "Deep Throat" of Shelby American) had sent it to Mike.

The proceedings in North Carolina became a source of major consternation. First of all, the lawyer's memo was terribly damaging in that it suggested Wayne lie. Second, Deichmann's secretary had been on vacation and did not know where all of his Shelby files were located, so he asked me for copies, and I faxed what I had from my files. Shelby letters and memos came from both me at my home and Shelby in Las Vegas. Mike was double checking to make sure he had them all.

When the state submitted its inquiry, it used all the fax copies I had sent Mike. They had my own fax number on them. Therefore, I was the one who "leaked" the information. I was aiding and abetting the enemy. Since all the documents that I had sent Mike were already in his and every other dealers' files, I didn't feel like a turncoat, especially since I had not even seen the infamous legal memo.

Not long afterwards, I received a call from another Venture attorney, Dave Moore, who was "of counsel" to one of Venture's law firms. He asked if he could come to Los Angeles and interview me with a court reporter present. It would not be a deposition and I would not be under oath. I agreed and said I could be under oath if he wanted. We met at the Marriott Hotel by Los Angeles International Airport, and for about three hours I answered his questions. I also gave him copies of everything that I had in my files that pertained to Shelby. I just emptied all my Shelby computer files and handed them to him.

At the close of the session I was certain he believed I had not sent the purloined document to Deichmann. He asked me who might have sent it. While I did not know for sure, I stated there were potentially 100 people at Shelby American who would have sent it to him.

I explained that Mike had taken up station in Las Vegas and had been the most productive and enthusiastic seller of the car. He had befriended everyone at Shelby American. When he took prospective buyers on plant tours, everyone greeted him and helped him out. In return, Mike bought lunches, beers, loaned his new Corvette, and his money, and, in general, had become just about everyone's best friend.

When it became apparent that Venture was planning to upset Mike's program and cause him grief, the troops were annoyed. Anyone who had had anything to do with Mike could have been a willing provider of the infamous legal memo. Venture had come in like Attila the Hun and wiped out everyone's best friend.

The lawyer just looked at me for a minute while he digested what I told him. Then he said, "I think I understand."

Chapter Fourteen

More Confusion

With the big meeting over, the dealers went home with mixed feelings. Some felt they had come to Las Vegas for no good reason and that Larry Winget was going to do what he was going to do no matter what they said. Others took a wait-and-see position. If the promised minutes of the meeting came out as was agreed, then business could move ahead as planned. While the dealers waited, Shelby American and Venture personnel agonized over what had to be done.

The issue of the car dealers that had ordered at reduced prices had not been resolved. While the agreement at the meeting had been that the Series 1 would be priced at $165,000, Venture, after thinking hard, decided if the dealers were to make money, Venture should as well, and it decided on a price of $175,000.

They had discussed the retroactive price increase and believed they had come to a resolution, but it was not yet in writing. Furthermore, the issues of the cost of paint stripes and color changes were still up in the air.

Mike Deichmann was out of the picture but had kept in close contact with his customers, and many other dealers' customers came to rely on him for information as well.

Since I was no longer on the scene, there was no one to answer dealer questions. The brunt of the responsibility fell on Wayne Stoker and, to a lesser extent, Gary Patterson. While Sarah Moore should have been in the loop because she had been in the forefront of customer relations, she was kept out in the cold because she had been a prime suspect in the case of the leaked legal memo.

Wayne had a fine financial head, but he was not much of a public relations man nor was he always good with customers. His instincts were good, but his manner was often abrupt. He had the additional problem (not his fault) of being unable to speak with the full authority of the mother company. In addition, without resolution of the major issues, he really had nothing to say. As hard as he tried, it was almost impossible for Stoker to placate the long list of owners and dealers who were calling constantly.

Compounding the difficulty was the fact that Venture had not yet responded to the dealers with the final written minutes of that session. And no new sales had been generated in the year 2000.

When the meeting memo finally came out, the uproar started all over again. The agreement, according to Venture, was not the same as the agreement according to the Series 1 dealers. Instead of the price being $165,000, it was now $175,000. There was no definitive resolution on the cars that dealers had ordered at the early and low price.

Mike Juneau, the most active dealer after Mike Deichmann, was annoyed. "Fly to Las Vegas, waste a couple of days, make agreements, wait a month, and find out the trip itself was wasted," was his take.

The resolution would take even more time, but what was finally offered to the dealers was convoluted in that it rewarded those who decided not to continue and forced those who were willing to accept the terms to agree to less revenue.

The agreement allowed those who insisted that they be allowed to purchase the cars at the originally agreed-upon price to do so. However, they would not be able to continue as dealers. In simple terms, those who had made deposits on cars at the original $99,975 price were able to have their five cars for which the retail price was $99,975 and the price to the dealer was $79,975.

Those dealers who wanted to continue with the program would only be allowed one car at the $99,975 price. The balance of their original order of five that had been ordered in their dealerships' name would be sold to them at $109,975, the wholesale price that had been set by Venture for those cars.

All cars as of that moment were to be sold to dealers for $154,975 with a suggested retail price of $174,975. Venture had also agreed not to go into the retail business (i.e., to sell cars directly in competition with the dealers).

The proposed agreement put the dealers in a dilemma. If they opted out of the new program, they stood to make a lot of money. A few dealers had sold only one or two cars. The price of the car to them was $79,975. The new retail price of the car was $174,975. This meant that there was a *potential* profit of $95,000 on each of their unsold cars.

Those dealers who decided to go with the new program and who had sold five or more cars would have to settle for participating at the new retail price. The program rewarded those who had not done a good selling job and presented an uphill battle to those who had worked hard to sell the cars. Venture had set back the science of economics by at least a century.

A further outcome of the April 2000 meeting was an agreement about the $20,000 dealer commissions: $10,000 would be paid at the time of delivery and the balance paid after Shelby American had delivered 250 cars. Winget signed a personal note guaranteeing the additional $10,000 commission to be paid after 250 cars had been delivered. At that time, the production schedule indicated that 250 cars would be delivered by year's end.

As a result of the new rules, 17 of the original group of 23 Olds dealers remained involved.

While the dealers seemed to think that a retail price of $174,975 was high, it was still possible to sell the car at that price. Car dealers are optimistic by nature and most figured they could do the job.

For Mike Deichmann, though, the die was cast. He decided he did not want to be paid half his commission. He wanted it all. He had earned it, had invested a lot of money in his sales efforts, and wanted to be repaid. He sued for the full amount of his commissions.

Just as Joe Tignanelli stated, when somebody sues his father-in-law, he sues 'em right back. True to form, Larry sued Mike for unlawfully interfering with Shelby American business. The theory of the countersuit was that by stirring up the other dealers and the press, Mike had caused Venture to lose business.

George Berejik, the Oldsmobile dealer from Needham, Massachusetts, dropped out. He had not sold many cars, yet he arrived at the conclusion he could not be involved because he had not been told the truth. He loved the car and the idea of the whole program, but enough was enough.

There were a few elements missing from the equation. The first was when delivery would really begin. The second was the quality of the cars. The third question and the biggest unknown was this: what would the market say?

Sales had come to a screeching halt when the idea of a retroactive price increase bubbled to the surface. Dealers took a wait-and-see attitude with good reason. Any sale that was made prior to the final decision about the retroactive price increase was a potential headache. The dealer would either have an unhappy customer, a lawsuit, or just plain egg on his face.

Since the discussions of the price increase had begun in August 1999 and the dealer meeting was not held until April 2000, sales momentum disappeared. Enthusiasm that had been built up slipped away because the meeting that had originally been talked about for January was pushed further and further out until it happened months later.

One good thing happened. By May, Wayne Stoker began to issue checks to me for my past labors.

After organizing the production line and the assembly process into what, according to all reports, was a first-class operation, Nelson Gonzalez returned to Detroit and to an advisory capacity for Shelby.

Nelson's front-office duties were turned over to Wayne, and the manufacturing program was turned over to Brent Fenimore for the Series 1 and Bob Marsh for the Cobra. Bob and Brent were named business unit managers with responsibility for all aspects of the two programs. Bob Zientek was there to counsel and steer the troops through the major problems and to keep Venture informed.

While the cars were coming together, there continued to be problems with tops. None had been delivered, and major top reengineering was being done. Cars were ready to go, but the tops were not.

Initially cars were to be held in the plant until tops were available. As the tops became further delayed, Shelby American had to revisit that decision. Cars were to be delivered without tops and someone was to drive to customers' homes to fit the tops when they became available. It was hard to believe that, after all this time, the tops were still a problem. To be sure, the top was not an easy product to build. It had to collapse into a very shallow well and it had to be light. Naturally, cost was a significant factor.

Before the tops were finally delivered, Venture had to agree to pay a considerable premium over and above the originally agreed-upon price for the redesign and reengineering involved in making them fit. This added further to the financial woes of the program.

Since I had officially resigned as of mid-March 2000, I thought I was now out of the loop and would get no more Sunday morning phone calls from anxious customers and dealers. I had never before fully appreciated the value of a good Sunday morning sleep. Then again, it was still some time before I could count on that.

Chapter Fifteen

The Fun Never Stops

Even though I was officially out of the loop, my phone did not stop ringing. I had not been replaced at Shelby American, and there were just not enough people on hand at the plant to respond to all the phone calls or answer all the questions.

To top it off, I was now getting phone calls from the press. I had been an affiliate member of the Los Angeles Motor Press Guild for many years and, therefore, knew most of the local representatives of the press.

Fortunately, I had not been involved in the famous April dealer meeting, so I could not report on what happened. Besides, that was a rather inflammatory meeting, and I did not want to put myself in the position of having any comment whatsoever about the proceedings. As upset as I was about the idea of a retroactive price increase, the Series 1 was a potentially great car— possibly Carroll Shelby's last car. Many fine and dedicated people were working to build it, and any bad press could well sink it. I had five years invested in the success of the program and was not interested in watching its demise.

I easily sidestepped having to answer the question of "what happened?" I just told the press that there was a list of dealers in the latest *duPont Registry* ad, and they could easily obtain firsthand information from someone who was actually at the meeting.

Naturally, I had very strong opinions about the program and its players. I had not done a good job hiding them, but there was no reason to supply grist for the reporters' mill. Even though I was no longer with the program officially, my loyalty to Carroll and the concept of the Series 1 never wavered.

One of the better things that I did after departing the Series 1 program was to take a vacation with my wife, Mary. It was all pleasure—*no business*—but we did swing through New Bern, North Carolina, and spent a few days with Mike Deichmann. By then, Mike was more friend than business associate.

After a few days with Mike in New Bern, it became apparent why Mike was so upset about the concept of a retroactive price increase on the Series 1.

While he had sold cars all over America, he had sold a number of them to his friends in New Bern, and a retroactive price increase would have put him in an absolutely untenable position in his hometown. Mike had grown up in New Bern and had taken over his father's Oldsmobile dealership. Nearly everyone in town knew him. When he walked down the street, just about every shopkeeper would shout out "Hello!" as he passed. The idea of having to go back on his word to these people was unthinkable. He had taken their money and given his promise that they would get Shelby Series 1 automobiles for a contracted price. This may have been a man who was rich, but contrary to Nelson Gonzalez's vicious comment, Mike Deichmann had not become rich "by not being totally honest."

Mary and I spent the rest of our trip on the beaches of Sarasota, and for the first time in a few years, I was not plagued by dozens of phone calls that started with, "Where in hell is my car?"

Aside from a few calls from a few of the dealers and some buyers who had become friends, my telephone was relatively quiet about Shelby matters for a number of months. Aside from my curiosity about what was going on, my life appeared to be back to normal.

Then out of the blue in mid-June 2000, I took a call from Wayne Stoker. He asked if I would consider coming back to help them out. I was surprised, to say the least. I figured my hard-line stand against the price increase would have shut me out completely. I told Wayne that I would consider it, but a lot of changes had to be made. A few days later, Carroll called with the same question: would I come back? While I had no doubt that Wayne's invitation was sincere, I had no idea whether he had the weight of the organization behind him or if he was just desperate for some help. Carroll's call was confirmation that at least Carroll and

Wayne agreed. If Carroll wanted me back, I would have to give it serious thought.

I wrote a letter to the two of them that outlined what I felt was necessary to sell the cars. It was simple. The price had to be lowered to something within reason. Trying to sell a car that came on the market at $100,000 for $175,000 and without any improvements was a sure road to oblivion.

The issue of how many cars were to be built was a big one. Dealers were not convinced that Venture would build all 500. The price of the stripes on the car remained a troublesome issue. After being told that the stripes were $1,200, some customers were now being told that they might be $3,100.

There were other issues too, including what was to become of the conflict with Mike Deichmann. Naturally, Mike was my friend and I believed he was entitled to his commissions. But more than that, the other dealers viewed the dispute between Mike and Shelby American/Venture as symbolic. If Mike would not be paid, they were not convinced that they would be paid. I asked that the difficulties with Mike be resolved.

After submitting my letter to Wayne and Carroll, all was quiet for a time. Then, after a month, Carroll began to call me periodically with updates. "Hang in. I want you back, but I have to get the details cleaned up first," was the message. Since I had no place to go, I just went about my life.

The next message from Carroll was to the effect that he had to convince Larry Winget I would be a loyal and trustworthy employee. "Be patient," he said. In late September 2000 I called Larry Winget's secretary and set up a date to meet with him in Detroit. We had never met to discuss anything, and my decision as to whether I went back to help out depended on Larry and his reaction to me and to my suggestions about what had to be done.

In Detroit, after killing the morning with a prolonged breakfast with Jim and Margaret Brophy, who helped produce one of the early Series 1 brochures, I set off for lunch with Joe Tignanelli and a "pre-Larry briefing." During lunch, I asked Joe a question that had been really burning my curiosity. "Why in hell did Venture, a company that grew by leaps and bounds through smart acquisition, buy Shelby American, a company that even the most cursory of investigations would reveal to be a mess?" There had obviously been little or no due diligence.

His explanation was that shortly after the Shelby deal was put on the table, a major opportunity arose in the form of the purchase of

Peguform, a German company that was a clone of Venture. It was a major deal and a huge opportunity for Venture. The legal and accounting staffs became totally consumed with making it work. In the interim, the details of the Shelby deal fell through the cracks. In the total scheme of things, the Shelby deal was a nickel-and-dime operation, and the Peguform deal was millions upon millions.

However, having made the purchase and having found it less than perfect, Venture moved to take remedial action at a snail's pace. The original promise was that Venture would infuse enough capital to make the company work. What it did instead was put in money only when a crisis arose. That meant that Shelby American was always behind the curve. In the end, this approach must have cost Venture millions of dollars as workers were laid off and rehired and parts were purchased at high rates because of low volume. The deployment of this piecemeal approach cost time, money, and a lot of grief.

Then came the meeting with Larry Winget. He told me that he intended to build all 500 cars, and Venture was looking into the pricing issues and the need for a supercharger. He also described his vision of the future for the Shelby/Venture relationship.

He explained his reason for wanting the company. He believed that future cars would be built of composites and that he wanted to have a showcase for Venture technology. It all made sense to me, but I was waiting for the key questions about my loyalties.

Then he slipped the question in quickly and almost glossed over it. It came as, "I understand that you had some difficulties with the way we were planning to do business." Before I could respond, he went on to discuss something else.

I had to catch myself. I had to be sure that he knew where I was coming from, and I guessed that he handled the question in such a way as to make sure that I would speak my piece. I think he was testing me, challenging me.

As politely as I could, I asked him to back up, that I felt a need to make myself clear. He acted surprised and told me to go ahead. I told him how I had spent three years telling customers and dealers that Shelby American was solvent, the cars were going to be built, and all contracts were going to be honored. That was what Don and Carroll told me, and that was what I passed along. I also stated that by instituting a retroactive price increase, Venture threatened to turn me into the biggest liar on the face of the earth and that my only defense was that I could and would not present or support that position to our constituents—the dealers and customers.

He looked at me and cleared up the entire matter with one sentence: "You cannot lie to people." That was the end of the subject. We shook hands and off I went, back to California, once again under Carroll's spell.

After catching up on sleep, I headed back to Las Vegas for a fact-finding mission and to reacquaint myself with the goings-on at Shelby American.

A lot had changed. They were actually delivering cars. While a few cars had been delivered the previous August 1999, no more made it into customer's hands until the following August 2000. There were just too many problems and, of course, no tops. The lack of tops had been such a holdup that the company had decided to ship cars without tops and to retrofit the tops when they became available.

Now cars were going out with tops and Terry Jack, a production supervisor, was on the road in a van loaded with convertible tops for those cars that were delivered without them. Bob Marsh was now running the Cobra program and was heavily involved in the sales program as well as manufacturing. The biggest surprise was Wayne. When Nelson had departed, he had appointed Bob and Brent to major supervisory positions, and he had entrusted Wayne with the role of caretaker.

I had been leery. Wayne was, after all, an accountant. In addition, he had shown some pretty dark moods and little sense of humor. But Wayne knew exactly how the business ran and had come to the job because of his respect for Carroll Shelby and his accomplishments. By giving him some room to maneuver, Nelson had released every good instinct in Wayne. While he was under terrible pressure to control the finances and put Shelby American on an even financial keel, Wayne had found time to laugh and also learned that there were problems of note other than his own. He had also determined that even though the Venture financial people had said "No" to just about everything, he had to take action anyway if anything was to be accomplished. He quit asking for permission and acted in what he thought were the best interests of all parties. Yes, Wayne stepped up to the plate when we needed him.

Wayne became the glue that held the place together. After watching him for a few weeks, I came to the conclusion that he might have become a darned good automobile executive had he been thrown into the pot a few years earlier. Everything would be perfect, so long as he didn't try to use his public relations "skills."

With Terry Jack on the road with tops, it was also a good time for him to try to correct some of the other problems that many of the early cars developed. Transaxles in particular caused many headaches. Initial assembly problems at the transmission factory caused grief. There were shifter linkage problems and oil leaks. Numerous transmissions were replaced.

Because of all the delays, pricing problems, and initial quality problems, customers had expected more rough treatment. When Terry Jack found a transmission problem, he just called and had one shipped to the right location and installed it. It was a refreshing note from a company that heretofore seemed to totally ignore its customers' needs. While there was a warranty, the transmission was not covered in the policy, but between Shelby and Roy Butfoy Transmissions, no customer's faulty transmission went without repair, correction, or modification.

The warranty was yet another source of grief. From the beginning we had planned to provide a warranty of 12 months or 12,000 miles, which seemed fair for a hand-built car with a limited production run. However, the best warranty obtainable was a six-month, 6,000-mile program. Big companies, such as GM, self-warrant their cars, meaning they take the financial responsibility for fixing and repairing defective work or parts. (The best way to keep warranty costs low is to build better cars.)

A small company, such as Shelby American, that intends to build only 500 units cannot afford to self-warrant. The solution is to purchase a warranty. A warranty is like an insurance policy. You either pay for a policy or set aside enough money to pay for the anticipated repairs. An actuary or adequate previous history dictates the anticipated cost.

In the case of Shelby American, there was not only no history but the nature of the car, a high-speed sports car, made warranty companies shudder with horror. While it is likely that a more extensive warranty could have been purchased, the price would have been extremely high. With the Series 1 program anticipated to be a giant money loser, spending a small fortune for a warranty seemed inappropriate.

When the warranty was announced to the owners and potential buyers, there was an outcry. It seemed inadequate and less than we had been touting. To its credit, Venture/Shelby never backed away from any serious customer complaint and, in some instances, shipped cars back to Las Vegas for repairs.

Dealers were of little help. Not only were Oldsmobile dealers among the worst to be selling the Series 1, the Oldsmobile franchise system was in such serious trouble that there were other things on the dealers' minds. This is not to say that the Olds dealers were bad dealers, but Olds dealers were used to selling conservative sedans to older Americans. They had little understanding about how to sell an expensive race car for the street. Most thought that if they could put one on the showroom floor, it would stimulate sales.

While it would help having a car on display, the kind of man who would buy a Series 1 would have a hard time making the connection between high performance and an Olds dealership. Car aficionados and race car people would just as soon be caught dead as to be found at "your father's Oldsmobile" dealership. Many Olds dealers were aware of the problem sales people had adapting to the specialty car and tried to direct customer responses to a designated salesperson. While this was a good idea in principle, in some cases the result was disastrous. Turnover in car dealerships is high, and auto sales personnel are a transient lot. A man or woman who either knew about the Shelby or was responsible for it might be gone in a week. Sometimes when a customer called, after seeing the dealership listed in an ad in the *duPont Registry*, and asked about the Shelby, the receptionist (who might be brand new to the job) or a salesperson would respond, "This is an Oldsmobile dealership, I don't know about any Shelby," or, "The man who handled the Shelby is no longer here."

In Milwaukee, Mike Juneau was a major exception. He loved the car and had sold cars to those among his clientele who were car collectors and enthusiasts. In anticipation of service problems, Mike set aside a considerable amount per car to cover what the warranty might not, or to do what he felt was necessary to make the car as close to perfection as he could. Terry Jack spent an extra few days on his top installation rounds to teach Mike's mechanics the intricacies of the Series 1.

With all the problems the Shelby Series 1 had in its development, there were still some good people determined to make it a success. How you define success is another matter.

Chapter Sixteen

The Snakes Keep Biting

C arroll Shelby has always been the darling of the motoring press. Over the years, he has cultivated the press and befriended just about every motoring journalist of note. It is a mutual love affair. He is extremely quotable, and he is accessible. For the time he shares with them, he is rewarded with all the press coverage he wants, and the editors reward their writers for getting a good story from Shelby.

As the Series 1 began to hit the streets, Carroll was afraid that one of the early cars would make it into the hands of an unsympathetic automotive reporter. The early cars were crude and severely overweight. Some of the first cars delivered weighed over 3,000 pounds with all the necessary fluids. This was a far cry from the initial 2,400-pound estimate and the final spec of 2,650 pounds. It was also an awful lot more bulk for the 4.0-liter Olds motor to propel to the speeds that were reported by *Motor Trend* in November 1998.

The first prototype generated a reported a 0 to 60 acceleration time of 4.4 seconds. As was noted earlier, this was an extremely light vehicle, and the recorded times had been adjusted for altitude and temperature. A totally objective test on an early production car would probably have indicated a 0 to 60 time of at least a second slower. This would be an obvious attack on the credentials of the car and a further impediment to sales. Remember: The first rule of Shelby cars is that they must be fast.

Carroll had always insisted that a supercharger was in the works, and he now pushed to get it ready for the press to review. It was Carroll's contention that once the supercharger was installed, the car would be so fast that its other faults would seem insignificant. I agreed. There are enough people who will pay anything for all-out speed so they can be king of the hill. Ever since the idea of a supercharger was mentioned, the Shelby office had been bombarded with questions of its price and availability. It was amazing the number of people who said, "Just get it for me, I don't care what it costs."

Venture, though, took some convincing. It would take another infusion of cash to do all the engineering work and testing to make the blower a reality, and Venture was not sure if it wanted to make any more investment in what it already considered to be a loser.

Although Mark Visconti had already done a lot of the planning, none of the actual work had been executed and tested.

Mike Edwards and Kirk Harkins were still at the Gardena facility, and they set out to create the supercharged Series 1 using the forbidden work they had previously done with Mark Visconti as the basis. With the car as compact as it was, very little space was available to add the supercharger, the intercooler, and the extra plumbing that went with the project.

The target was *Car and Driver* and its editor at large, Brock Yates. Carroll had specifically requested Yates. Over the years, Carroll and *Car and Driver* had somehow managed to be at odds with each other. *Car and Driver* always found a way to take a shot at Carroll, and Carroll reciprocated by never missing the opportunity to denigrate *Car and Driver*. The exception to the animosity was Yates who had a long and solid friendship with Carroll.

Car and Driver was a major and well-respected automotive magazine. Therefore, whatever *Car and Driver* had to say about the supercharged Series 1 was critical. Over the past two years, Shelby had been ducking all the magazines until the car was ready to withstand the critical eye of experts. Since *Car and Driver* had been asking for a car, Carroll thought the least risk would be to have his friend Yates involved.

While Carroll was personally making the arrangements for the *Car and Driver* test and for a *Motor Trend* test two weeks later, Mike and Kirk were struggling to get past the development problems in order to have a car ready. Once again, press deadlines took precedence over mechanical preparedness, and the car showed up at *Car and Driver* with an untried and untested clutch. While the engine developed big horsepower, over 500 on the dynamometer, it was of little use when the clutch was not up to the task.

In a nutshell, the *Car and Driver* test was another disaster. While the tact and editorial efforts of Brock Yates helped soften the blow and highlighted the potential of the car, there was no way to hide the fact that the clutch failed. If that was not bad enough, when the clutch was replaced with a heavier-duty version, the car burned a piston, the first and only regular engine failure ever reported in a Series 1. A second car fitted with the supercharger had been standing in the wings. This car was only able to manage a couple of attempts at speed before it, too, fried its clutch.

After all the delays and hard work, *Car and Driver* referred to the Series 1 as a "wonderful concept." That was little comfort to Carroll Shelby, knowing that the car was sporting a retail price of $175,000. Carroll was furious, at Shelby American for delivering such a bad car and at *Car and Driver* for the bad review. Sure, Carroll had no right to be pissed off at *Car and Driver* for doing its job, but Carroll was always pissed off at *Car and Driver*.

The weeks between the *Car and Driver* test and the *Motor Trend* test gave the engineers time to fit the right clutch and ensure that the engine was timed properly so it wouldn't burn another piston.

The *Motor Trend* piece was billed as a "High-Speed Shootout!" between nine high performance cars. The *MT* staff gathered the BMW Z8, Ferrari 360 Modena, Porsche 911 Turbo, Qvale Mangusta, Corvette Z06, Ford SVT Cobra Mustang, Dodge Viper ACR, Pontiac Trans Am Firehawk, and the Shelby Series 1. These were cars with serious performance pedigrees.

This time, in all measures of acceleration, the Series 1 was clearly the champ. It recorded a 0 to 60 acceleration time of 3.71 seconds and a 0 to 100 acceleration time of 9.27 seconds. Finally, the Shelby Series 1 was able to demonstrate what it could do. Unfortunately, total preparation was once again a bugaboo. While the Shelby had previously recorded 60 to 0 braking distances of around 100 feet, the test car, which had not had its brakes properly attended to only managed to stop in 129 feet, the worst of the lot from the car with the most potential.

Fortunately, Shelby fans are more interested in going than stopping. All in all, the *Motor Trend* piece was vindication. The car was blazingly fast and ran to perfection. So what if it didn't "stop to perfection?"

SNAKE BIT

A third article appeared in *Sports Car International* in the fall of 2000. *SCI* is a small, high-quality magazine geared toward the purebred car enthusiast. The editors approached Avery Greene, the dealer in Vallejo, California, about borrowing his car for a report. Avery was one of the first dealers to become involved in the program. He was enthusiastic and eager to provide his own car. Unfortunately, his was an early car and not necessarily representative of the best of the Series 1 program in terms of its fit and finish.

Fortunately, the *SCI* editors treated it fairly well, with the biggest negative being the price. The piece ended with this statement: "For 175 big ones, we can think of several cars we'd rather own." Unfortunately, Greene discussed the skimpy warranty and aired his beefs with the service operation. All of this raised more questions in the minds of prospective buyers and offset the good that had been written about the handling and the fun factor.

The magazine articles were all breaking about the time I returned to the Shelby fold in Las Vegas. It was an unfortunate way to become reunited. My assignment was to sell the cars, and some magazine editors seemed determined to make my job more difficult.

While Wayne, Sarah Moore, and Gary Patterson had done all they could when it came to responding to customer questions, sometimes there were no answers to be given. This made the problem even more difficult.

Besides the problems of the bad press, the fact that cars were being delivered caused an even greater impediment to sales. The cars that were now being delivered sold for $99,975. The current retail price of the car was $175,000. While there were many who bought the Series 1 because it was the new Shelby, others had purchased it because they were gambling on the fact that, over time, the price of the Series 1 would escalate, as had the price of the original Cobra. Those who had purchased original Cobras in the 1960s for $7,500 and held on to them were now looking at Cobras being sold at auction for prices that ranged from $150,000 to $400,000.

When the retail price of the Series 1 jumped from $99,975 to $175,000 in less than two years, some of the speculators figured that there was no need in waiting for future auctions, the time to sell was right now. Also, there were a few who were just disappointed in the rough and overweight early cars. Some of these cars also went on the used-car market.

A couple of the first resellers were able to obtain $160,000 for their vehicles, but the price rapidly dropped as the number of vehicles available increased. In early November 2000, a Series 1 sold for $112,500 at a collector car auction in Chicago. One appeared for sale on eBay with an $85,000 minimum reserve price but drew no bidders. The same vehicle finally turned up on a Porsche dealer's used car lot, where it sold for $80,000 after having been part of a complicated swap for a boat, another car, and something else.

After those extremes, the price seemed to settle in at around $125,000, with the classified ads in *AutoWeek* usually carrying one or two advertisements per week.

The two most recurring questions were, "When will I get my car?" and "Why is the stripe now $3,100 when I was told it would be $1,200?"

When I arrived back on the scene, the company was shipping cars on what appeared to be a regular schedule, so it seemed that it would be a simple matter to address the information gap by putting the delivery schedule on the Shelby Internet site. Not so fast. I was told to back off because of the lack of confidence in any kind of delivery schedule. The problem was in the paint process. While Shelby had worked with PPG to obtain the latest and best in equipment, the bodies were hell to paint. As a result, cars that had been shipped were coming back from dissatisfied customers, and we had a logjam on our hands.

The silver paint showed all the imperfections that would normally be hidden by a dark color. Little bits of dust showed up. Little fish eyes appeared. The irregularity of the body panels became more apparent. While some cars had been shipped, complaints about the paint were almost universal, and the cost of shipping cars back to the plant for refinishing became a matter of concern.

This problem had a number of causes. When Nelson Gonzalez took over the operation, he had to break the delivery logjam. He was adamant that cars were to be shipped. If he had not done so, the ensuing problems would have been worse, with even more delaying and fumbling. The system had to be able to function, and lame excuses could not continue to take precedence over performance. The urgency of moving the car deliveries off dead center was more important than perfection.

The tragic result was that many cars were shipped that should not have been. Inspectors overlooked details that, under normal circumstances, they would have corrected. Also, the body panels were still not coming to Shelby with the kind of quality and uniformity that was required to make assembly and painting a simple task. The last problem was the paint itself. Anyone involved with auto painting, either as a manufacturer or a buyer of a retail paint job, has heard of the difficulties concerning clean air laws. All the properties that make a car's paint shine and make it easy to apply are bad for the air. Since our collective breathing comes first, car companies and car painters have to struggle to learn how to overcome the problems of the new paints.

From the standpoint of cost and customer satisfaction, obviously something had to be done. An inspection of the cars that were ready to go (by this time there were more than 20) showed that we needed a serious rehab program. The painters had to stop painting new cars and rework those that were already painted. Therefore, a schedule of shipment could not even be considered until the logjam in the paint department was broken. At one point, 30 cars were ready to ship except for the fact that the paint had to be retouched.

Wayne Stoker was beside himself because Jim Butler, the Venture finance man in charge of the project, had removed the Venture cash life-support system. With such a backlog in the paint department, we could not deliver cars. If we could not deliver cars, we could not receive final payment. Without the cash from the final payments, we could not pay the bills or even make payroll. It was so ironic, since a major part of the problem with getting cars ready for delivery rested squarely in the hands of Venture, which was supplying the body panels that were a big part of the problem.

While Venture was working to improve the body panels, the Shelby American operation was suffering severely. Rather than acknowledging that Venture itself was part of the problem and helping to mutually solve the financial problems, Butler heaped invectives on Stoker.

Wayne solved the cost issue of the paint stripes with a stroke of common sense. When Gary Pniewski was onboard, he was adamant that it didn't matter what the customer had been told—the price of a paint stripe that ran from nose to tail was now $3,100. When the stripes were originally offered, they were $1,200, which was already a profit operation for Shelby. Customers then asked for variations, and the car that had been first shown in *Motor Trend* in 1998 had a stripe that ran over the nose. While this was a slight increase in expense, it was a pain to accomplish. With those two added elements, we had raised the price of the stripe to $2,500.

One of Mike Juneau's customers asked for the stripe to continue over the nose and over the tail of the car and to run back under the rear of the car above the exhaust pipes. At first, no one wanted to do this, figuring it would look strange. The customer insisted, and the results looked surprisingly good—so good that Carroll asked that his car be striped this way, too. Of course, that caused a stampede for stripes over the tail.

There were still customers who had been quoted $1,200 for the standard paint stripe and were incensed that Shelby would try to force them to pay double. To me, it seemed the larger penalty was having irate buyers. The extra money obtained for the original basic stripe would not make or break the program.

Before I could bring up the subject with Wayne, he came to me and said it seemed foolish to try to gouge an extra $1,300 from customers who had been told a paint stripe would be $1,200. This was an ongoing problem, and Wayne felt that everyone's best interests would be served by merely asking what the customer had been told in the first place. If he had been told $1,200, $1,200 it was, but the extra charge for putting stripes over the nose and tail would be $300 per area. There it was, sales logic and customer relations from an accountant turned auto executive.

We finally resolved other lingering problems. The producer of the ice-skating show settled for a Cobra, avoiding a lawsuit. The Playmate of the Year for 1999 was assigned a Cobra as per the original agreement, and the Playmate of the Year for 1998 was given assurances that her Series 1 would soon be delivered.

Shelby also dropped the services of Davey Hamilton as the driver/instructor on the delivery program. He was expensive, and his racing schedule made his availability questionable. Gary Patterson took over Hamilton's duties. While he did not represent a racing "name," Gary was a capable self-taught driver. With his knowledge of the road-racing course at the Las Vegas Motor Speedway and all of his time behind the wheel of the Series 1, his demonstrations of the car were thrilling and more than satisfactory for the customers.

The problems with the top continued to plague us. While we now had tops, fitting them was a problem. It was an exacting process and if a top was not raised and clamped down properly, it would leak profusely. One customer who lived in Florida had a particular beef. While he was a nice-enough guy and had purchased two cars on the theory he would "probably wreck one," he tended to be rather self-important.

One day, this gentleman called the Shelby warranty administrator. He was irate and screaming into his cell phone about how he was caught in a downpour, the car was leaking like a sieve, and he and his girlfriend were getting soaked. Dale Simmons, the warranty administrator, was an extremely empathetic man and his thought went immediately to how he could help this owner. With the thought in mind that he would get him immediate help, such as a truck to haul the car and a cab to get them out of the rain, he asked, "Where are you?" The answer was, "I am in my driveway." Dale's response was, "Why don't you just pull into the garage?" Silence from the other end.

We did ship his car back and replaced the soggy carpets and dried out the seats, but basically his problem was worsened by the fact that he had not properly raised the top, so it couldn't help but leak.

One customer purchased a car and asked for a very late serial number. Apparently he thought that the longer he waited for his car, the more faults would be corrected. He was right up to a point, but after about number 100, quality and consistency were pretty even. For some unknown reason, this particular customer decided his mission in life was to denigrate the car and the program. I wondered what his rationale was. If he succeeded in badmouthing the program enough, he would decrease the value of the car he had not yet received.

It was also strange because he went to every dealer in the network to purchase a car at a rock-bottom price. He finally succeeded in buying a car from a dealer who would kick back a large portion of his commission. I believe his purchase price was the lowest of any car sold.

While this customer waited for his car, he began to check with other owners and prospective owners. He began to log complaints and problems. He claimed to have amassed over 500 pages of notes about details of the car.

He asked for special considerations and collected photos of prototypes and the first cars that were delivered. He seemed to be looking for ways in which he could sue the company for not delivering his car the exact way some cars appeared in photos. The truth of the matter is that no two cars were exactly the same. If something was too difficult to accomplish and had no effect on performance or value, it was changed during production. Grommets were added here, gaskets and seals there. The car was, after all, hand built.

In the case of this antagonist, he was reported to have said, "I intend to sue the bastards." To what end, I never did figure out. He even started a website that appeared to be a source for collecting damaging data. He posed questions to Shelby American and complained that the company did not respond even though he had blocked Shelby American from access to the site.

He called customers, dealers, and Shelby personnel until finally most decided that he was a misguided pest and declined to talk to him. Besides, no one wanted to be quoted by him or have to testify based on answers he had elicited during his telephone conversations.

Serial numbers were an issue. All the Series 1 cars carried a CSX5000 code. CSX was a letter designation on all Shelby cars. Cobras were CSX2000 and CSX3000 series cars. Series 1s were CSX5000 series. All cars are supposed to be built in number sequence: CSX5000, CSX5001, and so on. However, many customers had requested special numbers, such as 5360, which might represent a birthday or an anniversary or whatever. The understanding was that they would just have to wait until their special number appeared in the build sequence to get their car.

When production became delayed, it was apparent that getting to a special high number could take years, so an effort was made to move all those customers who held late numbers to early numbers. This was not easy, and it was nearly impossible to tell someone that his car might not appear for months and months.

Nature abhors a vacuum, and in the absence of any designated leader (Wayne, while he was, in fact, in charge, had never been given the operational authority for the entire place), Brent Fenimore grabbed hold of all the authority he could. Brent was capable and bright, yet his ever-so-obvious power grab made work difficult for others.

Although Joe Tignanelli was the Venture man most in charge, he was rarely available, although he seemed to be most available to Brent. If there was a problem, Brent would say, "I just talked to Joe and he said. . . ." Or Brent would come to a meeting and say, "I just talked to Joe and here's what you are to do. . . ." It made life difficult for Wayne and anyone else who had problems he or she couldn't resolve. While Brent had the title of business unit manager for the Series 1, he was effectively regulating the activities of the company through manipulation of his contact with Tignanelli.

One cynic was heard to say that if Joe stopped in his tracks too fast, Brent's head would disappear up Joe's ass.

When I agreed to come back and help out for a while, it was to be for a period of six months. After I was back for about six weeks, it became apparent that the problems were so severe that I had little chance of success. I had insisted that the price be reduced. It was not. While the Series 1 was a fantastic car, it was priced way beyond the market. I had asked that the Mike Deichmann problem be resolved, and nothing had happened.

Strangely enough, when I had met with Larry Winget, he asked Tignanelli if the problem with the dealer down south (Deichmann) had been resolved. Joe answered, "We're working on it." Resolving the Deichmann deal was important because he had sold about a third of all the cars that had been sold. Mike's attorney now told him not to talk to customers. Therefore, all the calls Mike had fielded in the past were routed to me. It was difficult for me to do anything but talk to customers, which made efforts to unload the remaining cars almost impossible.

Carroll kept telling me to be patient, but I could tell he, too, was reaching a certain level of frustration. At least he had the confidence of being Carroll Shelby. Angry customers did not yell at Carroll.

The lack of coordination with the departments at Venture was incredible. The marketing department had decided to "help" Shelby American in the merchandising arena. We certainly needed help but not the kind that came with little or no discussion. The marketing guys incurred two huge expenses. One was for product literature, created in the best Detroit tradition of overkill: expensive photographer, super-glossy paper. The second area was merchandise: caps, jackets, T-shirts, golf shirts, sweatshirts. They ordered a variety of stuff to see which would sell best. That which proved popular would be reordered and stocked.

The problem was that Venture felt it had the authority to spend money in the name of Shelby American, and Shelby American had no budget. We couldn't pay the suppliers and had not become involved in a merchandise program because we didn't have the money. On top of that, the Venture people loved wearing Shelby gear.

Under most circumstances, it would be fair to ask that expenses be paid by those who incurred them, but that was not the case. Even though Shelby American was wallowing in its own red ink, Venture was adding to the debt in Shelby American's name with no understanding or agreement from Shelby American.

In early November 2000, Wayne and I went to Detroit to try to resolve some of the financial woes. Wayne worked for days to determine the whereabouts of every dollar and separate the critical debts from the not-so-critical.

The merchandising gear bill was one that we needed to clear up because the merchandising company was holding the goods and did not want to release any new stuff until the bill was paid. Further, we had been promising both Cobra and Series 1 dealers that we would provide them with Shelby-licensed merchandise to sell. Caps and T-shirts are good business and good advertising. We had been trying to fulfill the dealers' requests for catalogs and/or inventory. The company that Venture had hired could create the catalog and handle all distribution, but it had to be paid.

In our meeting with Venture's finance guy, Jim Butler, he agreed to give us some relief on that particular budget item and said he would get it paid as soon as possible. Wayne and I then met with the merchandising company and set up a program that would enable all the dealers to have merchandise to sell, contingent upon Butler coming through.

A Cobra dealer meeting had been planned for early November, timed to coordinate with the SEMA show. I had inherited the Cobra activity since Tom Conley had retired and since Bob Marsh was up to his ears building cars. He had been ordered to build Cobras at the rate of 250 per year despite the fact that only about 54 had been sold in 1999 and the 2000 total looked like it would reach about 71.

I had been involved in the last Cobra meeting as the person helping Conley. This time I was put front and center. I looked at the agenda and cancelled the meeting. It was exactly the same agenda with the same unanswered questions as the last meeting. One of the unanswered questions was about the merchandising stuff that had been one of the reasons Wayne and I went to Detroit to visit with Butler.

The rescheduled Cobra meeting was held on December 1, 2000. While certain aspects of the meeting were fine, it was a hodgepodge at best. We promised the dealers they would soon receive a merchandising catalog, so this item was off the agenda. As we should have known, Butler didn't pay the bill, and once again, Shelby American looked like idiots to those who were trying to sell the products.

Venture's lack of understanding of automobile sales was incredible.

Bill Walker, the Shelby man-at-large from Venture, was in and out of the Cobra program so many times we figured he was doing it for the frequent flyer miles. One day, he was in the middle of everything, the next day he was off on an assignment in Russia. One of his assignments was the co-op ad program. We had signed a dealer in Northern California who, like everyone else, contributed to the fund. However, because he was a late-comer to the program, his name was omitted from the bottom of the ad.

Unfortunately it was omitted, and omitted, and omitted. He was irate, and for good reason. Walker finally confessed why. Because the type was reversed out of a dark background, there was a charge for redoing the ad. Bill thought the charge was excessive and told the magazine to forget it. He also told me it was best to come forward with the truth; it was better to confess and move on.

In the meeting, he performed a mea culpa. That did not go down very well. The dealer who had been shortchanged was seething. The other dealers couldn't believe that the much-needed advertising for one of their counterparts was cut off because someone at Venture thought it was too costly to correct the problem. Advertising was an important part of the group's collective livelihood.

The other awful part of the meeting came when I (the designated bad guy) had to get up and tell the group that Venture had insisted on a sales objective of 250 units for 2001, and if they, the existing Cobra deal-ers, could not do it, many other measures would be taken, such as signing up many more dealers, selling the cars directly, and on and on.

It was tough stuff, and my heart wasn't in it, but I had been told that that was what Larry wanted and we had better do it "or else." The "or else" was a difficult issue. "Or else" may have meant that I might get fired. So what? Both Venture and Shelby had asked me to come back, hadn't they?

The implication that others felt in the "or else" was that Larry Winget might decide to shut the place down. I never thought he would shut it down. He told me he wanted it to be a success, and I had no rea-son to doubt him. The trouble was that too many of his people believed they should speak what they thought was on Larry's mind.

Fortunately Joe Tignanelli was in the meeting, and a lot of the heat went to him as the Venture representative who could speak for the own-ership. Joe immediately backed down. We would sell 125 cars because that was all Bob Marsh could build. Shelby would not sell cars directly to retail customers unless they were relatives or very close friends.

The Mike Deichmann saga was also a problem that would not go away. Mike had decided not to accept the agreement made at the April dealer meeting, in which the dealers agreed to accept half of their commissions on a car ($10,000) upon delivery and the remaining half after 250 cars had been delivered. Mike took the view that Venture could bankrupt the company at any time. By his calculations, he was owed $1,800,000, and he wanted it before Venture decided to fold Shelby's tent.

When he sued Venture, and Venture sued him, the standoff became a continuing saga. Because I had become a really good friend of Mike's, I was often asked to be the conduit for information because each side's attorneys had told the principals not to talk to each other.

I suppose it was the right thing to do from a legal standpoint, but it seemed so futile. Mike and Joe Tignanelli had become friends. Carroll and Mike had become good friends. It always seemed to me that a simple conversation among the three would make the problem go away.

At one point, the Venture attorney arranged to meet with Mike—in *South* Carolina. The lawyer chose South Carolina rather than North Carolina (Mike's home) because Mike had appealed to the state attorney general in North Carolina for help.

The meeting did nothing to help the problem. In fact, it made it worse. Mike had to travel to a relatively distant city (nothing is close to New Bern) to meet with the lawyer in a grubby hotel room. Rather than try to come to an agreement, the lawyer started the meeting by telling Mike what a wonderful guy Larry Winget was and how he had personally stepped in to save the company. Rather than negotiate with Mike, the lawyer lectured Mike on why he should be grateful to Winget for saving the program. Mike couldn't wait to get out of the meeting and into a shower.

Sometimes things happened for the strangest reasons. Phil Blackaby had become the official Shelby truck driver. Phil's business was that of hauling collector cars to and from auctions. Shelby had made an arrangement with him to drive the Shelby transporter when needed and recommended him as the man buyers should contact to transport their cars from Las Vegas to their homes.

Phil knew all of the major auction company principals and many of the nation's big collectors. However, he was a truck driver and not a marketing whiz. Because of his proximity to those in power at the auctions, the Venture people tended to view him as an expert on the subject. While Phil knew which auctions were the big and important ones for Shelby, he also knew which ones were good for him and for keeping his trucks filled with classic cars. It was also good for his business to bring participants in the form of cars to be displayed and not necessarily for auction.

After the disaster of the Chicago auction and the $112,500 price that was achieved for the Series 1 in November 2000, I was skeptical about getting anywhere near auctions. However, Phil convinced Joe Tignanelli that an appearance at an auction in Branson, Missouri, would be in the best interests of Shelby. Joe agreed, and Phil loaded a Series 1 on the truck and headed for Branson. As the guy in charge of sales, I should have attended. I felt that because we were turning down bona fide opportunities to promote the car, it seemed a waste of money to head for what was probably a wild-goose chase. Especially since Tignanelli and Bill Walker were both going to Branson, their expenses would wind up on our books.

Wonder of wonders, a Series 1 was sold at Branson. And, for the full price of $174,975. Even better yet, the buyer, a country-and-western fiddle player, said that he would gladly pay more for a special-edition car, a brainstorm that hit Tignanelli on the spot. Rather than pay $174,975, the buyer guaranteed a bid of $200,000 for a special edition Series 1 Shelby American would prepare for the Barrett-Jackson auction that was coming up in January 2001 in Scottsdale, Arizona.

The car was to be a one-off. It would have special brakes, special paint, a full-leather interior with carbon-fiber trim, and it would be the first car to have the special X-50 option, which was a special performance package that added 50 horsepower. Since no new cars had been sold for over a year, it was a great opportunity to show that the car was not dead in the water and that there was still serious interest in the Series 1.

The Barrett-Jackson auction was a Shelby triumph. Four of the highest priced cars sold carried the Shelby badge, and the Series 1 drew $217,080 including the commission. Brock Yates did the commentary for SpeedVision and atoned for the earlier brutalization of the car in *Car and Driver*. He stated that it seemed that the Series 1 had finally arrived and it was nice that Carroll was being so recognized for creating some of America's most desireable cars.

December 2000 was a significant month. On December 12, General Motors management announced that the Oldsmobile division was to be closed down. Under the conditions it announced, Oldsmobiles would continue to be sold as long as there was demand, and the current models would run through their natural business cycles. The announcement came as no surprise to most, but it was sad to think that the oldest automotive brand in America was gone. Most of the Shelby/Oldsmobile sales agents were not seriously affected. Most owned multiple franchises, and the Olds business had been slipping away for some time.

In addition, Wayne Stoker announced that as of the first of the year he would become a part-time employee. Wayne had taken a terrible emotional pounding, and he felt he just didn't need it anymore. He agreed to work two or three days a week as needed.

Venture saw no need to bring in another manager to coordinate the overall operation. Brent Fenimore, Bob Marsh, and Guy Childers, the comptroller, were left to individually deal with the Series 1, Cobra, and financial operations with no local leadership, direction, or coordination. The Las Vegas operation was now just a simple branch office operation responding to strings being pulled in Detroit.

It underscored the futility of the Series 1 project as far as Oldsmobile and its dealers were concerned. If there had been any shred of interest in the Series 1 project by General Motors or Olds, it disappeared with the Olds obituary. The Series 1 had become a bastard stepchild when John Rock departed, and now both parents were dead. Fortunately, any sign on the car that Oldsmobile was involved had been removed after only a few cars were built. (At one point the engine cover carried an "Aurora V-8" decal, but Carroll had insisted that it be removed after one too many disputes with Oldsmobile.)

Another major event occurred when Venture came to the conclusion that there were no new sales and the production crew was rapidly heading toward the end of the order bank. With the only cash being received from cars being finished and delivered, the fiscal picture was more than bleak. In mid-December, Wayne was asked, as one of his last official acts, to bring the entire staff together and announce that everyone was furloughed for the time between Christmas and New Year's Day. Included was notification that only about 60 percent of the workforce would be called back after the holidays. To further hang the scrooge label on him, Wayne was directed to cancel the Christmas party. Wayne was desolate and later commented that executing that order was one of the toughest tasks of his life.

By now it was apparent that cars could not be sold for $175,000. In addition, none of the things that I had asked for were being done. If anything, services and any help I might have expected were being reduced. I heard indirectly that Larry was disappointed because I had not been able to make any progress. That made sense to me. I felt I was wasting my time and his money.

I directed a letter to that effect to Joe Tignanelli, the Shelby watchdog. I also sent an e-mail to Larry Winget that related the same message. I heard nothing for a while. Joe did ask that I stay on board through the Barrett-Jackson auction. Eventually, Barbara, Larry's secretary, called and told me that Larry wanted to know what I felt had to be done.

I prepared a brief white paper elaborating on the concept that cars (both Cobras and Series 1s) should be built to order and that carrying an inventory was costly. I further suggested that a smaller production crew could be created of the best people from the Series 1 and Cobra programs. The idea was that Shelby American was a custom-car company and that buyers should have a greater involvement in what was being built for them. Start with a low base price and add options. Car companies have been doing this for years.

I heard nothing back, but the week following the Barrett-Jackson event, Larry Winget and some of his key executives came to Las Vegas to review what was going on and to come to some conclusions about how to move ahead. While everyone had prepared an agenda and gathered the facts about his or her own operations, the meeting became a rambling two-day affair that went from subject to subject without meaningful transition or conclusion.

The upshot was that there would be a combined work force, and, of major importance, the price of the car was reduced to $135,000 plus a commission of $7,000 to any dealer who sold one. Shelby would now sell the Series 1 directly to anyone who walked through the door.

There was a new pricing structure that enabled a prospect to build a car to his or her own specifications. The X-50 engine was added as an option, as was an all-leather interior, carbon fiber interior trim panels, body color choices, all the way up to a supercharged car for $215,000.

The meeting came at the end of January 2001. This was just in the nick of time for me. I had been having some serious back pains. They began in October and became progressively worse until, by the end of

January, I was hardly able to stand. I headed for surgery on herniated disks in early February.

While the downsizing was going on, Mike Deichmann's lawsuit stalled. Both Carroll and Tignanelli called me from time to time to see if I could find out what Mike would settle for. He felt he was owed $1,800,000 and had stated he would settle for $1,500,000. I just kept repeating that. Somewhere along the line Carroll got the idea that Mike would settle for $800,000, but he never discussed it with Mike until early March. Mike dispelled the notion, but the real issue was that Mike was the most effective salesperson. He had sold one-third of the cars, and Shelby desperately needed him back to clean out the rest of the Series 1s. Carroll knew that Mike was entitled to the money. Mike's case was almost airtight, and Carroll cursed "them goddam lawyers."

Depositions for the case were set for the third week of March 2001 in Las Vegas. I had been summoned for deposition along with Don Rager, Sarah Moore, and God knows who else. Many of Mike's customers had already been deposed by the Shelby (Venture, that is) attorneys. While I have no idea what they said, Venture was undoubtedly looking for someone to say that Mike had acted in some way that was detrimental to the program. This was a search for support of its countersuit—that he had harmed its business. That would be a tough case to prove against the man who had bragged in his advertising about the wonders of the car and that he, Mike Deichmann, was the largest Series 1 dealer in the country.

One claim was that Mike had generated negative press and that this impeded sales. While there was some negative press, it was not yet about the car. The press had been about the proposed retroactive price increase, and there were enough anxious customers and angry dealers willing to speak out to the press.

It had also been Mike's customers who wrote letters of praise about Mike, the car, and the program. Most of the press generated about the Series 1 and its problems came from a press-offensive by Venture to justify the price increase. There had even been a front-page story in the April 3, 2000 edition of *Automotive News* that carried news about the price increase and how it was justified. That story had been placed by Shelby/Venture.

Mike was the greatest champion that the Series 1 ever had. The claim that he was interfering with its success was preposterous. Of course, when it comes to our legal system, nothing is a sure thing.

Chapter Seventeen

The End is in Sight

The latter part of 2000 had seen dramatic changes in the U.S. economy that continued unabated into 2001. There was a general collapse in the technology sector led by the dot-com industry, which had been built on the inflated hopes of the viability of business on the Internet.

With that collapse, a lot of the surplus money that was being spent on expensive toys disappeared. Some of the dot-com money that disappeared put a few instant millionaires into the tank. A few of them were Series 1 buyers.

The general market slowdown meant that auto companies were cutting back production. Because Venture Industries depended on the auto industry's prosperity for its own prosperity, it, too, was forced to watch its pennies a lot more closely. The luxury of force-feeding the Series 1 program no longer existed, and the work force that had gone from over 100 to about 60 was cut back even more, until the total work force, including office staff, dwindled to about 40.

While the price of the car had been reduced from $175,000 to $142,000, now an added number of cars were on the market at prices well below $142,000. One of Deichmann's customer's dot-com shares fell from over $160 to under $16 per share. His Series 1 was one of the first items to go on his scale-back program, and there were many more financial casualties that led to expensive toys being sold off.

SNAKE BIT

Lou Adimare, the early buyer who had waited so patiently for his car, decided to dump it. He was reported to have accepted $90,000 to get out from under a car he decided he did not like.

Another of Mike's customers died, and the estate asked Mike to step in and help out. Suburban Olds put one of its cars on eBay with a $100,000 minimum, and there continued to be Series 1s in the classified pages of *AutoWeek* magazine.

While there were nibbles for new cars, the program was essentially stalled. The new X-50 engine option was popular for cars that were in the assembly process, but it did not attract new buyers to the fold. The supercharger had been developed, but it was not put into production and would not be available until there were at least 10 orders accompanied by a 50 percent deposit. The price of the supercharger installation was $35,000, or $27,000 for the do-it-yourself version.

Mark Visconti, the former chief engineer, figured he could develop and sell a supercharged car utilizing the bigger 4.6-liter Northstar engine for about $6,000 less, including a suitable clutch, and he planned to solicit Series 1 customers to see how many would be interested.

Despite all the noises about settling with Mike, depositions for the case continued. Both sides deposed Mike's customers. Mike's depositions were to demonstrate that he had been an effective salesperson and, therefore, worthy of the commissions. Venture's attorney was trying to prove Mike had tried to torpedo the program.

I went Las Vegas on March 21, 2001 to give a deposition.

Mike was there, and that meant another night or two of fun, Deichmann-style, in Las Vegas. A couple of great meals at Piero's more than compensated for the six hours of questioning that I endured by both attorneys. Since I had been around the program from the beginning, there were many questions I could answer for both sides. However, since most of the business orders had been issued by Don Rager, my deposition could only point out what I had been told and had then related to dealers and customers, including Mike.

Mostly, the questions centered on the issues of what Mike had earned and how. Had he been told he would earn extra commission by purchasing the rights to sell cars at a lower price before price increases were instituted? Had he forwarded money into the company in times of need? Indeed he had.

While I could give my understandings on these matters, it was Don Rager's testimony the following day that was the capper. For all his dodging on many issues, Don stood tall when it came to backing everything I had testified to and that Mike had claimed. Yes, Mike had put in money when Shelby needed it. Yes, Mike had been the most productive dealer. Yes, Mike had earned the extra commissions. Yes, those commissions had been promised to him.

As had happened many times before, the Shelby/Venture attorneys recommended a settlement. All parties had too much to lose by procrastinating. Again, Mike was told there would be an offer on the table "next week." Next week turned into next month, and despite many calls from Carroll to Mike that the deal was on the way, nothing happened until late May 2001. Carroll Shelby desperately wanted Mike back on board. Mike had been the most enthusiastic and prolific salesperson, and without Mike or someone like him, the program would continue to lose ground.

If Mike came back to the program, it would be after all problems, both legal and product, had been resolved. The other dealers knew this, and some felt there would be no end to the miseries until Mike's situation was clarified. By now, the program had gathered enough bad publicity to cast an air of gloom over the operation.

Deichmann's claim against Shelby had been for $1,800,000, including the extra commissions due him plus some of his expenses. Because of all the delays, problems, and negative publicity, Mike's customer base had dwindled to the point where the commission due him had dropped to $1,300,000, and Mike told Carroll that he would settle for $1,000,000.

In mid-May 2001, the Venture attorney tendered Mike an offer for $600,000. Part of the settlement offer included a clause that Mike would drop all Series 1 activity. This was obviously counter to any deal that Carroll wanted to see. Mike was not only perplexed about Carroll's involvement but about the size of the offer.

Mike's next move was, as part of the rejection, to have his attorney advise the Shelby/Venture attorneys that the next round of depositions would soon be scheduled in Detroit and among those to be deposed would be Larry Winget, Jim Butler, and Nelson Gonzalez.

In addition, Mark Visconti and Wayne Stoker were to be deposed. Obviously, Wayne had all the details of all dealer financial transactions, and Mark had vital testimony about the federal certification of the car and what the effective dates of those certifications were.

Everyone involved—customers, dealers, employees—had been told that all the cars had to be either completed or well along in the production process by the end of 1999. Cars were still being completed in May 2001, and no paperwork had been filed with the EPA asking for extensions of the previous standards.

The ramifications of this were obvious, and certainly if the facts about the certification or lack thereof ever reached the EPA, there could be serious problems. In addition to the normal certifications, the supercharger had finally been approved (within the company) for release as an option. With the supercharger in place, the price of the Series 1 was now up to $215,000. But, since the supercharger had not been part of the original certification package, it could only be added as an aftermarket installation, and Shelby American was offering it as a "factory-installed" option.

There was also some question about the certification of the X-50 engine option now being offered. Former Olds employees who had racing experience with the Aurora V-8 that claimed 370 horsepower was possible, but the engine ran "dirty" and would not pass emissions tests.

Jim Butler of Venture denied (to Mike's lawyers) that Shelby/Venture was selling the supercharger directly, but the offer of a supercharged car was clearly on the Shelby website, and an article in *AutoWeek* (May 14, 2001) quoted a press release from Shelby that offered a supercharged car for $215,000.

The obvious dangers of the Visconti and Stoker depositions set off some alarms, and Carroll again called Mike and suggested the $1,000,000 was doable but that Mike would have to take half up-front and the balance over time. The Shelby/Venture attorneys claimed there was not enough ready cash available to pay Mike the full sum at once. This was hard to fathom, since Venture was a company that did over $2 billion in sales and was owned solely by Larry Winget, who also owned 75 percent of Shelby American (Carroll owned the balance). Again, Carroll put the proviso in that Mike had to come back and help sell the cars, a statement that contradicted the clause that accompanied the first settlement offer of $600,000.

In the meantime, the case against Deichmann by Venture was continuing into the discovery stage, and Mike was deposed in mid-June 2001. The Shelby/Venture position continued to be that Mike Deichmann had harmed the Series 1 program by interfering with the business of the company. Deichmann had supposedly done this by calling attention of the press, other dealers, and customers to the attempted retroactive price increase.

This was really a reach. Even if Mike had fought against the retroactive increase, he had done so because, if Winget had instituted the price increase, the entire operation would have been tied up in litigation. As it was, the retroactive price increase was never put into effect. While the Series 1 program was dying, it was not dying in a barrage of customer lawsuits.

Sales of the Series 1 were still virtually nonexistent. There were plenty to choose from on the resale market. One independent agent ran an ad in *AutoWeek* offering to buy Series 1s for $90,000, and there were plenty for sale in *AutoWeek* and the *duPont Registry* with retail prices from $129,000 to $134,000.

While Mark Visconti was long gone, Kirk Harkins remained with Carroll Shelby assembling Cobras for special customers of Carroll. Mike Edwards hung on as well, doing various engineering assignments.

In July 2001, a customer who had purchased the X-50 engine option called to report he had placed the car on a dynamometer and the horsepower delivered to the rear wheels was 270. The number on the certificate accompanying the engine package promised 370 horsepower. Normally, there is a 10 to 15 percent loss of horsepower through the drivetrain when a car is dynamometer tested. So, the X-50 package on the Series 1 should have produced about 320 horsepower on the dynamometer. This fact sent everyone scurrying to find out what the problem was.

The Playmate of the Year for 1998 eventually got her car. She turned around right away and offered it for sale on eBay. The last apparent bid for her car, which was autographed by her and by Carroll Shelby, was around $130,000. The ice-skating fiasco was also resolved with one Cobra. The special Jeff Hamilton Series 1 jackets, which had become a hot issue, ceased to exist and only early buyers were able to claim that part of the prize. The delivery program, in which the buyer was flown to Las Vegas and provided track time and driving lessons, also fell by the wayside.

Millard Design, the Australian design firm that had been purchased by Venture, closed its doors. Gary Millard had been the one who had warned Don Rager and me that an association with Venture would destroy the nature of Shelby American as it had Millard Design.

SNAKE BIT

The August 2001 issue of the *duPont Registry* carried seven ads for the Shelby Series 1 with prices ranging from $155,000 down to "no reasonable offer refused." Some of the ads had been placed by dealers, some by customers.

And, wonder of wonders, Mike Deichmann and Venture/Shelby came to terms in July 2001. Those in Detroit who knew how Venture usually responded to lawsuits against them claimed Venture would eventually settle. Venture settled when all other options were exhausted. It seemed to be more in defiance than anything else. Every action was like a squeeze play at home plate.

Chapter Eighteen

It Ain't Over 'til it's Over

A t this point, the story isn't over—but it is. A major wrench was tossed into the equation when in mid-2001 a potential customer called the EPA to ask, if he bought a car, could it be certified? This then caused the EPA to check its records, and it learned that the car's certification had expired at the end of 1999.

A call to Mac Yousry at Global Certification, who had initially performed all the required certifications, revealed that he had not been engaged to do any certification beyond 1999. Clearly, the cars were in violation of the various clean-air laws, and the EPA and CARB (California Air Resources Board) began investigations.

While certification was required for the time after 1999, it was problematic since no cars were sold. It is not known whether the decision not to recertify was a business decision based on a wait-and-see attitude about future sales or merely an oversight, but the result was the same. The cars had to be recertified or they could not be sold.

While there was a lot of finger pointing and accusations about the EPA investigation, it was actually a good thing. The ongoing debate within Shelby/Venture about whether or not to put more money into what appeared to be a losing effort was now front and center. In the end, Shelby American decided to end the Series 1 production run. The cars were nearly all manufactured and delivered by Brent Fenimore and his crew by March 2002. The high point for sales had been 285, but that had declined because of customer fears and because Venture wanted to recover as many of the low-priced cars as possible so they could be resold at a higher, profitable price.

Shelby achieved the ability to sell cars equipped with superchargers installed as aftermarket equipment. So far, about 50 Series 1 buyers have taken advantage of the supercharger option.

Two-hundred-fifty delivered was the number that made the dealers who remained in the program after the "big meeting" of April 2000 eligible for the second half (the second $10,000) of the commissions due them for the sales they made. Wayne Stoker had placed the money in escrow for the dealers when the car was delivered and the final payment received. Jim Butler released the money from escrow, but it did not go to the dealers. Instead, the money went to pay bills and other business obligations.

Although a few buyers were unhappy and sold their cars, most were extremely pleased. The Series 1 was a rare automobile with a vast performance potential. Best of all, it was a Shelby. If the balance of the 500 cars is never built, the approximately 250 owners of the Shelby Series 1 will have an uncommon treasure.

It is easy to find heroes in the Shelby Series 1 saga. There was no shortage of enthusiasm, spirit, and talent that went into the creation of the car. From Peter Bryant on through Mark Visconti, Mike Edwards, and Kirk Harkins and his crew, there was dedication and a single-minded determination to build a unique, high-performance vehicle. When the final configuration was approved, the car went from plans to a drivable prototype in 18 months, a miraculous achievement.

This may have been Carroll Shelby's last car, and as the only one built from scratch, it should have been a great one. His only failure in the program was that he did not protect himself and his good name. He remained too detached from the detail, perhaps by design. He let Don Rager run with the show. If Don tripped and fell, it would have been Don's fault, and Carroll could claim little involvement. As it was, Carroll's name was on a product of questionable viability, and Carroll Shelby is a very proud man. For better of worse, the Series 1 "ain't no Cobra."

We may excuse Carroll's shortsightedness by the fact that he suffered through a failing kidney and a transplant operation, as well as the tragic loss of his wife, during critical times in the Series 1 development. It is hard to imagine anyone keeping focused on anything other than those all-consuming problems.

Neither Carroll nor Don Rager did enough to learn about Venture, the ultimate buyer of the company. A little due diligence on their parts might have revealed the nature of their prospective partner. Shelby American needed cash and, secondarily, a loyal long-term partner. They got a talented but eccentric and overbearing organization instead.

Mike Deichmann deserved more than he got. He single-handedly took up the slack in sales. His enthusiasm and persistence helped keep the Shelby doors open when they might well have been closed. He personally spent more on advertising and marketing the car than Shelby American did. If you are looking for a true hero, you need look no further than Mike.

Wayne Stoker bled Shelby Guardsman Blue trying to keep the company finances in order. He finally had to choose between the program and his health, and wisely, he chose his health. His contributions were enormous and all positive. Wayne left the Shelby operation in late April 2002 to take on a prestigious assignment for the Mormon Church.

Brent Fenimore matured and became a balanced production executive and had at least as many hours, and certainly as much blood, in the project as anyone. It is hard to find anyone among the devoted band of Shelby loyalists who did anything but give his or her best.

Gary Patterson came aboard as a purchasing agent for the Cobra and evolved into the entire sales and marketing organization. Gary just plain loved fast cars and being involved with them. From his perspective, he had the perfect job. He got to take customers on a racetrack and demonstrate the high-speed characteristics of Cobras and the Series 1. Nelson Gonzalez once told Gary he was "an expensive luxury." Nelson was wrong. Gary was an inexpensive necessity.

Don Rager was certainly both a hero and an impediment. With a sharp mind and no experience in car building, he got the Series 1 program up and running. That was the hero part. However, he used half-truths, sleight of hand, and distortions to move the program ahead. He tried too hard to become the hero, a new version of Carroll Shelby. They say that the truth works best, but I wonder if the Series I would have been anything more than a pipe dream if we all knew the truth in the beginning.

Don exhibited bad judgment with his promotional madness. Playboy Bunnies, ice-skating shows, *Wheel of Fortune*, and the myriad other schemes and promotions came back to bite him and everyone else with their cost and the bad feelings they ultimately generated. His promises of delivery and production dates were a farce. His insistence on involvement in every detail turned the day-to-day operations into a waiting line outside his office. Coupled with his health problems and the personality cycles induced by his many medications, Don Rager became an unstable leader when we desperately needed a sure hand.

While the car showed every promise of keeping to its heritage as a race car for the street, Rager's decisions to add amenities such as electric windows, a stereo, air conditioning, and a convertible top changed the nature of the car. It is difficult to say whether or not sales were better because of these creature comforts, but the car was heavier and provided less performance than the original concept. Race cars don't have all that stuff, and the car became neither fish nor fowl. It was neither a race car for the street nor an overly fast sports car.

Worst of all, Rager was intent on becoming Carroll Shelby, complete with cowboy boots and hat. His insistence on keeping Carroll out of the loop also had a detrimental effect on publicity and credibility.

Unfortunately Don Rager's health problems have worsened. At this time, his replacement liver is giving out, and the infectious skin conditions that have plagued him have not subsided. Still, Don is a fighter and will hang on as best he can.

Don was a man with a vision. He set out to achieve that vision, no matter what. While it is easy to dismiss him for his faults, it is difficult to do anything but praise his determination and guts.

General Motors surely could have applied some of its expertise and support. The success of the Series 1 program would have cast GM in a more favorable light with auto enthusiasts, even with the demise of Oldsmobile. The Series 1 would have shown that GM was a car company that cared about the kinds of cars that make people say, "Wow." Once it settled on a brand-management system, it isolated the traditional "car guys" as unfortunate leftovers from the past. These car guys have always understood that cars have emotional value and cannot be sold like bars of soap.

In early August 2001, GM took a big step forward by hiring former Chrysler president Bob Lutz, as vice chairman and apply his product expertise to GM. Lutz was reported to have been an admirer of John Rock. Had Lutz been a force at GM when the Shelby project was getting underway, there is no doubt in my mind that the Series 1 project would have been viewed differently within GM.

John Rock must share some of the blame as well, not because he made any bad decisions but because he didn't make enough decisions. Had he jumped in with both feet at the outset the results might have been much different. While he was around, his advocacy was not forceful enough, and he didn't use the leverage of his office to secure agreements within GM that would lead to a successful conclusion to the program after he departed.

In fairness to John, he probably did not have the ability to make those decisions. I believe he succeeded in sneaking the program through. He had been designated a dinosaur by a new wave of General Motors management, which was determined to erase all traces of the past and instill new ways of thinking into a steel-and-rubber business. Because GM market share is and has been on a downward slope, it is hard to say whether or not the new way of doing business is working. Time will tell, as will the new influence of the "car guy," Bob Lutz. Without John Rock's advocacy and because the guard had been changed, it was difficult for anyone at Oldsmobile to step in and make the program work. The Series 1 program was a career breaker for those who were too closely involved with it. The upper echelons of GM frowned on it. Those Oldsmobile people who remained involved in the project were at a low level and not decision makers. They had no power to force decisions or gain access to GM resources. As enthused and committed as they were, they were merely drones working to fulfill the Shelby/Oldsmobile contract and do it quietly so as not to be blamed.

The Oldsmobile dealers surely share some of the blame. While some of them knew what they were getting into, many of them took a wait-and-see attitude. If the car appeared, they would make efforts to sell it. Customer deposits were desperately needed to keep the cash coming in, and only a rare few bothered to dig in and help. At the same time, only a limited few actually knew how to sell the car or even bothered to learn. It was almost as if, suddenly, dump trucks had appeared at Rolls-Royce dealerships and the salespeople were asked to get to work. ("What in hell do I do with these things?") The reach was enormous, and a salesperson accustomed to selling comfortable sedans to suburban matrons had no idea about how to attract customers to, and close a sale for, an expensive and exotic sports car.

Because of the itinerant nature of car salespeople, there was a constant turnover at the dealerships that handled the Series 1. Even if a potential customer did call, he was often left on the line while a receptionist looked for someone who had any idea of what the car really was.

John Rock had spelled out all of those dealership issues. When he identified the original group of potential Series 1 dealers, he had been quite explicit as to what Shelby might expect. However, one of the reasons for the existence of the cars, as far as Oldsmobile was concerned, was to try to breathe life into some dealerships. Therefore, while the Olds dealers carried some blame for the malaise of the program, they were only partially at fault. They were culturally out of their league.

I believe that the biggest enigma was Larry Winget. Strangely enough, he was the man with the most to lose and the most to gain. He reportedly invested $50,000,000 into the success of the Shelby American Series 1 program. In one way or another, it was all his own money because Winget personally owns Venture Holdings, which owns Venture Industries, along with myriad other companies including Venture Nevada, which owned Shelby American.

In his own area of expertise, Winget could probably be described as a genius. He began with a small company, merged with another, and bought other companies until he commanded an empire. That, however, did not make him a genius at managing a specialty automobile company.

It appeared to those of us close to the program that had Winget done what he said Venture Industries would do when it bought Shelby—invest enough resources to complete the Series 1 as quickly and as professionally as possible—the car could have been delivered in a timely manner, and the Series 1 could have been promoted as a success.

Instead Winget vacillated. His money trickled in with no apparent plan. The expertise of Venture was never applied in a timely manner. The body panels that were supposed to be his showcase became one of the bugbears of the program. Also, his decision to build the chassis in-house caused huge delays and put the program in possible violation of government regulations. The body panels that Venture was to provide should have been first-rate. They were never the showcase products that Larry Winget envisioned.

All the original Shelby decisions were derided and turned aside as Venture people took charge and asserted themselves as the experts. As they became more deeply involved, it became apparent, even to them, that while they didn't agree with all the early decisions, some had been correct decisions and had been made for good reason. Months passed while Venture people refigured each decision and eventually came back to some of the original Shelby positions. But we could never recover those crucial lost months.

Worst of all, Winget isolated himself from the realities of the marketplace. His attempt to retroactively raise the price brought sales to a screeching halt. His delays about the next steps and the constant revisions to the price and pricing policy further destroyed dealer and consumer confidence. The price he demanded for the car, $175,000, was well above the market's level of acceptance, and when the price dropped to $142,000, there were enough dealers and customers who had their own cars for sale that even the lower price did not attract buyers.

His personal feeling that the dealers were making too much money while he was losing money destroyed any chance of creating a clear and cohesive marketing program. While he may not have liked the idea of having dealers, there has yet to be a car distribution system that could live without them. I believe Larry Winget made many of his decisions based on bad advice, and he was, in the main, only involved when someone dared to approach the Mighty Oz with a problem needing his personal response.

While Winget did invest vast sums, they could have been used in a manner that would have heaped praise and glory on Carroll Shelby and Venture Industries.

There was one last bite of the snake.

In the fall of 2002, *Automotive News* reported that Peguform, the German company that Venture Industries had purchased, had applied for bankruptcy, claiming that Venture was "repatriating" too much money to the United States to pay off debt. This resulted in Peguform being unable to pay its suppliers. With Peguform protected by the German courts, cash stopped flowing back to the United States, leaving Venture with all of the debt and no Peguform cash or profit to ease the burden.

In March 2003, Venture filed for Chapter 11 protection in the U.S. Bankruptcy Court in Detroit, Michigan. Also in March, Carroll terminated his relationship with Venture. Right to the ownership of Series 1 parts is unresolved and in dispute.

Carroll formed Shelby Automobiles Inc., and continued to build and sell the beloved Cobra. In August of 2003, Carroll and the Ford Motor Company joined forces once again to undertake a new program to apply Shelby performance magic to Ford vehicles.

Acknowledgments

I wrote this book because it all seemed so unbelievable and because when I began to relate all the madness, all I got were nods of disbelief from my listeners. As I became further emerged in the process, I realized how much time and energy so many people had put into the Series 1. Some of the efforts were misguided, and some were right on the money. In the end, all efforts were part of a crazy story.

While I can't acknowledge everyone who participated, I would like to give special thanks to these people in particular.

Vic Olesen got me into the mess, and he gave me counsel when I needed it. It was a grand adventure but it cut into our morning coffee sessions for about three years.

Mike Deichmann became a great friend. The story would have been dull without him, and the whole adventure would never have gotten off the ground. Unfortunately, he was bitten by the Series 1 snake, and his enthusiastic efforts on behalf of the Series 1 were tossed to the winds.

Mark Visconti, along with Kirk Harkins and Mike Edwards, created what could have been—should have been—a world-class sports car. They hung tough all the way and did their best to avoid being caught up in and brought down by the problems.

Gary Patterson's constant enthusiasm and commitment were vital parts of any success the car enjoyed.

Craig Robinson, while not mentioned in the story, was the one man on the Series 1 production team who would not accept the fact that the cars could not be built. He refused no challenge, fought off all excuses, and pushed harder than anyone else to get the Series 1 produced. For his efforts, he was laid off.

Wayne Stoker lived through it all and made the most of it. He also made sure that I was paid what was due me. (Thank you, Wayne.)

Bob Marsh's job was never clearly defined. He kept getting new assignments but did the best he could to make something happen. He eventually steered the revitalized Cobra program into a viable reality.

Tom Conley was always there with moral support and friendship.

Sarah Moore brought sanity to my trips to Las Vegas. Her friendship, sense of humor, organizational skills, and home-cooked meals were a blessing.

Don Rager. He was almost as much of a pied piper as Carroll. If he had not done what he did, nothing would have ever happened: good, bad, or otherwise. No Don, no car, no story.

And nobody, but nobody, would have given a damn about any of it had the car not been a Shelby. So thanks, Carroll.

And, of course, my wife, Mary, who took me to LAX every Monday morning and picked me up at LAX every Tuesday night and who always listened to my tales of Shelby in Las Vegas. She never could comprehend the silliness of it all until she helped me with this manuscript.

Series 1 Dealers

Tom Emich – Emich Oldsmobile, Tucson, AZ
Bill Coulter – Coulter Oldsmobile/Cadillac, Phoenix, AZ
Kent Browning – Browning Oldsmobile, Cerritos, CA
Avery Greene – Avery Greene Motors, Vallejo, CA
Lisa Schomp – Ralph Schomp Automotive, Littleton, CO
Michael Brockman – Connecticut's Own, Milford, CT
Bill Fischer – Fischer Oldsmobile, Stuart, FL
Cliff Findlay – Findlay Oldsmobile, Las Vegas, NV
Walt Otto – Otto Oldsmobile, Albany, NY
Rick Dorschel – Dorschel Oldsmobile, Rochester, NY
Mike Deichmann – Trent Oldsmobile, New Bern, NC
Bud Schoenleben – Bud's Oldsmobile, St. Mary's, OH
Anthony Ferrante – Ferrante Oldsmobile, Vandergrift, PA
Chris Holler – Holler Oldsmobile, Winter Park, FL
Mark Harrison – Ed Martin Oldsmobile, Anderson, IN
Todd Archer – Edwards O'Neil, Council Bluffs, IA
George Berejik – Berejik Motors, Needham, MA
David Fischer – Suburban Oldsmobile, Troy, MI
Greg Ryan – Ryan Oldsmobile, Billings, MT
George DeMontrond – DeMontrond Automotive, Houston, TX
Ragnar Pettersson – Valley Oldsmobile, Mt. Vernon, WA
(Pettersson purchased the dealership from Greg Hinton, the original participant)
Mike Juneau – Arrow Oldsmobile – Milwaukee, WI

These dealers were part of the original group with the program but decided to end their participation:

Vic Noe – Dean Bailey Oldsmobile, Tulsa, OK
Todd Meier – Meier Oldsmobile, Dallas, TX
Neil Gerald – Gerald Oldsmobile, Naperville, IL

Index